Inspector of Irish Fisheries

Inspectors of Irish Fisheries report, 1870

Inspector of Irish Fisheries

Inspectors of Irish Fisheries report, 1870

ISBN/EAN: 9783741104756

Manufactured in Europe, USA, Canada, Australia, Japa

Cover: Foto ©ninafisch / pixelio.de

Manufactured and distributed by brebook publishing software
(www.brebook.com)

Inspector of Irish Fisheries

Inspectors of Irish Fisheries report, 1870

REPORT

OF THE

INSPECTORS OF IRISH FISHERIES

ON THE

DEEP SEA, COAST, AND INLAND FISHERIES OF IRELAND,

FOR

1870.

Presented to both Houses of Parliament by Command of Her Majesty.

DUBLIN:
PRINTED BY ALEXANDER THOM, 87 & 88, ABBEY-STREET,
FOR HER MAJESTY'S STATIONERY OFFICE.

CONTENTS.

REPORT

OF THE

INSPECTORS OF IRISH FISHERIES

ON THE

DEEP SEA, COAST, AND INLAND FISHERIES OF IRELAND, FOR 1870.

TO HIS EXCELLENCY JOHN POYNTZ, EARL SPENCER, K.G.,

LORD LIEUTENANT-GENERAL AND GENERAL GOVERNOR OF IRELAND.

MAY IT PLEASE YOUR EXCELLENCY,

We, the Inspectors of Irish Fisheries, in conformity with the Act of Parliament, beg to submit our Report on the Sea and Inland Fisheries of Ireland for 1870.

THE SEA FISHERIES.

This branch of the fisheries was only intrusted to us in the latter part of 1869. We were unable for the reasons stated in our Report for that year to furnish statistics as to the number of men and boys and craft wholly and partially engaged in fishing.

We experienced considerable difficulty in obtaining full information on those points for 1870. Up to 1869 the coast was divided into thirty-eight divisions, each being under the charge of an Inspecting Commander, on whom devolved the registry of men and boats. No portion of the coast was left unguarded.

The Coast-guard were therefore enabled to ascertain with comparative ease and certainty the number of persons engaged in fishing and the craft employed. From 1868 to 1869 changes took place which threw considerable obstacles in the way of our obtaining accurate statistics.

The registration of fishing vessels and their crews was transferred from the Coast-guard to the Custom House.

The divisions of the former were changed from thirty-eight to thirty-one, most of the limits being altered and extended.

The number of Coast-guard was so much diminished that different parts of the coast were left wholly unguarded, in one place alone for twenty-five miles. Although a small penalty attaches to the non-registration of boats, and that the duty devolves on the Coast-guard, when opportunity occurs, to see that the law is carried out, still from their diminished number and total withdrawal from some portions of the coast, the strict enforcement of the registry regulations became impossible, and several boat owners neglected to register.

Having pointed out to the Admiralty the difficulty we would have in obtaining information, unless instructions were given to the Coast-guard to ascertain the number of boats with their crews, whether registered or not, on the unguarded as well as the guarded part of the coast, orders were issued to afford us the co-operation we requested. Even with the assistance given to us the operation has been a slow, and, in some instances, an expensive one to this department.

As the services of the Coast-guard could only be afforded when not engaged on other duty, the issuing of this Report has in consequence been delayed considerably beyond the time that it would otherwise have appeared. Although we are confident that the returns now presented are as perfect as it is possible to make them, considering the difficulties we have had to contend with, still we deem it well to observe that we apprehend that the crews returned as belonging to the craft only partially engaged in fishing are calculated to convey an exaggerated idea of the actual number. The mode adopted frequently in reference to this class, both by the Customs and Coast-guard, appears to be to register about the number that would be likely to be required to man a boat in the event of its going to fish; supposing, therefore, as often occurs in a locality, that there are six boats, but only available crews for four of them, the number of fishermen which would appear on the registry would be twenty-four, whilst in reality only sixteen existed, allowing four to each boat.

After minutely inquiring into the number of boats, and the crews required for them, along the coast, the Coast-guard return 164 more boats than were registered at the Custom House, but 58 less in the crews, clearly showing that they must have averaged the latter in a different way from the Customs.

We have come to the conclusion that fully one-third may be taken off the 26,374 men returned as partially engaged in fishing, and that 18,000 is nearer the correct number than 26,000.

The number of fishermen returned in 1846, and previous years, represented we believe the actual number, as the greater population enabled every boat to obtain a crew when required. The last Report of our predecessors on the Sea Fisheries, that for 1868, stated that the number of vessels and boats engaged that year was 9,184, and men and boys 39,339. The number of the former in 1870 was 8,909, and of the latter 38,629, showing in the two years a decrease of 185 in the craft, and 710 in the crews.

The following table shows:—

NUMBER of VESSELS and BOATS, MEN and BOYS, EMPLOYED in the COAST FISHERIES, from 1840 to 1871, inclusive.

YEAR.	Vessels and Boats.	Men and Boys.	YEAR.	Vessels and Boats.	Men and Boys.	YEAR.	Vessels and Boats.	Men and Boys.
1846	19,883	113,073	1855	11,251	47,864	1863	11,375	48,601
1848	19,652	81,717	1856	11,069	48,774	1864	9,300	40,946
1849	18,100	71,505	1857	12,758	53,673	1865	9,456	40,802
1850	16,247	68,380	1858	11,833	52,101	1866	9,444	40,063
1851	14,756	64,612	1859	11,881	50,115	1867	9,333	38,444
1852	11,789	58,863	1860	13,483	55,630	1868	9,184	39,339
1853	12,381	49,206	1861	11,845	48,624	1870	8,909	38,629
1854	11,079	49,237	1862	11,590	50,220			

Thus it will be seen that the vessels and boats are now less than half, as compared with 1846, and the crews reduced to nearly a third.

Hitherto no information was afforded as to the number of vessels and boats, and men and boys solely, nearly, and only partially engaged in the fisheries.

We have, however, been able to ascertain that there are solely engaged in fishing—231 first-class vessels; 1,118 second ditto, or boats; 470 third ditto, or boats; or a total of 1,819; and 8,150 men and boys. Nearly altogether employed in fishing—63 first-class vessels; 448 second ditto, or boats; 373 third ditto, or boats; or a total of 884; and 4,104 men and boys. Only partially engaged in fishing—54 first-class vessels; 2,615 second ditto, or boats; 3,627 boats; or a total of 6,296 boats, and 26,374 men and boys. The latter number as already stated being much exaggerated. Besides this we find that the Coast-guard, through misconception of the orders issued by the Board of Trade, have, in some instances, entered boats wholly engaged at salmon fishing as sea-fishery boats.

The greater portion of the boats and men and boys returned as only partially engaged in fishing seldom fish for more than a few days in the year. The boats for the most part are used for cutting and collecting seaweed, carrying sand and turf, conveying passengers and agricultural produce, &c.

When opportunity offers, the owners collect a crew from amongst their neighbours, frequently farmers' sons, and go out for a few hours' fishing. In some instances this does not occur a dozen times in the year; but if even on only one occasion, the boat is deemed a fishing boat, and her chance crew put down as fishermen, although they may have followed the occupation only for a single day during the entire year. Relatively, the capture of fish is now much less than before the famine, by the boats only partially engaged in fishing, on account of the deterioration in the craft and gear, and consequent inability of the owners to follow their calling properly.

Putting aside the large diminution in the number of boats since 1846, it is not too much to say that on a comparison of equal numbers of the boats partially engaged in fishing before that period, with the number now returned under that head, it would be found that the former fished twice as much and captured twice more fish than the latter.

In our first Report (1869) we fully stated the cause of the enormous decline that has taken place in the number of boats and persons engaged in fishing pursuits, viz.: the famine of 1847–8–9, and subsequent years of distress, and pointed out the only remedy which we considered could be successfully applied to arrest further decline, and place the fisheries in a prosperous condition. Another year's experience fully confirms the opinion which we have already expressed to your Excellency, that "no great improvement can be looked for in the sea fisheries until loans are advanced to a portion of the fishermen for the repair and purchase of boats and gear."

Having visited every part of the coast, and fully informed ourselves of the condition of the fishermen, we unhesitatingly pronounce that if much longer time is allowed to pass without our suggestions being carried out, fishing industry will nearly expire on half the coast. Every day's delay will add enormously to the difficulty of restoration, as boats and gear get out of repair, and the owners abandon the pursuit—in many instances their little tracts of ground become absorbed in the larger farms near them—and there is less opportunity for the youthful portion of the sea-coast population becoming acquainted with the mode of managing boats or capturing fish.

Already in many places the coast may be traversed for miles, even where good shelter exists and fish abound, without a boat being seen. This deplorable state of things is certain to increase if a helping hand be not extended to save this important industry from perishing. Ten or twenty thousand pounds, judiciously expended now—not as a gift, but as a loan—would do far more good than a million given away in half-a-dozen years hence. Indeed, no amount of money, if things be suffered to take their present course, could in that time accomplish what might now be done by the outlay of a few thousands, certain to be again nearly all refunded to the State.

Numerous instances have come to our knowledge of industrious fishermen being prevented from adequately pursuing their calling for want of a little money to procure materials, for which they could give satisfactory security.

It is not too much to estimate that if men such as these were aided, within a few years fully a million's worth more of fish would be afforded to the public than there is at present, that the above additional amount would be put in circulation, tending to promote various other industries, the extinction of an important class would be stayed, and a valuable nursery for the Royal and Mercantile Marine preserved.

That loans could be easily and inexpensively administered, and that little or no loss would be likely to be incurred, if due care were observed by the department charged with their administration in obtaining proper security, is fully proved by the operations of "the Society for bettering the Condition of the Poor of Ireland."

To free grants we would be strongly opposed, and consider that much of the benefit likely to result from loans would be marred unless their repayment were strictly enforced.

As the large influx of herrings which set in on a portion of the east coast, and mackerel on a portion of the south, are often erroneously regarded as an indication of the general state of the fisheries of Ireland, we deem it well to call attention to the fact, that owing to the numerous indentations the coast line is estimated at upwards of 2,500 miles.

The length of coast along which the more important herring and mackerel fisheries are carried on does not amount to 250 miles, and the value of the capture, nearly £300,000, amounts to fully two-thirds of all the fish taken around the coast. When, therefore, it is considered that on the remaining 2,250 miles of coast not more than £130,000 is taken, it will be understood why an equal amount of cured fish has to be imported from Norway, Labrador, Canada, Newfoundland, and Scotland, to supply the requirements of the people. As will be seen in the Appendix, the Cornish, Manx, and Scotch boats must have taken by far the greater quantity of the herrings captured on the east coast. The return from Howth states the highest number of boats of each country that fished as follows:—Manx, 95; Cornish, 92; Scotch, 34; Irish, 67.

The same may be said of the mackerel fisheries, so far as regards English and Manx boats, as it appears that at Kinsale for 1870 there were fishing there 95 Manx boats, 25 English, 18 French, and 58 Irish.

During this year there were 197 English and Manx boats against 70 Irish, and the French vessels had increased to 49, most of them double the tonnage of the Irish craft, besides being as a rule better equipped and manned, and able to proceed distances to fish which the Irish boats could not attempt. This superiority may be mainly attributed to the aid given by the French Government to the forwarding of their fisheries.

The Commission on Oyster Fisheries having, in compliance with your Excellency's desire, furnished you with a Report on the state of the Sea Fisheries, so far as they came under their observation when conducting the former inquiry, we deem it well to give the following extract from their Report on the subject of loans, as it fully bears out our statement, and is valuable as expressive of the opinion formed by two independent English gentlemen of great competency who formed a portion of the Commission :—

"It would appear that since 1800 Scotland has received for the promotion of her fisheries fully a million and a quarter sterling more than Ireland.

"We entertain little doubt that if Ireland were only *lent*, on satisfactory security, for the promotion of her sea-coast fisheries, a like sum to that which Scotland has received in excess of Ireland during the last ten years for the same purpose, or even if the Fishery Department were authorized to lend annually a sum equal to that which is voted for Scottish over Irish fisheries, that the latter would, in ten years, without loss to the State, be placed in so flourishing a position as to require little, if any, further aid. Should something of the kind not be done to arrest the present rapid decline of the fisheries it is inevitable that they will sink still lower. We cannot, however, believe that any Government will continue to neglect so obvious a duty as the attempt, at least, to render as available as possible the rich field for increased industry offered by the surrounding seas.

"In the last ten years alone there has been a decrease in fishing craft of 2,697, and in the crews of 10,776 persons. If not arrested in the way we have suggested it is inevitable that this decline will go rapidly on, and that every delay will enormously increase the difficulty of restoration.

"The great change from tillage to pasturage now going on in Ireland renders it the more desirable that anything likely to afford other employment should be availed of.

"Unfortunately, Ireland does not possess the same mineral resources as England and Scotland, or the same advantages of capital, commerce, and manufactures; therefore it is the more incumbent that those on whom the duty devolves should endeavour to render available to the people every industrial resource which Ireland possesses.

"Rarely, perhaps, was there given to any Government such an opportunity of doing so much good at so little risk of loss.

"With the example of what the French Government is doing for its fisheries, and remembering the aid which has been and still is rendered to the Scotch fisheries, it seems incredible that those of Ireland should be left to their fate.

"That the poverty of the coast population, caused by dire visitations of Providence, has alone prevented them from benefiting to the full extent of the plenty contained in the surrounding seas, is proved by the eagerness with which they have taken advantage of every encouragement to engage in fishing pursuits which has been offered to them.

"We feel bound to repeat that we believe nothing of value can be accomplished for the Sea Fisheries until effect be given to the strong recommendations of the two Commissioners and of the Select Committees of 1849 and 1867, combined with the advice of some of the most experienced officers of Government, so as to aid, in the manner suggested, the fishing population in pursuing their avocation with success.

"Should the Legislature lend the assistance sought, and thus enable the willing labourer to provide himself with the implements of his craft, we anticipate that this declining pursuit will ere long be converted into a flourishing industry."

A reference to Appendix 1, containing the report from the Inspecting Commanders of Coast-guard, shows the excellence of the character of the fishermen. No conflicts have taken place between persons pursuing different modes of fishing; and around the entire coast they are described as sober, honest, peaceable, well-conducted, and industrious.

As a proof of their industry, capability, and honesty, we may mention that on the east coast some of the Manx boats are commanded by Irish skippers, and have Irish crews. Several Irish fishermen having no boats of their own go to Scotland and hire themselves to Scotch boat owners during the herring season. An extensive net manufacturer at the Isle of Man frequently gives nets on credit to the east coast fishermen, and has invariably been repaid.

Owing to the precarious nature of the fishing on a large portion of the coast, the possession of a little land is most desirable to the fishermen, to occupy them during the long intervals that they are often prevented from fishing by tempestuous weather.

We find the fishing communities that have got on best are those combining a little farming with fishing. The importance of sustaining the small class of fishermen following both avocations, cannot be over-estimated when the fluctuating character of the large fisheries is taken into consideration.

From time to time large shoals of herrings, mackerel, and pilchards have set in on particular parts of the coast, continue sometimes for years, and then almost totally disappear for a long period—sometimes never re-appearing again.

In 1870, the herring fishery on the east coast was considerably below that of the previous year. The mackerel on the south was unusually abundant, whilst in the present year, notwithstanding that 118 more vessels were fishing, the capture was fully a third less as compared with 1870.

More than 100 years ago pilchards set in on the Cork coast in enormous quantities. After some years they entirely disappeared, but have lately re-appeared again in vast shoals, having probably abandoned the coast of Cornwall, where the take is said to have fallen to less than half what it was some years ago; that of 1870 was better, however, than for some previous years. Unfortunately, however, the people are unable, for want of sufficient appliances for the capture and cure of this fish, to avail fully of the riches brought to their very doors.

The following brief sketch will give a general idea of the nature and extent of the fishing on the Irish coast:—

From Dublin to Waterford trawling operations are carried on by from thirty to forty trawlers, which supply the Dublin market. When an excess of superior fish takes place, which does not often occur, it is sent to England.

The Nymph Bank, which extends along this coast, is said to abound with fish, but, owing to its distance—in some places thirty miles from shore—few vessels venture so far. A large quantity of herrings are taken on a part of this coast, where also are situated the principal oyster banks off Arklow and Wexford.

From Waterford to Cork, the take of every description of fish is insignificant. At Dungarvan there were formerly 100 hookers engaged in the capture of hake and ling. Not more than six are now occasionally engaged. The almost extinction of the fishermen of this place is attributable in a measure to their not holding land.

When adverse times for the fisheries came during the famine, having nothing else to fall back on they were obliged to succumb, whilst in the same bay the fishing community of Ring, holders of a little land, survived, attributable in some measure, too, to the judicious loans advanced to them by the Society of Friends, which they honestly repaid.

From Cork to Cape Clear the great feature is the mackerel fishery, of which Kinsale is the head-quarters. During 1870 the take was considerable, but owing to insufficient means of transit the fish on some occasions sold as low as two shillings per hundred. Once, indeed, it is said that a boatload was offered for nothing as there was no ice to preserve or steam-boats to carry away.

Since then, however, ample provision has been made for conveying to England, ten steamers being sometimes employed—two of which were put on by the aid of Lady Burdett Coutts, who also some years since conferred considerable benefits on the fishermen of Cape Clear Island.

Nearly 100,000 boxes, containing 120 each, of mackerel were sold at Kinsale in 1870 at prices varying from two shillings to thirty shillings per hundred and twenty.

A good deal of herrings occasionally appear off this part of the coast where they are supposed by some to strike first, but the capture is inconsiderable, owing to the boats not being adequately provided with herring nets.

From Cape Clear to the Shannon, considering the number and excellence of the harbours, the various good trawling grounds, and the vast shoals of fish which set in occasionally, the number of boats, particularly trawlers, is very small.

Bantry Bay, Kenmare Estuary, Dingle Bay, and Brandon Bay, offer great inducements for trawling, which is, however, prohibited for the present in the latter.

Along this part of the coast, for the last few years, immense quantities of pilchards have appeared; comparatively few have been taken for want of suitable nets.

The fishermen have a strong objection to take them in the nets they have, alleging that the oil exuding from the fish is injurious to the net. The nets in Cornwall are said to be prepared in a peculiar manner to prevent this.

Much money might be realized if the fishermen had suitable nets, and if a few curing houses were established to press the oil from the fish and prepare them after the Cornish mode for foreign markets.

A serious drawback to the development of the fisheries along this part of the coast is the difficulty and high cost of transit to the large markets.

Tralee Bay is the only place where oysters are found in any quantity. The produce has much fallen off from over dredging and export of small oysters.

From the Shannon to Galway the fishing is very insignificant, such as there is being chiefly carried on by Curraghs, or canoes covered with canvass, carrying usually four men. The usual mode of fishing is by long and short lines for the capture of cod, ling, pollock, bream, &c.

In Galway Bay, although, in compliance with the protests and opposition of the Claddagh fishermen, a large portion of it is closed against trawling, the condition of the fishermen has not improved, and they are decreasing in number. The Inspecting Commander reports that restrictions are no longer necessary, and that the Claddagh men are not now opposed to it.

Some of the best oyster fattening beds exist on the Clare coast, and some few natural banks, but the produce much diminished.

From Galway to Sligo there are few points where fishing is carried on, except by canoes, owing to the exposed nature of the coast, and the sudden and severe tempests to which it is subject.

At Inishbofin Island a small fishing company was lately established for the purchase of fish, which is most abundant; as the terms of co-partnership precludes the company from the purchase or hire of boats or fishing-tackle, or to make loans for same, the poverty of the islanders prevents them from taking anything like the quantity that might be taken if they had sufficient appliances. At Clew, Blacksod, and Broadhaven Bays good natural oyster banks exist—much deteriorated from over dredging and taking away small oysters.

From Sligo to Lough Swilly. A few trawlers in Sligo and Donegal Bays—the restrictions, by nearly general consent, removed from the latter without any ill effects since resulting. The remainder of the fishing in those bays is carried on by small boats usually engaged in line-fishing, and occasionally seining. Along the coast of Donegal, up to Lough Swilly, very little fishing carried on by the few small boats that occasionally go out. The coast is wild and stormy.

At Sheephaven some years ago a fishing company was established, which lasted only a short time, although abundance of fish were caught.

In Lough Swilly a few trawlers obtain employment, and sometimes large shoals of herrings enter; there are, however, few boats provided with nets.

In Sligo Bay and Lough Swilly some oysters are got, but the supply has largely decreased.

From Lough Swilly to Belfast Lough. In Lough Foyle there are a few small trawlers and line-fishermen. On the remainder of the Derry and Antrim coast little fishing is carried on. Good banks are said to exist some distance out to sea, but too far for the description of boats in general use to venture. The fishing in Belfast Lough confined to some eight trawlers and a few linesmen; both appear to get on harmoniously since the removal of restrictions on trawling more than a year hence. A few trawlers fish off Groomsport.

From Belfast Lough to Dublin (which completes the circuit of Ireland) no fishing of importance, until Ardglass is reached; from thence to Dublin is the principal scene of the herring fishery of the east coast. Ardglass, Annalong, Kilkeel, Balbriggan, Skerries, and Howth being the principal harbours from whence herring vessels are fitted out and sheltered, the highest number of craft engaged in 1870 was under 300, the majority of which were English, Scotch, and Manx. Curing establishments have from time to time been attempted at Howth, but all failed.

This was mainly attributable to two causes—first, when the herrings appear on the Irish coast, which they usually do much earlier than on the Scotch, the price for them in the fresh state is more remunerative than curing them; secondly, it is alleged that on the Irish coast the herring is much too fat to render it desirable for curing.

Although excellent trawling grounds exist along the east coast, prohibitions extend from Howth to St. John's Point, in the county Down, to the great loss of the consumer. Around the entire coast, of which we have given the foregoing rapid sketch, nothing deserving to be called curing establishments exist; here and there a few fish are salted, the greater part intended for almost immediate use. The absence of curing houses frequently deters the fishermen from going out, as, in the event of a large take, there are often no means of disposing of the surplus after the immediate wants of the neighbourhood are supplied.

As already stated, the people even on the coast have to depend for cured fish on supplies from Scotland, Norway, Newfoundland, Labrador, and Canada.

Trawling.

During the year we removed trawling restrictions only from Donegal Bay, being anxious to proceed slowly and cautiously in reversing the acts of predecessors with regard to the prohibitions imposed by them on trawling. No collisions whatever between trawlers and persons pursuing other modes of fishing have reached us from the places we have opened—Lough Swilly, Belfast Lough, Kenmare Estuary, and Donegal Bay. As the opinions we expressed in our last report respecting restrictions on trawling are strengthened by our experience since, we propose, as soon as other engagements allow, to make inquiries in conformity with the 32 and 33 Vic., cap. 92, into the expediency of making further alterations.

Oyster Fisheries.

The produce from the Oyster Fisheries, so far as the sum realized, continues about the same, under £50,000 a year, half of which is realized from the Arklow and Wexford Banks. Although no total failure of spatting can be said to have occurred on any of the public beds, so far as ascertainable, for some years, still the deposit of spat in some places for the last two years has been very trifling.

Nearly everywhere there has been over dredging and too great an exportation of small oysters. The desirability of buoying off portions of certain banks, so as to prevent dredging for some time, and thus to enable them to recover, and the prevention of the exportation of oysters under a certain size, are now engaging our attention.

During the year we have granted only one oyster licence. Very little appears to have been done in the way of production by the holders of licences, some of which we shall probably deem it advisable to withdraw in consequence.

The inclosed system of cultivation has not in any instance been attended with a success worth mentioning. The attempts, as a whole, have been a failure.

The Report of the Royal Commission on Oyster Fisheries, in all of which we concur, has been so recently laid before your Excellency, that we deem it unnecessary to go at present into further length on a subject so fully dealt with in that Report.

SALMON AND INLAND FISHERIES.

With regard to the salmon fisheries, we are glad to be in a position to say that our anticipation of improvement, as expressed in our last report, has been fully realized.

The past year has been one of progress in all that relates to these fisheries. The take of fish has been greater than in 1869, and in many places probably much more than for previous years, and there is still every reason to expect that this improvement will go on steadily, as the laws for the protection of the fish during the spawning season, and the regulations which we are empowered to make to prevent over capture, are firmly administered. The quantity of fish sent to the London market from Ireland has been greatly in excess of that exported in any year since 1866, and, though this may, to a certain extent, be taken as an evidence of the productive character of our salmon fisheries, it should be borne in mind that in consequence of the increased means of transport to all parts of England, it only bears a very small proportion to that which finds its way to most of the local markets of England, while the quantity sold in the markets of this country cannot be ascertained, though it must be considerable. The great *desideratum* is the supply of fish to the public, and this has been steadily progressing; and, as we said already, with every prospect of continuing to do so.

In addition to the evidences of progressive improvement to which we have referred, we adduce a few instances of the increased and increasing value of the salmon fisheries of this country:—

A few years ago about four miles of a river was sold in the Landed Estates Court for £5,000. The same property has been lately valued at over £45,000.

A portion of another river (not exceeding six miles) has been lately sold in the same court for upwards of £45,000.

These were what may be called commercial fisheries, though at the same time there are very valuable angling waters attached to them.

Rents of commercial fisheries have in many instances more than trebled. Fisheries have increased for the same properties from £2,400 to £4,500, from £300 to £1,200, and from £30 to £140 a year.

Many other instances of the increased values of the commercial fisheries might be given, but the foregoing will be sufficient to show the great and improving value of this branch of the salmon fisheries.

It may, however, be said that this is accomplished at a sacrifice to a certain extent of the fisheries in the upper waters. The following schedule of the increased rents of upper water fisheries will prove the contrary. We dissent from the theory advanced by some, that the increased value of commercial or tidal fisheries is no proof of a general prosperity. We hold that no branch of the fisheries can be in a thriving condition, or be permanently benefited, without the other being proportionately improved. The prosperity of the tidal fishermen must, to a great extent, depend on the upper waters being in a good condition, and on the cordial co-operation of the riparian proprietors; while the latter depend almost wholly on the tidal fishermen for providing funds to protect the fish during that part of the year when its protection or otherwise, must prove of the most vital consequence to all interests.

In the upper or freshwater portions of *one river alone* in Ireland, rents have increased to the following extent:—

Old rents.	Present rents.	Old rents	Present rents.
£4,	£30	£30,	£100
£40, £75, £120,	£330	£30,	£120
£20,	£120	£10,	£120
£50,	£150	£40,	£260

Many instances of other rivers might also be given to show the greatly increasing value of the upper water fisheries, and it is very probable that this value will go on increasing, as the demand for fisheries is so great that it is with difficulty even a small portion of waters can be had in almost any locality.

We do not think we exaggerate the value of the salmon fisheries when we estimate them as being worth over £400,000 a year.

Although the past season, being probably the driest on record, was most unfavourable to the angler, yet in many rivers angling has been prosperous; on the whole, however, it cannot be put down as having been a good year for angling. This could not be attributed to deficiency in the quantity of fish, but, as we have stated, to the unusually dry weather which continued almost throughout the whole year.

The upper waters have been better stocked with breeding fish than for many years past, and we have every reason for believing that in most of the districts, increased protection has been afforded.

No doubt very grave offences are committed, particularly in the destruction of breeding fish far up in the country, but the number of these offences are yearly diminishing, and we hope that by a firm, at the same time temperate enforcement of the laws, which are generally sufficient to meet almost any case that may arise, these offences will steadily diminish. There is no offence deserving of more severe punishment than that of killing fish during the spawning season. It not only tends to destroy a most valuable resource, but poaching has a most demoralizing effect on those pursuing it. It is, therefore, gratifying to us to be able to say that wherever it is known and felt that the laws will be rigidly enforced, offences have diminished, and it should be a great encouragement to the authorities to enforce the law in places where such offences are not now uncommon, when it is known their doing so must eventually have the tendency of preventing other crimes which are sure to follow the poacher's life.

The funds at the disposal of the Boards of Conservators are insufficient for effectual protection in many localities, but we are in hopes of seeing those funds largely augmented by a revision of the licence duties and the valuations of fisheries, while the formation of angling clubs in most of our good angling rivers will prove of the greatest possible advantage to both upper and lower waters.

In most, if not all of the rivers in Ireland, where an exclusive or several fishery is enjoyed in the lower waters, the proprietors consider it their advantage to protect at their own cost the fish in the upper waters during the spawning season, independently of the amount they have contributed in the shape of licence duty; and this is done altogether independent of the riparian proprietors.

In one river we have been informed that the tidal proprietor expends nearly £1,000 a year on protection, in addition to his licence duty, which is also considerable.

Taking all the circumstances connected with the present state of the salmon fisheries, their production and value, and the increasing interest displayed in their protection, into consideration, we look with confidence to the future, believing that unless some exceptional causes should occur, we may anticipate continued prosperity.

Close Seasons.

When we came into office we found that a decision which had been made by our immediate predecessors, in accordance with a precedent by their predecessors, in one district, had the effect, according to the opinion of the Law Officers, of invalidating the order made by them with respect to the close season fixed by that order. It became our duty, therefore, to look into the orders affecting the various districts in Ireland, and we found that analogous errors had been made with regard to other districts.

We are not empowered under the Fishery Laws to change the season in any river unless on the application of some person or persons interested in the fisheries of that river or district. On receipt of applications, and after the fullest inquiries by evidence on oath, we have during the past year made changes in the following districts, viz.:—Wexford, Waterford, Lismore, Killarney, Limerick, and Ballina.

It would be impossible for us to give, in a report like this, even an abstract of the evidence taken in each district, but the meetings at which the evidence on this subject, and on which we came to our decisions, have been held in every district at places the most convenient for all parties. In some districts we have held meetings in as many as nine different places, so anxious were we that all interests should be fairly represented. In weighing the evidence, which is almost invariably one-sided, according to the locality in which it is given, we have considered the nature of the river, its capabilities, the extent and number of engines used thereon, the time at which the fish are in their best condition for the market, the fair time that should be allowed for fishing with all kinds of engines, so as to allow a fair distribution of the fish throughout the length of each river, and, above all, to insure a sufficiency of breeding stock without which all efforts for the improvement of the salmon fisheries would be in vain. In our decisions, which we believe have given satisfaction to the parties most deeply interested, we have thought it prudent to curtail the season for netting at the latter end of the season as much as possible, with the view of preventing the capture of the autumn fish, which are invariably the best breeders. We do not, of course, pretend to say that some of our decisions give universal satisfaction. We did not, and could not, hope to please everyone, but expect that a few years will prove the sound policy of our decisions, and we anticipate that the few who now think they may be immediately injured by the changes we have made, will hereafter admit the correctness of our views. Except in one river, the Slaney, we have not permitted netting in the month of September, and there it is allowed until the 15th of that month, while we prohibited it up to the 9th of April, in consequence of the vast number of slats or spent fish that used to be taken in that river. The old Acts of Parliament fixed a much later season for netting in that river than we have allowed, but the freedom from netting later on in the year will secure a large stock of good breeding fish. Indeed, had we fixed a season for this river according to our own inclinations, and not according to the evidence, we would have prohibited all netting during September.

In Waterford district we have fixed the season for netting in tidal and upper waters from 16th February to 31st August. The season previously fixed had been for one portion of the tidal waters, viz. the Waterford harbour, the same as we have fixed for the entire of the tidal waters, and for the rest of the tidal and upper waters, from 1st March to 31st August. The law officers of the Crown having given their opinion that we had only power to prescribe one close season for the tidal portion of a particular river, and had "no power to make an arbitrary division of a river, and fix divers close seasons for different portions thereof," compelled us to make the opening of the season uniform on the 16th February, as it would have been unjust to have deprived the harbour fishermen of working in the latter portion of that month.

In Lismore district the alteration made from the old season is to allow all netting to commence on 16th February, instead of 3rd of March as before, and prohibiting it after 31st August, instead of 15th September.

In Killarney we have allowed one river (the Waterville) to commence on 1st January, instead of 10th as formerly, and to close on 16th July, instead of 31st as before. In no district probably is there such a variation of the natural seasons for fish in the various rivers. Two rivers, the Laune and the Maine, discharge into the same estuary, their mouths being little more than half a mile asunder. In the former the finest fish are found in January, in the latter no good fish are seen until May.

In Limerick we have allowed netting to commence on 1st February, instead of 12th as formerly, and we have stopped all on 15th July, instead of 12th August as before. This greatly extended close season has been forced on us by the fact of so many engines being now, and since 1864, used in the tidal waters of the Shannon; and it was the only means we could adopt to prevent an overcapture or to secure a sufficient stock for the upper waters. It no doubt appears hard to prohibit netting so early in the tidal waters, but we feel convinced that the hardship, if at all real at present, will not be permanent, as the escape of such a large quantity of fine fish after the 15th July to the upper waters will, if protected there during the winter, secure an ample return in a few years. It is not unreasonable to assume that the 8lb. fish of August, which to the tidal fisher is only worth at the most 6*d.* per lb., or 4*s.*, if allowed to escape, will, after depositing its spawn, and return again from the sea in the spring, be at least 16lbs. weight, and worth 2*s.* 6*d.* per lb., or £2. These are not exaggerated estimates of increase in either weight or value. The tidal fishermen will have the first fruits of this, and it is to be expected that in the meantime the rod fishers, after 15th July, will have a good harvest for the remainder of their season, when all nets are removed.

In Ballina we have prohibited netting in tidal waters between the 12th August and the 16th March, instead of 19th August and 4th February, and in the upper waters between 31st July and 1st February, instead of 19th August and 4th February as formerly. We have made a considerable curtailment of the netting in this district, and indeed it is only fair to say that the proprietors of the estuary or tidal fishing freely gave up this time, believing it would be eventually for the benefit of the river to curtail the season; but that it was proved to us that except in the months of February and March the Ballina weirs, since the opening of the Queen's gap in 1863, caught very few fish, and that to deprive the proprietors of fishing during these months would in reality have the effect of almost extinguishing their property, we would have considerably curtailed the season for netting in the upper waters at the commencement of the year, as we believe, when the netting is carried on in this river at that time of year, a considerable quantity of slats or spent fish are killed. Fortunately, however, for the river, few proprietors net early in the year. The weirs are in the upper or fresh waters, but they cannot take spent fish, and we were therefore forced to allow the netting in the fresh waters to commence much earlier than we would have wished, not having the power, according to the opinion before referred to, to make a regulation for it different from the weirs.

The foregoing remarks have reference exclusively to all the changes we have made in the seasons for netting during the year 1870, and we now proceed to make a few observations on the seasons for angling.

In 1842 the Act of Parliament fixed a uniform season for the whole of Ireland, not only for angling but also for netting. The principle of uniformity was found to be most erroneous, and inflicted grievous injury not alone on individuals, but on rivers; in the one case, by not allowing the fish to be taken in its proper season and finest condition, and in the other by allowing it to be taken at a time when it was not only perfectly unfit for food, but when its capture was most destructive to the river. The Commissioners, after a few years' experience of the evil effects of this system, made changes more approaching to the natural requirements of each river, until the Act passed in 1863 again fixed a uniform season for angling to be from 1st February to 1st November; and by some oversight the power to change this season, if required in any district, was not provided in the Act, while the power to change the season for netting was retained in the hands of the Governing Department. So matters remained, not, however, without complaints from nearly every district in Ireland of the evil effects of continuing the season open generally throughout the country so late as the 1st of November, until the Act of 1869 passed giving us similar powers of changing the season for angling to that we had already possessed in reference to netting. These powers we have exercised during the year 1870 in the places enumerated before, and we think it as well to append herewith a schedule showing the seasons which existed in these districts previous to the Act of 1863, and those fixed by us in 1870:—

—	Seasons previous to Act of 1863.	Fixed by Act of 1863.	Fixed in 1870.
Wexford,	1st April to 28th September, and 1st March to 28th September.	1st Feb. and 1st Nov.	1st March to 30th September.
Waterford,	1st March to 28th September,	do.,	1st February to 15th September.
Lismore,	14th February to 9th October,	do.,	1st February to 30th September.
Killarney,	18th January to 15th September,	do,	1st February to 30th September.
	Maine and Inney, 1st May to 28th September.	do.,	Maine, 1st March to 30th September.
	Currane, 1st April to 15th September,	do.,	Laune and Carra, 16th January to 30th September.
Limerick,	12th February to 15th September,	do.,	1st February to 30th September.
	Between Kerry Head and Dunmore Head, 1st April to 15th October.	do.,	For rivers between Kerry Head and Dunmore Head, 1st April to 15th September.
	Feale, Geale, and Cashen, 1st May to 15th October.	do,	Feale, Geale, and Cashen, and Doonbeg, 1st May to 30th September.
Ballina,	1st February to 19th August,	do.,	1st February to 15th September, and for Palmerston and Easkey Rivers, 1st June to 30th Sept.

These seasons have been settled by us with the concurrence of, we may say, all the persons who have any substantial or vested interests in the districts, and we have no doubt they will prove most beneficial. The general feeling throughout almost the whole country is, and has been for the last six years, that angling has been allowed to be continued too late. We have not extended it, as may be seen by the changes above, into the month of October; and there are indeed only a very few rivers in Ireland where angling in October will be advocated by any person having any *bona fide* interest in the river. In these few rivers, and wherever it is satisfactorily proved to us that angling may with safety be allowed, we shall, of course, admit it during that month.

It is not our province or wish to discuss in a report to your Excellency the merits or demerits of a uniform season for fishing in all rivers; but we cannot help saying that the trial having been made in 1842 with all kinds of engines, and again in 1863 with rods and lines, has completely proved the fallacy of the doctrine, and showed its absurdity, and that the only true mode of acting is to fix for each river such a season as is suitable to its character.

In the Appendix will be found a Schedule of Close Seasons in every district in Ireland, up to the 1st January, 1871.

By-Laws.

The Act of 1842 empowers us from time to time, as may become necessary, to make and ordain such by-laws, rules, orders, and regulations as shall seem expedient for the more effectual government, management, protection, and improvement of the fisheries, and from time to time to repeal, rescind, or vary the same, and substitute others in lieu thereof, and to impose and prescribe any conditions and restrictions for the regulation of the fisheries and the preservation of good order among the persons engaged therein, and in relation to the times and seasons at which the taking the several species of fish shall commence and cease, or the times and places, or the manner at and in which any net or engine to be employed in the fisheries shall be used, and also as to the description and form of nets to be used in the fisheries, and the size of the meshes thereof, or to the prohibition thereof, or of any practice whatsoever tending to impede the taking of fish, or to be in any manner detrimental to the fisheries or to any other matter or thing which shall in any manner relate to the government and protection of the fisheries.

The same Act provides that no by-law shall be in force until approved by your Excellency in Council, and that any person feeling himself aggrieved may appeal to your Excellency in Council.

During the past year we have made a number of by-laws affecting the fisheries in particular localities, an abstract of which will be found in the Appendix.

Although the law does not prescribe any particular steps to be taken before making a by-law, we have made it a rule not to enact any without first calling a meeting in the locality of the persons interested in the fisheries, and taking evidence on oath as to its necessity or propriety; and at such meetings we have always taken care to inform the public that any person feeling himself aggrieved had the power of appeal to your Excellency.

In no case, however, save one, has any appeal been made against any by-law we have made, and in that case we merely continued one made by our predecessors, prohibiting the use of nets in a certain portion of the Bandon river, county Cork, for a period of three years.

Even in this case, although it was apparent to us, that the by-law made by our predecessors, prohibiting netting in a part of the river for three years, had not been in force long enough to prove its efficacy on the fisheries of the river, and that it should be continued for a further period of three years, we took no steps towards this object until we had called meetings both at Bandon and Kinsale, received evidence on oath, and made ourselves perfectly familiar with all the circumstances of the river, and the effect of the use of nets in that part of it where it was proposed to prohibit them.

The Committee of the Privy Council, after hearing counsel in opposition to the proposed by-law, unanimously recommended that it should be sanctioned.

The power of making by-laws, such as is given to us, is one which requires great care and circumspection in exercising. It is one, however, that is absolutely necessary to be invested in the Governing Department, as it would be utterly impossible for Parliament to enact laws that would be applicable to the circumstances of each locality or river; and when that power is controlled by the right of appeal, injury to individuals is not likely to arise; while either the permission or the prohibition in the by-law is likely to be for the benefit of the fisheries in general of the locality, and if it should afterwards prove that it had not the desired object, we have the power to alter or repeal it.

In addition to the by-laws given in the Appendix to which we refer, we received during the past year applications for a great number of others, but, on inquiry, the evidence adduced in support of their necessity was not in our opinion sufficient to warrant us in acceding to the requests, and we therefore declined granting them, or adjourned the hearing.

These by-laws, as we have before said, were made under the powers given to us by the Act of 1842. The Act of 1869, however, conferred on us additional powers in other respects, on which we now beg to offer a few observations.

The Definitions of Mouths of Rivers and Estuaries.

The 10th section of the Act of 1869, 32 & 33 Vic., c. 92, directs that the Inspectors shall, in addition to their other duties, as soon as they conveniently can, make local and other inquiry into the expediency and necessity of altering, amending, or repealing any definition of the boundaries of the mouth or estuary of any river, or of making new definitions of the boundaries of the mouths or estuaries of rivers. We presumed that the duty of defining mouths of rivers and estuaries which was imposed on our predecessors had been exercised with all the care that was necessary for such an important work, and therefore, although, as far as our duty was concerned, the law was mandatory, we made no move in the matter at first until we had received applications from parties interested to alter, amend, or repeal any of the definitions heretofore made.

The first received by us was from the owner of the Bush River, in the county of Antrim. The definition of the estuary of that river made by our predecessors had the effect of prohibiting the use of two bag-nets which had been in operation for a number of years some distance outside the mouth of that river. They were owned by the proprietor of the river, and were erected in a several fishery.

To alter or repeal any act of our predecessors called for the greatest care on our part. But when this was probably one of the most difficult subjects that could be brought before us to determine, it required more than ordinary care on our part. We therefore consulted the best authorities as to the definition or meaning of "an estuary of a river."

We all inspected the place, afterwards held a public meeting in the locality and received evidence on the subject, and, after going fully into the question, we unanimously decided that it was our duty to repeal the definition made by our predecessors. We were much aided by an important opinion which had been received by the proprietor from the ablest legal authority in England, and we subjoin for your Excellency's information the following copy of the case and opinion which were laid before us.

Case and Opinion.

1. The Salmon Fishery (Ireland) Act, 1863 [26 & 27 Vict. c. 114,] contains the following provisions:—

s. 3. "After the passing of this Act no bag-net shall be placed or allowed to continue in any river or the estuary of any river, as such river or estuary has been defined by the Commissioners of Fisheries, or shall be defined by the Commissioners under this Act, or within a distance of less than three statute miles from the mouth of any river as defined as aforesaid.

"Any bag-net placed or continued in contravention of this section shall be deemed to be a common nuisance, and may be taken possession of or destroyed; and any bag-net so placed and continued, and any salmon taken by such bag-net shall be forfeited; and in addition thereto the owner of a bag-net placed or continued in contravention of this section shall, for each day of so placing or allowing the same to be continued, incur a penalty of not less than £5 and not exceeding £20.

"But no person shall incur any penalty under this section in respect of any bag-net if he removes the same within fourteen days after the passing of this Act. Provided always that no bag-net now legally existing shall be liable to be abated or removed, or be deemed illegal under this Act by reason of its being within three miles of the mouth of a river in the whole of which, including all tributary rivers and lakes upon its course, the proprietor of such bag-net has the exclusive right of catching salmon."

The 5th section empowers the Commissioners to inquire as to fixed nets.

The 6th section provides that where any fixed net other than a bag-net prohibited by that Act was in use at the time of the passing of the Act, and any person claims to have erected the same in pursuance of the Act of the 5th and 6th Vict. c. 106, the Commissioners may, on proof being given to their satisfaction that such fixed net has been erected in pursuance of the said provisions, certify to that effect, stating on the certificate the situation, size, and description of the net, and the person who has the right to erect the same in pursuance of such last-mentioned provisions.

The 17th section is as follows:—

s. 17. "Notwithstanding anything contained in the Salmon Fisheries Acts, or any definition of the Commissioners acting in pursuance of those Acts, the Commissioners under this Act shall mark out, by reference to maps or otherwise, what are to be the boundaries of mouths of rivers and estuaries, and the boundaries between the tidal and fresh water portions of every river, for the purposes of this Act and the said Salmon Fisheries Acts, with power, where several streams flow into a common mouth or estuary, to declare that the outlets of such streams form separate mouths or estuaries. The Commissioners may also define the point or points of mouths of rivers or estuaries from which distances are to be measured under this Act and the Salmon Fisheries Acts."

2. At the time of the passing of the Salmon Fishery (Ireland) Act, 1863, Sir Edmund Macnaghten was the sole proprietor of the river Bush, in the north of the county of Antrim. The river Bush is a small river, some fifteen or sixteen miles long. In the latter part of its course it averages fifty or sixty feet in breadth, and at its ordinary level has about sufficient water to supply two mills. It falls into the Atlantic ocean at the west side of an open bay something under an English mile in breadth.

3. Sir Edmund Macnaghten was also the owner of a several fishery extending along the sea coast for a short distance to the west, and for several miles to the east of the mouth of the river.

4. In the open season of 1862, and at the time of the passing of the Act of 1863, Sir Edmund's tenant had two bag-nets legally erected, one on the west and the other on the east of the mouth of the Bush, the latter being distant about three-quarters of a mile from the river mouth.

5. In August, 1864, the Commissioners under the Act of 1863 held a local inquiry into the title of those who claimed the right of erecting fixed nets.

6. At this inquiry Sir Edmund Macnaghten established his title to the several fishery in the sea as claimed by him, and he also proved to the satisfaction of the Commissioners that he had the exclusive right of catching salmon in the whole of the river Bush, including all tributary rivers and lakes in its course. The Bush was the only river in Ireland in which such a right was then established before the Commissioners.

7. In the result, however, this proved a very barren success. What the Commissioners gave with one hand they took away with the other. For they so defined what they termed the estuary of the river Bush as to include Sir Edmund's bag nets on both sides of the river mouth, which were the only two bag-nets within three miles of the mouth of the Bush. And by a singular coincidence, which made the case appear the harder, the line bounding the estuary, as defined by the Commissioners, was found exactly to fall along the line in which the eastern net had been set in the open season of 1863.

8. In their first report of 1864, the Commissioners stated the principles upon which they had acted in making their definitions in the following words:—

"The 17th section empowers the Commissioners, according to their opinion (in which, however, all do not coincide, Mr. Morris differing), to mark out, by reference to maps or otherwise, what are to be the boundaries of "mouths of rivers and estuaries," and we have given as much time to this duty as we could spare from our judicial inquiries.

"The objects with which these definitions are made are to be found in the 5 & 6 Vic., c. 106, s. 27; 13 & 14 Vic., s. 44; and in the 3rd section of 26 & 27 Vic., c. 114. The first two of these Acts prohibit the use of draught nets within half a mile seawards, coastwards, or inwards of the mouth of any river which is less than a quarter of a mile in breadth between the banks; and in case of dispute as to the position of the mouth, the then Commissioners were empowered to fix its position. In some instances of narrow rivers this was done.

"The last-mentioned Act, 26 & 27 Vic., c. 114, s. 3, prohibits, as just stated, the use of bag-nets within estuaries or within three miles of the mouth of any river.

"We have held meetings and taken evidence in the following districts, giving in each case as long and wide notice as possible, both of our visits and of the purpose for which it was held. Those districts were:—1. Waterford; 2. Lismore; 3. Cork; 4. Bantry; 5. Kenmare; 6. Drogheda; 7. Ballycastle; 8. Coleraine; 9. Londonderry; 10. Letterkenny; 11. Donegal; 12. Sligo; and 13. Limerick. The proprietors were generally represented by counsel, and much evidence was given as to the natural features of the different rivers. We met with a conflict and great diversity of opinion as to the rules which should guide us in fixing these definitions, and therefore we think it may be expedient to explain the principles upon which we have acted.

"First, as regards estuaries:—

"There was no object in determining the limits of estuaries under the fishery laws until the recent Act was passed; but a definition of an estuary was given by the 1st section of 13 & 14 Vic., c. 88. It is there declared that 'the words estuary or bay shall include and extend to any harbour or roadstead.' We have here a statutable definition, but there may be, and are, many places where a natural estuary is to be found, although there is no harbour or roadstead in the locality. In these cases we have defined the estuary according to the physical characteristics of the locality.

"It is difficult to give an abstract definition of an estuary. The dictionaries generally describe it as an arm of the sea, but we consider that reference must be made to a number of features, all of which need not be found to exist in each case, but that the presence of a majority determines the limits. An estuary may in general terms be described as the area in which the fresh and salt waters of the river and sea commingle. The features by which this may be limited and defined can be ascertained by examination and evidence. The tests are those which show the influence of the fresh water; and so long as that influence has power to affect and mark itself definedly upon the ocean we consider the estuary to extend. This fresh water influence may be detected by analysis, by taste, by the presence in the estuary of marine vegetable, and animal forms of life, by the formation of the land at the mouth of the river, and beyond the mouth; by the banks or bars formed in part by the deposit brought from inland, in part by the conflict between the river and the ocean currents, and by the channels cut and kept scoured by the outward discharge of the inland waters. No one test is sufficient, but none should be disregarded; for instance, a river in time of flood may be traced five, ten, fifty miles at sea by the discoloration of the pure ocean water. The trace of such colour should not extend the estuary to that distance, but on the other hand such evidence of the presence of the fresh water must not be lost sight of in determining the limits of an estuary.

"The catchment basin of the river whose estuary has to be determined is to some extent an index to the size; but on the other hand, a river that is confined between headlands at its junction, and after its junction with the sea, may demand a larger estuary than another of equal or even greater size which runs straight into the sea. In the last case the volume of the fresh water spreads over the open ocean; its trace, except in floods, is almost instantaneously lost, and the power and velocity of its current are overcome. A bar is not uncommonly thrown up outside the mouths of these rivers, and this, together with the set of the tides, the distance to which the fresh is traceable in floods, and the volume of fresh water discharged, are the points which must determine the limits of the estuary. But in the rivers which are confined within headlands, the *fauces terræ*, as they have been termed in the Scotch courts, compress the descending stream, and, by preventing its expansion, give endurance to its strength. Further, the fresh water, which in the open-mouthed river is carried along the coast by the tide and swallowed in the sea, is in the confined river dammed back by each flood-tide until, in the freshes of large rivers of this description, such as the Ness in Scotland, and the Shannon in Ireland, the area is filled with water almost fresh at a part which in dry weather is occupied by the pure salt sea; and in these cases it is common to find the ebb tide running on the surface seven or eight hours, and even almost continuously, instead of dividing the twelve hours with the flood; so that during the flood tide a ship of twenty feet draught will be riding to the flood, and a vessel of half that draught heading the contrary way, under the influence of the descending fresh-water current.

"Thus, though the catchment basin of a river must be considered in determining the extent of its estuary, the formation of the land at the river's junction with the sea to some extent overrules that test.

"The tests by which the mouth of a river should be fixed are similar to those just mentioned, but they must be more strongly marked. We commenced our inquiry under the opinion that the mouth was to be placed at the spot where at low water of spring-tides the inland current met that of the sea; but an examination of the great number of rivers included in the districts we have named led us to modify that opinion. In some rivers, such as the Annagassan and Boyne, such a test would place the mouth of the river during all conditions of tide but that of low water at half a mile to one and a half miles in the open sea; and we have therefore taken the river, tidal and fresh, to end where its banks are lost, or where they expand so much that the space between loses the character of a river channel, and we have fixed the mouth at that spot.

"The estuary will in this view, which we have well considered, and submit with some confidence is the true one, extend from the limit of the fresh and tidal waters to the limit of the tidal and salt.

"The mouth may be more or less up or down this area, discharging the fresh or the mingled fresh and salt water into the outer portion of the estuary.

"In such a case as the Foyle, the mouth of the river will be where Lough Foyle spreads broadly out and receives the inland waters of the river, the basin or lough forming the body of the bottle, of which the river is the neck. In such a case as the Shannon, confined by banks almost until the Atlantic is reached, the mouth of the river and the estuary will be almost coterminous; but, in all cases, if our view be right, something of the estuary, be it small or great, must extend beyond the mouth of the river."

9. It was understood at the time, and indeed it appears from the passage quoted above, that Mr. Morris, the legal commissioner, dissented from the views of his two colleagues, as expressed in the report.

10. It will be observed that the Commissioners in their report lay down this principle, that every river necessarily has an estuary, and in each case they proceeded to look for the estuary outside the river mouth according to certain tests so vague and elastic that no person could tell, with any approach to certainty, before the decision of the Commissioners was given, what part of the sea coast or what part of the sea would or would not be defined to be within an estuary. In some instances, indeed, though not in the case of the Bush, the Commissioners, following out the principles laid down by them were compelled to mark out the estuary of a river by an arc or segment of a circle projected into the sea beyond the line of the adjoining coast.

11. Sir Edmund Macnaghten was advised that the majority of the Commissioners had miscarried, in so far as they had departed from the ordinary meaning of the term "estuary," and that the definition of the estuary of the Bush ought to be repealed, inasmuch as that river falls into the open sea and is lost in the ocean as soon as it touches the salt water, and therefore had not any estuary in the sense in which that term was universally understood before the Commissioners' report. He was, however, advised that no appeal lay from a definition of the Commissioners, however erroneous it might be, and that even the Commissioners themselves had no power to review their own definitions when once made.

12. Under these circumstances Sir Edmund Macnaghten appealed to the Queen's Bench in Ireland on the only ground which seemed open to him, namely, that inasmuch as he was proprietor of the whole river, and so within the saving clause of section 3 his bag-nets were legal, although they were in what the Commissioners defined to be an estuary. The Bench, however, dismissed the appeal, though under the circumstances without costs.

13. Since the decision of the Queen's Bench Sir Edmund's lessee has fished with draught-nets set in the old Irish fashion, a mode of fishing held to be legal both by the Queen's Bench and the Common Pleas.

14. In the last session of Parliament an Act was passed (32 & 33 Vict. c. 92) which transfers all the powers of the Fishery Commissioners to a new body styled the Inspectors of Irish Fisheries. That Act contains the following section:

s. 10. "The Inspectors of Irish Fisheries shall in addition to their other duties as soon as they conveniently can, make local and other inquiry into the expediency and necessity of altering, amending, or repealing any definition of the boundaries of the mouth or estuary of any river, or any by-laws heretofore made, or of making new definitions of the boundaries of the mouths or estuaries of rivers, or new by-laws relating to fisheries in Ireland, and if on such inquiry they shall be satisfied of such expediency or necessity it shall be lawful for them, subject to the approval of the Lord Lieutenant in council, and on appeal to him in council to alter, amend, or repeal any such definition, or any of such by-laws, and to make such new definitions or by-laws as they may deem expedient, and all the provisions relating to by-laws, and to an appeal against the same contained in the Acts incorporated with this Act shall apply to definitions and by-laws altered, amended, repealed, or made under the provisions of this Act."

15. Sir Edmund Macnaghten has written to the Inspectors stating that he considers himself aggrieved by the definition made by the Commissioners under the Act of 1863, and asking when the other duties of the Inspectors would permit them to inquire into the case of the Bush, and whether they would hear counsel on his behalf as to the meaning of the term "estuary of a river."

16. The Inspectors have sent a courteous reply, stating that due notice will be given of the inquiry, and that although they do not decline to hear counsel they would consider whatever might be urged by Sir Edmund himself or any person on his behalf.

17. Under these circumstances it becomes necessary to consider how far the principles laid down by the Commissioners under the Act of 1863 are correct.

18. The Act of 1863 contains no definition of the expression "estuary of a river," but by sec. 44 it provides that the Act, so far as is consistent with the tenor thereof, shall be construed with the Acts relating to salmon fisheries in Ireland, and the definitions of words and expressions now in force in the said Salmon Fisheries Acts shall apply to the same words and expressions when used in that Act. No definition of the expression "estuary of a river" is to be found in any of the Salmon Fisheries Acts. The 13 & 14 Vic. c. 88, s. 1, enacts that "the words 'estuary' and 'bay' shall include and extend to any harbour or roadstead." But this definition seems inapplicable to the expression "estuary of a river."

19. The following definitions are to be found in the principal dictionaries:—

Facciolati. Æstuarium ii. n. [ἀνάχυσις *Strab.* 3. p. 140.] locus est in maris littore ubi terra recedit sinumque facit marinis aquis modo refertus modo vacuus ex inundationibus freti ita dictus quod aqua ibi æstuat et ebullit utpote in angustiis clausa ex accessu et recessu maris. [*A place on the sea shore where the land recedes, and at same time forms with the sea water, at one time borne inwards, at another outwards from the strait, so called because in it the water heats and bubbles, inasmuch as it is enclosed within a narrow space from the flux and reflux of the sea.*] *Festus.* Æstuaria sunt omnia quæ mare vicissim tum accedit tum recedit. [*All are estuaries where the sea alternately flows and ebbs.*] *Plin. Ep.* 9. 33. Adjacet mari navigabile stagnum ex quo in modum fluminis æstuarium emergit quod vice alternâ prout æstus aut repressit aut impulit nunc infertur mari nunc redditur stagno. [*Stagnant water close by the navigable sea, from which, as a river, the estuary takes its rise, which, as the case may be, the summer heat either withholds or sends forth; at one time borne onwards, at another returned to the stagnant water.*] *Plin.* 5. 1. Affunditur aestuarium e mari flexuoso meatu. [*An estuary flows from a winding sea in motion.*] *Id.* 3. 26. 30. Illyrici ora mille amplius insulis frequentatur natura vadoso mari aestuariisque tenui alveo intercurrentibus. [*The Illyrian coast, with more than a thousand islands, nature is seen in the flowing sea and estuaries running between in the narrow channels*] *Cæs. B. G.* 3. 9. Itinera concisa aestuariis [*The marches cut short by estuaries.*]

Johnson, 1755. Estuary. n. f. Æstuarium, Latin. An arm of the sea. The mouth of a lake or river in which the tide reciprocates. A frith.

Todd's Johnson, 1827, gives the same meaning and the following example:—

"Soon after which the river swells into a great estuary, and in sight forms the Bristol Channel."—*Swinburne of South Wales.*

Webster, 1832. Estuary. n. L. Æstuarium, from aestuo, to boil or foam; aestus, heat, fury, storm.

1. An arm of the sea; a frith, a narrow passage, or the mouth of a river or lake where the tide meets the current, or flows and ebbs.

20. The word estuary is not defined in Hale, de Jure Maris, but in that work, Bk. 1, cap. iv. 2, there is the following statement of "what is to be taken to be an arm of the sea":—

2. For the second that is called an arm of the sea where the sea flows and reflows, and so far only as the sea so flows and reflows, so that the river of Thames above Kingston, and the river of Severn above Towkesbury, &c., though they are public rivers, yet are not arms of the sea. But it seems that although the water be fresh at high water, yet the denomination of an arm of the sea continues if it flow and reflow as in the Thames above the bridge. 22 Ass. 93. Nota que chescun eu que flow et reflow est appel brus de mere cy tantavint come il flow.

21. There is not, it is believed, any decided case containing an authoritative exposition of the meaning of the term estuary of a river. It may, however, be useful to refer to the Scotch fishery cases noted in the margin*. Before the recent enactments on the subject, by the Scotch law which was contained in several old statutes, fixed engines were prohibited in rivers and in certain places described by the phrase "wateris quhair the sea ebbis and flowis," and similar expressions. These expressions were held not to extend to the open sea, but were treated generally as identical in meaning with the expression estuaries of rivers. As stated in the judgment of the House of Lords in Kintore *v.* Forbes, 3 Wilson and Shaw, 260, "The whole body of the Acts taken together refer not to the sea coast but to rivers and the continuations of rivers." The result of the cases seems to be that the question whether a fixed engine was in a situation prohibited by statute was a question of fact depending on the circumstances of the particular case, and to be determined in each case by the verdict of the jury. But it was held in the case of Horne *v.* Mackenzie, before the House of Lords (6 Clark *v.* Finnelly, 628), that the test suggested by Lord Cockburn in his charge to the jury, which was, that "The thing to be looked at is the fact of the absence or the prevalence of the fresh water, though strongly impregnated with salt," was "erroneous, whether treated as an exclusive test or as one of great importance for consideration."

22. Although Lord Cockburn's charge to the jury in Horne *v.* Mackenzie was disapproved of by the House of Lords on the point above mentioned, it is thought desirable to direct counsel's attention to the following passages from it, which are to be found in 6 Cl. & Fin. 631 to 635, as expressing in clear language, subject to the above mentioned correction, what is generally understood to be the meaning of the term estuary of a river:—

"Now, assuming the machines to have been used, the point is, whether they were so wrongfully? There are many circumstances which might have made the use of them wrongful; but the only ground on which they can be held to have been so under these issues is, that they were placed in illegal situations. Hence the full question put to you is, whether salmon were wrongfully fished by means of these engines 'placed in situations prohibited by law.'

"It may naturally occur to you as odd, that a question so much involved in law should be put to you. But it was unavoidable. Because, though a court may give the legal rule which permits or condemns these machines, according to circumstances, the determination of the circumstances, that is, of the facts to which the rule is to be applied, is the proper province of a jury. I shall therefore begin by giving you as much of the law as is necessary, and shall then leave you with such observations as may appear to me to be proper, to apply this law to what you shall think the true import of the evidence.

"I say, as much as is necessary; for it is not necessary for the determination of this particular case that I should give, or attempt to give you a catalogue, or a description of all the circumstances even of situation, under which stake-nets may be lawful or the reverse; many of them having no application to this case; and it is needless to incumber ourselves with legal matter that is superfluous. Nor shall I trouble you by any observations either on the history or the policy of the law. These may be useful to lawyers by assisting them to put the right construction on disputed statutes, but they are of little or no use after the construction of these statutes is fixed; and least of all to juries, who, without any reasoning on the subject, must take the law as they receive it from the court.

"Now I have to lay it down to you in the first place, that the statutes as explained by decisions make these machines unlawful if they be placed in what is usually known as a river in the ordinary sense of this word. You have heard enough in this case to let you know that science and investigation may discover rivers where the uninformed eye cannot or does not trace them. Of this case I shall speak instantly. All I now say is, that this apparatus is prohibited by law, if it be placed in a river.

"In the second place there are many rivers which only join the ocean through a frith, or through a long land-locked valley where the fresh and salt waters meet. In this situation it will probably depend upon external appearances whether ordinary observers will say that the space is occupied by the sea or by the river or by both. If it shall be so fully and distinctly occupied by the flowing fresh water as that it is really a river, though the common river features may be periodically effaced by the tide, it comes under the preceding rule; that is, being still a river these machines are unlawful.

* Dalgleish *v.* D. of Athol, the Tay case, 5 Dow. 282. Kintore *v.* Forbes, 3 Wilson and Shaw, 261. Horne *v.* Mackenzie, 6 Cl. and F., 628. Ross *v.* D. of Sutherland, 3 Bell, app. c. 315.

"Moreover, rivers have estuaries; that is, spaces intermediate between the strictly proper river and the strictly proper sea. Through these partly fresh and partly salt estuaries, though its ordinary river features may be impaired, or at high tides even obliterated, the river still does in truth exist and operate; though its existence be only continued amongst sands and shoals, through which it has to work its way struggling with the tide. Now these structures are also unlawful in these estuaries. Not that estuaries are specially mentioned by name in the statutes; neither are friths. But the estuary is a part of the river and is included under this word. The mere name is of little importance. The thing to be looked to is the fact of the absence, or of the prevalence of the fresh water, though strongly impregnated by salt. Now, where this fresh water prevails, though in the estuary these structures are illegal; and they are not only unlawful (meaning always within the ebbing and flowing of the tide) when placed in the channel of the estuary that is always covered with water, but they are so also if they be placed on the sands which are left dry by the ebbing of the sea.

"In these two situations, viz., in the river or in its land-locked estuary, the contrivances are illegal. There are two situations of a different description in which they are lawful.

"For in the third place some rivers terminate without passing through any frith or estuary, and are lost in the open ocean almost so soon as they touch the salt water. In this case stake nets are not prohibited if they be placed away from the immediate mouth of the river, though situated where the sea ebbs and flows. The ebbing and flowing won't of itself render them unlawful, because they may be within the sphere of this phenomenon, and yet in the pure and undoubted sea.

"In the fourth place there are examples in which the junction of the fresh water and the salt does not take place, as in the case last put, at the edge of the open ocean, but far up in the land where the river loses itself in arms or in bays of the sea. These portions of the ocean become what are called arms of the sea, merely because they happen to be inclosed within ridges which guide their waters into the interior; but this circumstance does not make these arms identical with estuaries. They are the sea; and, being so, these machines, if placed in or on arms of the sea, as distinguished from the estuaries of rivers, are not unlawful. What shall be held to be an arm, and what an estuary, is a question of fact for you. All I say as to the rule is, that if there be an arm distinct from an estuary, then in that arm, or, in other words, in that portion of the sea, these fixed traps are not illegal.

"The substance of these rules is merely this, that to make the particular engines with which we are now dealing unlawful, it must be proved that they are in a river, or in its estuary, whether within the channel or on the sands made dry by the ebbing. It is the pursuer's business to prove that they are so placed. If he shall fail the defenders may have nothing to do; but if, not content with relying on the pursuer's failure, the defenders choose, they may show, and they have tried to do so, that their structures are truly in the sea, whether the open sea or on one of its arms or bays, and if so, they are lawful.

"In short, a river does not lose its legal protection in reference to salmon fishing, merely by being met by the advancing tide, provided this be within what are called (though usually by two Latin words) the jaws of the land, and provided the relative size of the river, and the other circumstances, shall satisfy a jury that on the whole the space is river, including in this term its estuary. And, on the other hand, the sea does not lose its privileges merely because a river flows into it, or flows through one of its arms or bays where the tide ebbs and flows, provided the relative smallness of the stream, and other circumstances, shall satisfy a jury on the whole the space is sea, and not river or the continuation of a river through its estuary."

23. A copy of the map issued by the Commissioners, which contains the estuary of the Bush as defined by them, accompanies this case.

Counsel is requested to advise:—

1. Whether the principles laid down by the Commissioners in their Report of 1864 are correct, or in what respects they are incorrect, and particularly whether the Commissioners were correct in laying down the proposition that every river necessarily has an estuary?

2. What is the meaning of the expression "the estuary of a river" in the Salmon Fishery (Ireland) Act, 1863?

Opinion.

1. We think the principles laid down by the Commissioners in their report of 1864 are not correct. We think that the Acts of Parliament give no special or unusual meaning to the term "estuary of a river," either expressly or impliedly. We think that the influence of fresh water is not the test nor even one of the tests by which to decide where the estuary ends to seaward. We think the limits of the estuary must be decided to landward by the extent of the sensible influence of the tide, and to seaward by the configuration of the land on either side of the channel. We think the estuary, of a river must always be part of the river, and that the provision in 13 & 14 Vic., c. 88, s. 1, that the word "estuary" shall include and extend to any harbour or roadstead, means simply that an estuary properly so called shall not cease to be one because it happens to be also a harbour or roadstead. The phrase "estuary of a river," which appears for the first time in the 26 & 27 Vic., c. 114, was probably used *ex cautela* to meet the possible contention that certain portions of particular rivers must be considered not as rivers, but as arms of the sea. We think that there may be rivers, the configuration of the land on either side of which is such that they have no estuary.

2. We think the "estuary of a river" in the Salmon Fishery Act, 1863 (Ireland), means the portion of the river affected by the flux and reflux of the tide, extending downwards as far as it is confined between banks which have received their configuration from the joint action of stream and tide.

As far as we can judge from the ordnance map and the enlarged map before us, and from the explanations given, there is nothing here in the nature of an estuary beyond the moderate enlargement of the river as it enters the bay, which the Commissioners have (erroneously as we think) included in the estuary.

R. Palmer.
George Mellish.
Alfred Wills.

Lincoln's Inn,
28th December, 1869.

In addition to this, we consulted the best authorities we could find on the subject, viz.:—*Worcester's Dictionary*, the *Encyclopædia Britannica*, the *English Cyclopædia*, *Richardson's Dictionary*, &c., and it struck us that our predecessors, in defining the estuary of this river by drawing a line fully half a mile seaward of its mouth across a deep bay into which the river suddenly debouched and was lost, were to a certain extent misled by the word "estuary," in the Act of 1842, being defined to "extend to a harbour, and a roadstead, and a bay," and did not draw the distinction between the word "estuary" in the Act of 1842, and the words "estuary of a river" in the Act of 1863, which latter Act for the first time prohibited the use of bag nets in "estuaries of rivers."

The next application received by us was to alter the definition of the Palmerston or Cloonaghmore River, in the county of Sligo, and we took exactly the same steps as in the former case, and unanimously decided on altering the mouth of the river and estuary.

We trust it is needless to say that in making our inquiries into these questions we totally excluded from our consideration the effect our decisions would have on any modes of fishing either inside or outside the mouth of the river or estuary; but confined ourselves strictly to defining, to the best of our judgment, geographically, what we deemed were the mouths and estuaries of each river; and we were gratified to know, that if we erred, the right of appeal having been given by the statute of 1869, in the same manner as in the case of by-laws to anyone feeling aggrieved, and which had not been given in the statute of 1863, under which the definitions were made by our predecessors, would have a fair opportunity of obtaining a decision from the highest tribunal in the country on the correctness or otherwise of our views. We therefore took care at our meetings to make all persons acquainted with this right, and our disposition to facilitate in every way in our power any appeal against our decisions. No appeal was, however, made, and the effect in these two cases—the only ones in which we have performed this duty during the past year—has been to restore four bag nets that had been legally erected for a great number of years previous to 1863.

Fixed Engines.

The Act of 1869 having imposed a penalty of £50, and a further one of £20 a-day on any person erecting, using, or fishing with a fixed engine for the capture of salmon without having obtained a certificate from the Special Commissioners for Irish Fisheries, under the provisions of the Salmon Fishery Ireland Act, 1863, or a certificate from us in regard to such fixed engine, we issued, as soon as possible, certificates for all fixed engines which had been declared by the Court of Queen's Bench, on appeal, to have been legally erected, no certificates for such having been issued by our predecessors. In addition to these, we have held inquiries during the past year, and granted certificates for twenty-three fixed draft nets, commonly called in the north of Ireland "the half tram," which we found under the decision of the Court of Queen's Bench, in the case of Stewart *v.* Cubitt, and in the Court of Common Pleas in the case of Williams *v.* Boyd, to have been legally erected as fixed engines of some description or other during the year 1862, under the provisions of the Act 5 & 6 Vic., c. 106, which alone authorized the use of fixed engines. These description of nets, which are in reality nothing more than ordinary draft or seine nets, were never considered fixed engines until the decision of the case of Stewart *v.* Cubitt. We also, under the same authority, issued a certificate for one stake net in the place of a bag net, which had been erected in Cork Harbour previous to the Act of 1863, but subject to any complaint that might be made after to its erection, on the part of the public, on the grounds of injury to navigation or a nuisance to the public rights of fishing. No complaints have, however, reached us since its erection.

It is right for us here to mention that no new fixed engines have been established by our acts. We are bound to give certificates wherever it has been proved to us that fixed engines have been erected under the provisions of the Act of 1842, during the open season of 1862, and anyone feeling aggrieved has the right of appeal against our decisions. Only two notices of appeal have been given, and these are not contesting the facts as to fixed engines having been legally erected in 1862 in these places, but the rights of the parties to use them, and other slight technical legal grounds.

A schedule of the certificates issued for fixed engines up to the 31st December, 1870, will be found in the Appendix.

Fishing near Mouths of Rivers.

The 44th section of the 13th and 14th Vic., c. 88, enacts that it shall not be lawful for any person, save the proprietor of a several fishery within the limits thereof, at any time to use nets for taking salmon *at the mouth* of any river where the breadth shall not exceed a quarter of a mile statute measure, *or within half a mile from the* mouth of *any river*. As soon as the mouth of a river has been defined, it is the practice in many places for the proprietors of the land adjoining to lay claim to the exclusive fishing, and use nets within the prescribed limits, on the plea, which we believe in the majority of instances could not be sustained in a court of law, that they are the proprietors of a several fishery. We have no power to inquire into the titles of such parties, nor do we advocate that such an important power as deciding in such cases whether a several fishery exists in the place should be given to us, but we do think that, inasmuch as the jurisdiction of magistrates to impose the penalty for the *primâ facie* offence against the statute is ousted by the question of title being raised, no one should be allowed to fish in such places until they had satisfied a court of common law that their claim was *bonâ fide*, and that a several fishery existed in the place. At present in many places the effect of the definition of the mouth of a river is simply to prevent the public fishing where they had probably done for many years before, and conferring on the person claiming the several fishery a monopoly, thus counteracting the benefits contemplated by the statute to a river in preventing the use of nets within half a mile of its mouth.

Fish Passes.

During the past year we have built two fish passes over mill weirs on the River Suir at a cost of £98. They are reported to be working well, and are efficient. Not the slightest injury to either the dams or the effective working power of the mills has been caused thereby. We have also made an alteration in the fish pass on the Galway weir. The course we adopt in such cases is to have a survey made by our engineer at the cost and charges of the person or persons applying to have the fish pass built. When the form of pass has been designed, and plan and specification prepared, copies are sent to the persons interested, including the owner or occupier of the mill, and we hear any objections that may be offered to them. If there are no valid ones, and the money to cover the expense of the work is deposited in our hands, we enter into a contract with some competent builder for its execution, taking security not only for its completion in accordance with the plan and specification approved by us, but also that no injury should be done to the dam.

In addition to these passes, we have had surveys of many more weirs in Ireland prepared, and when money is provided we shall have the necessary passes built.

During the past year complaints have been received of the inefficiency of the fish passes erected by the Commissioners of Public Works on the Athlone and Tarmonbarry weirs on the River Shannon, and also that passes have not been built on the other weirs erected by them in that river.

With regard to the first, we took every pains to ascertain, not only by personal inspection, but by public inquiries, at which we took the evidence of a number of witnesses, if these complaints were well founded, and we found they were, and reported the result to the Board of Public Works. It is quite true that these passes, viz., those at Athlone and Tarmonbarry, were built by the Board of Works according to plans approved by our predecessors. The law, however, directs that all dams placed in rivers since 1842 should be so built as to allow of, in one or more parts of the same, the free run or migration of salmon *at all periods* of the year, *and* that such provision for the free passage of the fish through such dam, shall be made at the expense of the person forming such dam, *and* in such manner as the Commissioners shall approve.

There are here three distinct provisions—1stly, that there shall be fish passes in all new dams, which would allow the free migration of salmon *at all periods of the year*—2ndly, that these shall be built at the expense of the person forming the dam—and 3rdly, that they shall be built in such manner as the Commissioners of Fisheries approved. The two latter provisions were complied with in the case of the passes built at Athlone and Tarmonbarry, but the plans approved by our predecessors, and on which the Commissioners of Public Works acted, did not secure the first; and we therefore considered, that inasmuch as all the provisions of the Act were not complied with, the public were not concluded by the approval given to such plans, and that the penalty provided by the statute for non-compliance with its provisions, might be enforced at the suit of any one feeling himself aggrieved. In this interpretation of the law, however, it appears according to the opinion of the law officers, we were incorrect; and unless money is now provided by persons interested in the fisheries of the Shannon, for the erection of efficient fish passes on these weirs, matters must remain as they are. We are, however, in hopes that the necessary funds will be forthcoming for an efficient pass at least over Tarmonbarry weir.

With regard to the weirs on which no passes have as yet been built, viz., those at Roosky, Jamestown, and Knockvicar, we considered it prudent that, although plans of passes for these weirs were prepared some years ago, and even so lately as the summer of 1868, by directions of your Excellency's predecessor, our engineer should in consequence of the defects in the other passes, go again carefully over the whole of the weirs and revise his plans. This has been done, and they have been furnished to the Board of Works, and it is hoped the passes may be now carried out, and that they may prove efficient.

There is no provision of the acts which ought to be more strictly carried out than that relating to obstructions to the free migration of salmon, and we are in hopes that in a few years efficient fish passes will be built over every obstruction in Ireland.

Mills and Gratings.

By the 32nd and 33rd Vic., c. 9, it is enacted that the exemption from compliance with the provisions of the 76th section of the 5th and 6th Vic., c. 106, which requires that gratings shall be placed in watercourses leading the water to and from mills, during the ascent and descent of salmon, and lattices during the descent of fry, shall extend only to such cases in which, and for such periods during which, it shall be proved to our satisfaction that such exemption is necessary for the effective working of the machinery.

This imposed on us a work of more than ordinary labour, care, and attention. The mills are numerous in the country, the trade is a very close one, in the majority of cases little profit arising, and they are most important resources of the country, which should not be lightly considered even for the advantage of the fisheries.

It became, therefore, our anxious desire that while we were doing all in our power for the protection of the fish, we should not do anything to cause injury to the milling power of the country. The erection of lattice work would have caused in most cases a serious injury, and we have not enforced it, except in cases where turbines are used, and the law is peremptory in this respect. With regard to gratings, we have given exemption in every case where it was proved to our satisfaction they would have been injurious to the effective working of the mill, and we are not aware of a single instance of having compelled their continuance after they had been put up, when injury was proved. We can now, therefore, state that, notwithstanding all the outcry against this clause, no injury has been done to the milling power, while it has proved most advantageous in many cases to the fisheries.

Local Management, &c.

During the past year the triennial elections of Conservators have taken place, and we are happy to say that no complaints of irregularity at them have been made. The elections took place in the month of October last, and the regulations we had formed for their conduct were issued in June preceding. These regulations will be found in the Appendix.

We are, however, constrained to refer here to a matter which occurred in one district, and which if overlooked, or allowed in other districts, may have the most injurious effects.

The 8th section of the 13th and 14th Vic. c. 88, directs that when any moneys shall be received by the treasurer of any district in respect of licence duties, or rates for the period or term in which the then next election of Conservators is to take place, such moneys shall, until such election, be carefully retained by such treasurer, and shall after such election be paid over by him to, or to the order of, the new Board of Conservators, to be by them applied according to the provisions of the Acts.

In order to secure, as far as in our power lay, a strict observance of this most salutary provision, we issued to every Conservator, and clerk, and treasurer of a Board in Ireland a circular of which the following is a copy :—

4th day of May, 1870.

Circular.

To the Conservators of Fisheries in Ireland.

Sir,—I am desired to remind you that the 8th section of the 13th and 14th Vic. cap. 88, directs that the funds collected this year for licence duties and rates should be paid over to the treasurer of the district, and be carefully retained by him until the next election of Conservators, which should take place in October next ; and after such election, they may be paid over by him to the order of the new Board of Conservators.

The Inspectors beg that the present Boards of Conservators will take care that the above provisions of the law are strictly attended to, as they will feel it their duty to see that the funds of this year are handed over intact to the new Boards of Conservators to be elected in October next, as directed by the Act of Parliament.

Instructions relative to the elections will be forwarded in due course to the persons interested.

By order,

Alan Hornsby, Secretary.

It will be easily seen that the object of the Legislature in enacting the claues to which we have referred, was to place newly elected Boards of Conservators in possession of funds to meet the expenses of the district, without which, the salmon at the most critical period of the year, the spawning season, would be unprotected, as no funds could be collected from licence duties or rates till the following fishing season.

Immediately after the elections, a complaint was made to us by the newly elected Board for the Dublin district, that the funds paid into the treasurers' hands had not been handed over to the new Board, as directed by the statute.

We called upon them to comply with the law, which, however, we regret to say has not up to the present been done, and we feel it to be our duty, however unpleasant it may be, to state our strong opinion to your Excellency, that this contempt for the provisions of the law by any Board of Conservators or treasurers, should not be allowed with impunity, or the consequences to the fisheries may be most disastrous.

Newly elected Boards of Conservators cannot be expected, without funds, to run the risk of proceedings at law, which might involve them in heavy pecuniary liability. They may be composed of gentlemen who have no pecuniary interest whatever in the fisheries of the district, and who are simply giving up their time and attention gratuitously for the public benefit. It is therefore our duty to bring the matter thus prominently before your Excellency, as if it be passed over in this instance, the treasurer of any district hereafter, may, in the last year of his office of the Board of Conservators, retain all the public money received by him, and refuse either to comply with the provisions of the Act, or to give any account whatever of the money received by him, knowing that no incoming Board will undertake the liability of any proceedings at law to recover the amount; and when it is recollected that this is public money, and the greater portion derived from a poor class of fishermen who fish on the common law right, we cannot help feeling that it becomes the duty of the Governing Department to enforce the law.

This matter is of such vital consequence throughout the country we have felt it necessary to dwell on it at this length.

As a general rule, we find that Boards of Conservators are anxious to enforce such regulations as may tend to the advancement of the fisheries, and receive and give effect to any suggestions we may from time to time propose to them for the management of their district. The great difficulty, however, under which every Board of Conservators labours is a deficiency of funds for the protection and development of the fisheries. We think that this might be remedied to a certain extent by a re-adjustment of the licence duties and rates payable on fixed and several fisheries, for we know that at present there are many engines used in Ireland which are not at all taxed in proportion to their capability of capture, while there are others paying a higher rate in proportion to other more productive engines.

The raising of the licence duties on rods all over Ireland to £1, which has been accomplished during the past year, after considerable exertion, not only on our part, but that of many Boards in Ireland, will not only increase the funds at the disposal of the Boards, but will have certain other advantages. Heretofore the licence duty on rods was in some districts only ten shillings, while in others it was £1, and it was not an uncommon practice for some anglers to take out their licences in a district at the lower rate, wholly ignoring the interest of the district in which they fished, and which contributed to their sport. Indeed, so far was this carried in some places, that the riparian owners of fisheries in some districts, where the licence duty was £1, sent to Dublin, where the licenceduty was only ten shillings, for their licences, thus not contributing one farthing to the funds of the district in which they owned property and fished. This most unjust proceeding was naturally productive of considerable dissatisfaction. The equalisation of the licence duty will take away all inducement to act in the same way for the future.

The number of salmon rod licences issued during the past year was 2,787, and with the present licence duty this should increase the revenue fully £1,000.

The revenue last year *from licenses* exceeded that of any former year since the establishment of licence duties on fishing engines in 1849; and reached the sum of £7,511 13*s.* 4*d.* We believe this will be considerably increased during the present year, while the number of persons employed in 1870 amounted to 10,520, as compared with 9,629 in 1869, being an increase of 891.

In addition to this, there was received for moieties of fines, sales of forfeited engines, interest, &c. (independently of subscriptions), a further sum of £503 7*s.* 10*d.*, making a total revenue for the year of £8,015 1*s.* 2*d.*

In our last Report we referred to the question of the amount of duty payable upon the Poor Law Valuation on the fixed and several fisheries in the country as a means of increasing the sum available for, not only protection, but a further development of the fisheries by the opening up of new spawning grounds. This subject is receiving our attention, and we trust it will lead to the desired object.

In some districts, where the rivers are suitable for angling, societies have been formed by gentlemen for the purpose of securing more efficient protection by payment of water-bailiffs out of their own resources. We may instance two particularly—the Suir Preservation Society, and the Cork Anglers' Club. The former, in addition to the many advantages conferred by them on the fisheries of their river at a very considerable outlay, have provided the funds for building the fish passes last year, to which we have previously referred.

We strongly recommend the adoption of a similar course by the resident proprietors, wherever rivers are suitable. It would be attended with most beneficial results, and would tend much to overcome the difficulties arising from insufficiency of funds.

New Legislation.

However desirable it might be to have a consolidation of the present laws, which are scattered over so many Acts of Parliament, we believe the time has hardly arrived for this, and we think it would be much better to let the late legislation on the subject develop itself, and that short bills remedying defects and making any amendments that may be necessary should be passed from time to time, until there would at last be a code perfect in principle, from which a consolidation might then be prepared, which would not only be acceptable to the country, but be beneficial to the fisheries. It is quite true that so many Acts of Parliament in force on the subject have on many occasions led to confusion; but we think this is now greatly obviated by a short digest of these laws which has been prepared and circulated by Mr. Brady, and which will be found in the Appendix to this Report.

In conclusion, we can only repeat generally that the Salmon Fisheries of the country are at present a most valuable property—steadily increasing in commercial prosperity, and likely to continue so, and that we are indebted to the Coastguard and Constabulary for very valuable assistance rendered by both departments in enforcing the laws for the protection and improvement of the Irish Fisheries.

We have the honour to be,

Your Excellency's obedient servants,

THOMAS F. BRADY.
JOS. HAYES.
JOHN ALOYSIUS BLAKE.

Alan Hornsby, *Secretary*.

Office of Irish Fisheries,
12, *Ely-place, Dublin,*
13*th July*, 1871.

APPENDIX.

APPENDIX,

STATE of the REGISTRY of FISHING VESSELS on the COAST

No.	Name of Division.	Boundaries.	Registering Officer.	1st Class employed in 1878.			2nd Class employed in 1878.			3rd Class employed in 1878.		
				Vessels.	Men.	Boys.	Vessels.	Men.	Boys.	Vessels.	Men.	Boys.
1	Dublin, .	Howth to Greystones, .	John B. Creagh, Commander, R.N.	88	417	84	77	372	58	62	343	20
2	Arklow, .	From the breaches three miles north of Five-mile-point Station to the sluices three miles south of Cahore Station.	Vincent Williams, Commander, R.N.	-	-	-	293	1,053	21	46	301	13
3	Wexford, .	Morris Castle to Bannow, .	Edward Wilkinson, Commander, R.N.	23	126	-	178	751	22	40	189	-
4	Waterford, .	From East Bank of Bannow Ferry, county Wexford, to Ballyvoile Head, North of Dungarvan Harbour, county Waterford.	Hugo B. Burnaby, Commander, R.N.	9	30	8	148	406	16	44	76	5
5	Youghal, .	From Ballyvoile Bridge to Garryvoe,	W. R. Boulton, Commander, R.N.	6	84	2	92	480	23	26	127	1

No. 1.

of Ireland from 1st January, 1870, to 1st January, 1871.

Total employed in 1870.			Substance of Observations made by Inspecting Commanders of Coast Guards and other Registering Officers, up to the 1st January, 1871.	No.
Vessels	Men.	Boys.		
227	809	151	No improvement has taken place, compared with last three years, as to boats, gear, &c. Few fishermen hold land. No sign of improvement in the fisheries within the last year. No emigration has taken place among the fishermen. [illegible]	1
339	1,886	34	The fisheries, as compared with the last three years, appear to be improving at Wicklow, Arklow, and Courtown [illegible]	2
240	1,089	22	The condition of the fisheries in this district, in regard to boats, gear, &c., continues about the same as last year. [illegible]	3
196	609	29	The general condition of the fisheries, boats and gear, &c., much the same here during the last three years. [illegible]	4
124	651	26	There have no improvements taken place in this district as to boats and gear within the last three years. [illegible]	5

APPENDIX,

STATE of the REGISTRY of FISHING VESSELS on the COAST

No.	Name of Division.	Boundaries.	Registering Officer.	1st Class employed in 1870			2nd Class employed in 1870.			3rd Class employed in 1870.		
				Vessels.	Men.	Boys	Vessels.	Men.	Boys.	Vessels.	Men.	Boys
6	Queenstown,	From Ballycotton Bay westward to Ringabella Bay, including Queenstown Harbour.	J. Hall Robeck Commander, R.N.	7	36	1	81	306	6	101	364	31
7	Kinsale, .	From Myrtleville Point East, to Galley Head West.	J. W. Carter, Commander, R.N.	42	287	41	143	648	41	273	1,123	61

No. 1—*continued.*

of Ireland from 1st January, 1870, to 1st January, 1871.

Total employed in 1870			*Substance of Observations made by Inspecting Commanders of Coast Guards and other Registering Officers, up to the 1st January, 1871*	No.
Vessels.	Men.	Boys.		
			[illegible] at present. Conflicts do not occur between fishermen pursuing different modes of capture; they are orderly and industrious, and the able-bodied men are generally employed fishing. Trawling and the use of trammel nets [illegible] at Dungarvan and Tramore, but no [illegible] arise with the line fishermen. There are about fifty herring nets, of twenty fathoms long and three fathoms deep, [illegible] nets, of seventy fathoms long, one fathom deep, 120 trammel nets, of forty fathoms long, two fathoms deep. It is the general opinion that trawling disturbs the spawn. There are twenty trawl boats here, of from twelve to fifteen tons each, which work in from five to twenty fathoms of water, the size of mesh of trawl net from four to five inches. Trawl boats decreased in number since 1869. [illegible] trammel net, and line fishing boats number eighty-eight, of from half a ton to twenty tons. All fish caught sold in local markets. Plaice, sole, turbot, [illegible], hake, haddock, are captured by trawl, [illegible], herring, mackerel, pilchards, sprats by seine, and gurnet, [illegible], whiting, cod, by lines. A decrease of fish of all sorts, within the last five years, on this part of the coast, is generally reported. Loans of money would benefit the fishermen but it is doubtful whether security for its repayment could be obtained. The means of transit to market for the fish is good, and no complaints of the rates charged for same. There is accommodation for vessels up to twenty tons tonnage in Dungarvan Harbour, where there is an artificial pier. Increased accommodation for vessels is wanted at Helvick, and at Ardmore some kind of [illegible] is required. It would have been better to have left the registering of vessels with the Coast guard. Merchants and owners of boats give returns relative to the different kinds of fish and the quantities taken by them.	
189	706	38	There is an improvement in boats and gear in this district, during the last three years. Almost all the fishermen and owners of boats are holders of land of from three to seventy acres; the largest land holders are to be found in the neighbourhood of Ballycotton and Poor head. No improvement in the fisheries within the past year, the prospects of parties here, depend more on agricultural circumstances than upon fishing, except in few cases. The spirit of emigration still prevails. [illegible] employed, the chief inducement, probably would remain at home. Young unmarried people look forward to emigrating. The capture of fish has been less this year than the preceding year. There are four natural oyster banks, one at Pass Ferry, and one at Ashgrove in the channel between Great Island and the mainland, and two artificial beds in the Carrigaline River, they are in a good state, but not improving, the one at Pass Ferry is overworked, if it were given some rest it would prove a remarkably good bed. Steps have been taken to stock the beds for which licences were granted. No curing house for fish in this district. The fish is sold in a fresh state. No conflicts occur between [illegible] using different modes of capture, they are orderly, except when drunk. The able-bodied men engage in any work paying them best, and turn up—fishing, when fish are plenty—parking [illegible] when there is a good take, if it is to be had—and at farm work when it could be had. Trawling is practised in Queenstown harbour and at Ballycotton, where trammel nets are also used. Trawling has not given rise to contention with fishermen following other modes of fishing. A restraint ought to be put on the use of trawls inside Queenstown harbour, as the spawn of flat fish, which generally lies at the ground there, gets [illegible] owing to frequent trawling. The sizes of nets used are from seventy fathoms long and five fathoms deep, to 110 fathoms long and seven fathoms deep, [illegible], of which there are fourteen, about twelve herring nets of [illegible] fathoms long, and about eighty trammel nets, forty fathoms long. Trawling is not injurious except it be on spawn as disturbed by it. There are thirty-nine trawlers of from five to thirty tons, the size of meshes of trawl nets varies from one and a half to three or four inches from knot to knot, and the nets are generally from seven to ten fathoms long. Trawling vessels decreased in number since last year. About 151 boats, of from one to three tons, employed in seine, trammel net, and line fishing. The fish captured is sold in local markets or on the beach (as is done at Ballycotton). Sole, plaice, sprats, and herrings are captured by trawl, hake, pollock, bream, rock cod, ling, and haddock, by line, trammel, and seine. Pollock and bream are best in summer, hake in autumn, and in winter. In June and July the fish, excepting pollock and bream, are in bad condition, soad and mackerel are good in August. There has been a decrease of herrings and sprats on this part of the coast within the last few years. Loans of money to fishermen would certainly benefit them and improve the fishing, but it is difficult to say whether they would be able to procure security for the repayment. The means of transit for fish to market, for sale in and [illegible], if it were improved, it would lead to increased employment of men and boats. No complaints of high charges by means of rail. The natural harbours, Ballinacourty up the Ballycotton river, Whitegate, and Crosshaven, accommodate vessels up to forty and fifty tons. Ballycotton harbour is partially constructed, an outlay is necessary to provide accommodation and shelter there. The fishing interest on this coast would be much benefited by an outlay in this instance. The registry of boats not quite perfect in this district, some owners of boats register at the Custom-house, others at the Coastguard stations. The most accurate fishery statistical information can be had from returns of quantity sold in local markets, and when sold on the beach, as at Ballycotton, the Coast guard to ascertain the quantities, in doing which, the assistance of the older fishermen would be of value. The fishing along the east coast of this division would be much improved if steps were taken to complete Ballycotton harbour as a harbour of refuge for large boats, those boats owing to the want of harbour refuge, are laid up during the winter months, and the fishing is then conducted in small boats only.	6
447	2,003	147	The general condition of the fishermen about Kinsale is improving, also the boats and gear; but in other parts of this division there is no improvement. Some of the fishermen along the coast hold from five to six acres of land each, but none at Kinsale. There has been some improvement within the last year about Kinsale, where present prospects of the fisheries are good, but not so in other places in this division. No emigration from Kinsale, but in other parts of the district the fishermen, who only partially subsist by fishing, are glad to avail themselves of the offers of their friends in America, who generally prepay their passage to that country. Last year has been less productive in fish taken than the preceding year, except at Kinsale, where there has been an increased take in the mackerel fisheries as the modes of capture have improved; the system adopted by the Manx and Cornish fishermen having prevailed. Very few oysters here, only a few up the river. No natural banks. Supply not improving. No new banks discovered lately. No steps taken to stock private beds. The quality of oysters fine and small, they sell at 5s. to 6s. per hundred. Do not say what quantity sold. Some of the fish are cured at Brilly and Weddlemoll, and there are attempts made to cure fish at Kinsale, Courtmacsherry, and other places along the coast, with good results, for winter consumption. The principal part of the fish is sold fresh and sent to all parts of England and Ireland. There are fish curing establishments at Brilly, Kinsale, and Courtmacsherry, carried on successfully, and an icehouse, on a small scale, two miles from Kinsale, to the north, to save ice in frosty weather, also a store house for ice in Kinsale. No collisions between fishermen, they are all very peaceable and quiet, very orderly and industrious, the able-bodied men engage at tillage of land and other labouring works occasionally, except those at Kinsale, where they fish as much as possible. Trawling and trammel net fishing still exist, principally at Old Head, West, but no collision arising therefrom; restraints are unnecessary. Herring nets in pieces run from two sixty-five to thirty fathoms long, and five fathoms deep; where one of these reels share, from eighty to one hundred fathoms long, and from five to seven fathoms deep. Trammel nets in pieces about thirty fathoms long. Trawling is not injurious to the general interests of the fisheries. There are from eight to ten boats, principally from Cork harbour, of about from fifteen to twenty tons each, engaged trawling, the size of mesh of nets four and a half inches, and the trawlers work in from ten to twenty fathoms of water. The trawl boats are fewer in number this year than last year. About 801 boats of from two and a half to three tons engaged in trammel net, seine, and line fishing. Fish captured by trawl is sold in local markets, except at Kinsale, where it is generally exported, fish taken by other modes of fishing sold likewise in local markets, but a great quantity of it exported. Plaice, sole, and turbot, are captured by trawls, mackerel, [illegible], bream, pollock, sprats, herrings, and pilchards by seine nets, hake and pollock by trammel nets. Cod, ling, plaice, and haddock, by lines. Cod and ling are in best condition January to April, other fish in the summer. There has been a great increase of mackerel at Kinsale within the last five years; but in other parts of the coast a great decrease of all other fish. The fishermen would be much benefited if they were freed of the arbitrary regulations of the owners of boats and gear, who require them to work during the slack periods of the year without the slightest remuneration, either in money or provisions. The men have often to go to sea without provisions of any kind, and miserably clad, no comfort in the boats, and therefore no inducement to work well. The fishermen would gladly repay any loans of money given at such periods, as, when the mackerel arrives, it is caught in such quantities as to give a large share to the fishermen, which would enable them to repay any loans that might have been granted to them in the slack times. In such cases no security would be required, as vessels could repay themselves. The men would be very willing to accede to these terms. The means of transit for fish to market for sale are good, but the Railway Companies do not seem willing to suit the terms of buyers for its conveyance. On this account the buyers prefer to charter steamers to convey it to English ports direct, and find this mode of conveyance cheaper and more convenient. The natural harbours Glandore, Courtmacsherry, Kinsale, Oyster Haven, which could accommodate a large fleet of fishing boats, up to forty tons or more tonnage, all which harbours require an outlay for landing places for fish. At Courtmacsherry the piers are very bad for landing or making fast to, as they are all in a state of decay, and at Kinsale suitable accommodation very much required. Registry of boats perfect. The most accurate statistical information, as to the quantities and kinds of fish captured could be obtained by having a paid official to devote his whole time to it afloat and ashore, who should make periodical reports of the state of the fishery in the district. The local fishery at Kinsale is capable of much improvement. It is possible to assimilate it to the system adopted by the Manx and Cornish fishermen, both as regards internal comfort for the men in the boats, and pecuniary help during slack times of the year. Fittings and gear should be better looked after with a view to their completion and working capability. If a fishery saving's fund could be organized it would be a boon, especially if arrangements could be made to enable the fishermen themselves to become part owners either of the boats or gear or both. Kinsale being the principal port in the south of Ireland for the concentration of boats engaged in the mackerel fishery, it may be interesting to give the following few particulars with regard to that especial branch of the fishery trade. The number of boats from the Isle of Man, Howth, Cornwall, and elsewhere, which rendezvous in the harbour, has greatly increased during the season of 1870. To these are added the boats of the South of Ireland Fishing Company, and others belonging to local owners, making altogether from about 260 to 300 sail. The mackerel is generally caught in large quantities, and is disposed of chiefly to buyers from the English markets. In 1870 the proceeds of sales in the harbour amounted to nearly £100,000, the season continues from the middle of March to first June. The proceeds of each capture is divided as follows, at the end of the week:—In the Manx, &c., boats, the cost of provisions for the crew is taken out of the profits, the remainder divided, one-half to the owner, the other half to the crew, to be apportioned in equal shares. In the Kinsale boats a moiety is likewise given to the crew, the owners getting the other, while no deduction is made for provisions, therefore the Kinsale fishermen are thrown on their own resources for sea store which often leaves them very hungry, and without energy to work. The want of a suitable landing-place with an adjacent store and icehouse is a very great drawback to the successful packing, icing, and curing of the fish. Buyers are in consequence compelled to meet the boats as they return from sea, frequently proceeding ten to twelve miles off the land, and purchase the fish as they deem desirable while steamers are in waiting, on board of which the packing and icing is carried on till the cargo is obtained and sent off direct to Liverpool and Holyhead. Hulks are also engaged wherein to store the ice temporarily, which is a great inconvenience. A wharf, suitable at all times of tide, would be most desirable, and would afford the fishermen an opportunity of having a regular competition market where the buyers could attend and transact their business through brokers. Many of the Kinsale fishermen are still destitute during the winter, but they seem, generally, to have adopted more frugal habits, and their social position is more improved than of late years. This may be attributed to two causes:— 1st. The fishing has been better developed, and greater profits realized than heretofore. 2nd. Those who used to seek a refuge in the workhouse during late winters have been compelled by the Poor Law Guardians of the	7

APPENDIX,

STATE of the REGISTRY of FISHING VESSELS on the COAST

No.	Name of Division.	Boundaries.	Registering Officer.	1st Class employed in 1870.			2nd Class employed in 1870.			3rd Class employed in 1871.		
				Vessels.	Men.	Boys.	Vessels.	Men.	Boys.	Vessels.	Men.	Boys.
8	Skibbereen, .	From Galley Head to Snave Bridge at the head of Bantry Bay.	H. M. Dyer, Commander, R.N.	9	53	5	259	1,301	110	370	2,696	118
9	Castletown Berehaven,	From Snave Bridge, county Cork, to Kenmare Bridge, county Kerry	John C. Drew, Lieutenant, R.N.	–	–	–	53	214	10	638	2,202	163
10	Killarney, .	From Kenmare (S.), to Brandon Creek, near Limerick harbour (N.)	P. Mahony, Divisional Officer,	14	40	10	25	126	4	330	1,447	269

No. 1—*continued*.

of IRELAND, from 1st January, 1870, to 1st January, 1871.

Total employed in 1870.			Substance of Observations made by Inspecting Commanders of Coast Guards and other Registering Officers, up to the 1st January, 1871	No.
Vessels.	Men.	Boys.		
			union to recoup the ratepayers for their maintenance, and, therefore, during the winter of 1870 they took care to have something laid by out of their summer earnings to live upon, instead of entering the workhouse. This stringent measure of the Poor Law Guardians has had a most beneficial effect both on the social condition of the fishermen and the pockets of the ratepayers. It has also stimulated the fishermen to follow their avocations in other waters. *Many of them now go to Howth to prosecute the herring fishery*, a proceeding to which they had the greatest objection formerly. A provisional order from the Board of Trade has lately been obtained, and a Harbour Board constituted, which will be the means of causing some improvement, both in the accommodation of the harbour and the regulation of fishery transactions. From these facts it will evidently appear that the fishery at Kinsale is of very great importance and worthy the attention of the Government.	
627	3,444	333	Boats and gear are wearing out, and it does not appear that much new gear is being purchased to replace the old. Nearly all fishermen hold land from half an acre to forty acres each. An improvement is reported from Crookhaven, but from all other stations none. The present prospects are—that there will be a further decline in the take of fish, if capital is not invested in gear. There is only a slight emigration as compared with former years, the fishermen would remain at home if fully employed. Considering the several modes of capture, last year's take of fish has been about the same as the preceding. The general state of the oyster fisheries very poor, no large banks exist; there are a few oysters in the estuary of the river [illegible] and in Lough Hyne, which are not improving, and no new natural banks have been lately discovered. Dr. [illegible], of Dunmanway, has stocked some part of the ground in [illegible] Bay, for which he has a licence. The general quality of the oysters is fair—price [illegible] per hundred from public beds at the mouth of the river Ilen; the quantity sold within the year 1870 was less than 10,000. No curing establishment exists, but a considerable quantity is cured in the cottages for home consumption; most of the fish, however, is sold fresh in the local markets. No instances of conflicts of any kind have occurred between persons pursuing different modes of fishing; the fishermen are orderly and industriously disposed, and all the able bodied men are employed at fishing in summer and when not struggling on their farms. The practice of trawling and use of trammel nets exist in Ross Bay, [illegible] Bay, and Long Island Bay, and no contentions have occurred. Considers that the law should impose as few restraints as possible on these modes of fishing, where they interfere with one another, it is only fair that the trammel nets should have some protection from damage by the trawlers. There are in use about 250 pieces of herring net, each 100 feet long, ten feet deep (120 meshes), about forty pieces of mackerel net, 100 feet long, ten feet deep (twenty-eight meshes), about [illegible] seines, from fifty to 150 yards long, and twenty to forty feet deep, and about 450 trammels, 120 feet long and nine feet deep. Considers trawling the most effectual and economical mode of capturing all manner of bottom fish, and is of opinion it does very little, if any, injury to the other fishing interests, and the reasons for this opinion are the result of experience in all the various modes of fishing while employed superintending the Scotch fisheries. Trawling is practised by five or six boats of from twelve to twenty tons—trawl occasionally [illegible], in from four to fifteen fathoms of water, the number of trawlers is less than in preceding year. The number of boats employed in the seine, trammel net, and line fishing, is 476, tonnage from half a ton to thirty-five tons. The fish captured by these modes of fishing are sold in the local markets, those captured by the trawl are taken to Cork. The fish generally captured are:—By trawl—sole, turbot, plaice, skate, and haddock; by trammel—hake, cod, ling, and haddock; by seine—mackerel, scad, mullet, and pilchards; by drift net—herrings and mackerel; by line—cod, conger, ling, bream, whiting, pollock, and gurnet. Mackerel and herrings present in March, April, and May, [illegible] fish come into the creeks and harbours in summer. All fish in best condition from August to October. During the last five years there has been a decrease in the fish frequenting the coast, chiefly herrings. Considers it doubtful whether fishermen would be benefited by loans to repair and purchase of boats and gear, considers they would find it difficult to procure security for repayment of same. The means of transit of fish are bad, and would most likely if improved lead to increased employment of men and boats. Has not heard of any complaints of high charge for transit. The natural harbours in the division are:— Rosscarbery, for boats; Mill Cove, for boats; Glandore, vessels of 300 tons; Castletownsend, vessels of 300 tons; [illegible], boats; Baltimore, vessels of 400 tons; Sherkin, vessels of fifty tons; Cape Clear, South, vessels of fifty tons; Long Island Sound, ships of largest size; Skull, vessels of 100 tons; Ballydehob, vessels of fifty tons; Whitehall, vessels of 300 tons; Crookhaven, vessels of largest size; Dunmanus, vessels of fifty tons; Bantry, large ships. Formally constituted harbours—Cape Clear, South. Piers in fair repair, it would be well, however, that they were looked to. The registry of boats is not perfect, it being most difficult to enforce the registration under the present system, as the fishermen will not register unless they find themselves punished for not doing so. Thinks the statistics given are fairly accurate, but that portion of the coast extending from Dunmanus to [illegible] Bridge, near [illegible], in Bantry Bay, although within the limits of the Skibbereen division, is without a Coastguard station. Suggests that a man be sent along that portion of the coast, periodically, to collect fishery statistics. Thinks it would be a difficult matter in this division to procure accurate statistics, but it might be done by giving a small remuneration to the most intelligent fisherman at each fishing station, for keeping a record of these matters, and the Coast guard could collect and tabulate these returns. Fishermen require to be taught *the art of curing*, and until this is done the fisheries on this coast cannot be fully developed.	8
681	2,416	173	The fishermen are engaged in farming, except at times when the fish is in season, when they are continually engaged in fishing. The whole of the craft specified are engaged in fishing at the seasonable times, at other times they are made serviceable in any way—collecting sea-weed, sand, &c. The fishermen are in very fair condition. The fishermen are chiefly farmers holding about one or two acres of land each. Last year was not so favourable as the preceding one, but the fishermen are looking anxiously for better. Emigration is still going on, as it offers the fishermen the only means of bettering themselves, but if the opportunities were as good here they would remain at home. The take of mackerel has been better than for many years, pilchards very good, but no sale, sprats fair, other hand line fishing not so good. The oyster fisheries are in a fair state, no great natural banks in division, steps have been taken to stock the ground where licences have been granted for the establishment of private beds. The quality of the oysters is fair, price about 2s. per hundred, quantity sold not known. Fish has been cured at Castletown, Ross Cove, Bere Island, and Ballycrovane, and afterwards sold at the fairs and to jobbers for what it would fetch, there being no other way of disposing of it; but a great deal of fish is also sold fresh to jobbers from distant places. No curing establishments exist or [illegible]. No conflicts between persons pursuing different modes of fishing have occurred, the fishermen are all well disposed, and generally able-bodied men. Both trawling and trammel net fishing are carried on, no contention with line fishers, has formed no opinion on the subject of restraints. The number of nets used are about:— Eight trammel nets, 115 feet and [illegible], twelve score and [illegible],—from Bantry to Waterfall; twenty-four trammel nets, 160 feet and [illegible], thirty [illegible] and [illegible],—from Ardgroom to Kenmare. There may be twenty herring nets in use, averaging twenty fathoms long by ten feet deep; four seines, averaging each seventy fathoms long by fourteen feet deep, and twenty trammel nets, each averaging twenty fathoms long by ten feet deep. Trawling is considered injurious, on account of its destroying the spawn and fish lying on the ground, and is not practised in this division. The number of boats employed in the seine, trammel net, and line fishing is 528, tonnage 186. There are no local markets or means of conveying the fish to other markets, it is generally sold to jobbers from distant places. The fish taken by the seine are—mackerel, herring, pilchard, bream, and scad; by trammel net and line—hake, [illegible], ling, haddock, cod, and turbot. January and February are the best months for ling, haddock, and cod; May, June, July, August, and September are the best for seine fishing; the other months they are not so plentiful or in such good condition. There has been a great increase in mackerel but no great difference in other kinds of fish. Loans would be a good advantage to many if they were only able to find security. There are no means of transit of fish to market for sale, if there was, all kinds of fishing would be followed with much more spirit. There are no conveyances of any kind through this district. Between Kenmare and Castletown there are three good harbours, viz.:—Kilmakilloge, Ardgroom, and Ballycrovane; between Castletown and Bantry there are four natural harbours able to accommodate any kind of fishing craft, viz.:—[illegible], Glengarriff, Castletown, and Lawrence Cove. There are no artificial harbours, nor any in course of construction. The registry of boats is perfect, and the present system seems very good. Private persons—such as owners of seines—could give the best information as to the quantity and disposal of the fish captured. Assisting the fishermen with boats and gear, and providing some certain means of disposing of the fish taken, would improve the fisheries, and the condition of a very orderly and industrious class of men.	9
367	1,828	174	The general condition of the fisheries of this district is only indifferent. A decrease in boats and gear, &c., within the last three years. The fishermen generally all hold from one to thirty acres of land each. Salmon fishing very productive last year, but all other fishery produce only indifferent, and present prospects not encouraging. Emigration continues to a very great extent, and even full employment would not induce the fishermen to remain at home. Only salmon more productive last year than the previous year, a falling off in the take of all other kinds of fish. Only one known natural oyster bank in the division, which is at Kenmare, and which is slightly improving, as is also the supply. No steps taken to stock licensed ground with oysters. The quality of the oysters is good, and they sell at from 6s. 6d. to 7s. 6d. per 100. There is no fish curing establishment in the district. The fish are generally sold in a fresh state, but when there is a large take, the means of conveyance to distant places are so limited, that the fishermen salt what they cannot dispose of, for their own use in winter. There is an institution for the preservation of salmon at [illegible]. Not a single case of conflict or collision between fishermen in this division, during last year, they are orderly, and industriously disposed. Only able-bodied men, at any time, employed fishing here. Trawling is practised in Dingle bay, Kenmare river, and occasionally (in summer time), in Ballinskelligs bay, but does not cause any contention with the line or other fishers. The dimensions of nets used—probably from fifteen to eighty fathoms long, and from two and a half to fourteen fathoms deep. Trawling does not injure the general fishing interests, but there is a difference of opinion existing on the subject. There are sixteen trawl boats of from eight to forty tons each; meshes of nets from one and a half, one and three quarters, and [illegible] inches, trawling generally in from four to forty fathoms of water. The number of trawl boats at Kenmare is increased by two the last year, but a decrease of one boat at Dingle has taken place. There are about 516 boats of from one to four tons, employed in seine, trammel net, and line fishing. The fish caught by trawl mostly sent to Dublin market; the other fish usually sold in local markets, fish otherwise captured generally sold in local markets, except salmon, which is always sent to distant places. Brill, sole, [illegible], plaice, cod, ling, &c., are taken by trawl; hake, bream, gurnet, scad, herrings, pilchard, mackerel, whiting, &c., by nets and lines. The large fish taken by trawl, is in good condition from February to June, and net and line fish from June to November. There has been an increase of salmon, a decrease of herrings, and about the same quantity of other fish taken last year as compared with the last five years. Many fishermen would be benefited by loans, which would also advance the fishing to a great extent, for there is plenty room for improvement, but few could procure reliable security for repayment. The means of transit for fish to market for sale, are not good; if improved conveyances were provided for the ready sale of the fish, it would lead to an increase of men and boats in the fisheries. There are complaints of the high charges for conveying fish to market, a basket of fish weighing twenty or thirty pounds from Kenmare to Dublin costs from 3s. to 4s., and from Dingle to Dublin, about the same per cwt. The natural harbours in the	10

APPENDIX,

STATE of the REGISTRY of FISHING VESSELS on the COAST

No.	Name of Division.	Boundaries.	Registering Officer.	1st Class employed in 1870.			2nd Class employed in 1870.			3rd Class employed in 1870.		
				Vessels.	Men.	Boys.	Vessels.	Men.	Boys.	Vessels.	Men.	Boys.
11	Ballyheigue,	From Blennerville Bridge, Tralee, on the S.W., to Lake Castle, on the East.	Mr. W. Dolsh, ...	1	3	-	17	50	1	30	88	1
12	Kilrush, .	From Loop Head to Farrahy Bay, also from Loop head to Foynes.	Charles O'B. Hall, Commander, R.N.	-	-	-	8	16	-	100	400	-
13	Seafield, .	From Bettard, South, to Lucklean Point, North.	W. H. Wright, Divisional Officer.	-	-	-	-	-	-	81	290	-
14	Galway, .	From Lackglass Head to Mace Head,	George Harwood, Inspecting Officer.	7	10	22	245	880	11	114	304	-
15	Clifden, .	Dooaboy to Mason Island, county Galway.	C. E. Buckle, Commander, R.N.	20	63	-	608	2,306	26	429	1,006	6

No. 1—*continued.*

of Ireland from 1st January, 1870, to 1st January, 1871.

Total employed in 1870			Substance of Observations made by Inspecting Commanders of Coast Guards and other Registering Officers, up to the 1st January, 1871	No.
Vessels	Men.	Boys		
			[illegible] are Kenmare river, Port Magee, Valentia, Cahirciveen, Dingle, Ventry, and Smerwick, which are able to accommodate boats of any size and any number of them. There are no artificial harbours, but various small piers and coves are interspersed where local small craft belong to. A more perfect registry of boats cannot be obtained unless by a paid official, which would entail great expense, who should travel to the several landing places, and there obtain other statistical accounts of the fisheries also. If the means of conveyance for fish to market were cheaper and more expeditious, and a few companies formed at the principal fishing stations ready to purchase the fish when brought ashore, fishermen would be induced to exert themselves far more than they do now. Good order generally exists amongst them.	
51	189	2	The general condition of the fisheries of this district appears to be good. None of the fishermen hold land. There does not seem to be any improvement in the fisheries within the last year, nor is there prospect of any, apparently. The spirit of emigration still prevails, [illegible]	11
168	431	–	The general state of the fisheries in this district is very bad. The fishermen hold from three to ten acres of land each. No improvement in the fisheries last year, nor is there prospect of any. Emigration prevails, but it does not appear to affect the fishing. [illegible]	12
81	228	–	There is no improvement in the condition of the fisheries in this district. Some few fishermen hold about one-eighth of an acre of land each. [illegible]	13
388	1,988	88	The general condition of the fisheries, boats, gear, &c., remain in much the same state these last three years. Most of the fishermen hold land. [illegible]	14
1,119	3,978	39	The fisheries in this district appear to be declining, when compared for the last three years. Nearly all the fishermen hold from two to fourteen acres of land each. Within the last year there has been a very slight improvement in the fisheries in some parts of the coast, but present prospects are bad. The spirit of emigration still prevails here, [illegible]	15

APPENDIX,

STATE of the REGISTRY of FISHING VESSELS on the COAST

No.	Name of Division.	Boundaries.	Registering Officer.	1st Class employed in 1876.			2nd Class employed in 1876.			3rd Class employed in 1876.		
				Vessels	Men.	Boys	Vessels	Men.	Boys	Vessels.	Men.	Boys
16	Keel, . .	Doonbeg Head, East, to Doolena Head, West.	Robert George Gibbon, Inspecting Officer.	–	–	–	11	33	–	240	900	44
17	Belmullet, .	From Doolena Head to Buttar Point,	Duke Yonge, Lieut., R.N., .	–	–	–	..	–	–	410	1,514	[illegible]
18	Ballycastle (E).	Gap of Bartragh Island to Brandy Point.	H. S. Mandeville, Lieut., R.N.,	–	–	–	3	15	1	190	1,221	[illegible]
19	Pullendiva, .	Bartragh Island to Coney's Island, .	R. Benes, Divisional Officer,	–	–	–	–	–	–	57	235	–
20	Sligo, .	Strandhill Barracks to Donegal Abbey.	Geo. T. Morrell, Lieut., R.N.,	1	5	–	70	390	48	161	[illegible]	[illegible]

No. 1—*continued.*

of Ireland from 1st January, 1870, to 1st January, 1871.

Total employed in 1870.			Substance of Observations made by Inspecting Commanders of Coast Guards, and other Registering Officers, up to the 1st January, 1871	No.
Vessels.	Men.	Boys		
			Bay, and partly natural harbours at Bunown, Brandon, Dent Harbour, Clogane. There is undoubtedly abundant accommodation for a hundred times as many boats as are now employed fishing in the district. The registry of boats will be perfect within the next year, as the principle is being fully carried out here, but [illegible] that it is very difficult to obtain a perfect register of them. Statistical information might be acquired pretty accurately, concerning the kinds and quantities of fish captured, &c., from the fishermen when they come with their registers for examination.	
263	938	44	The condition of the fisheries, boats, and gear about the same in this division for the last three years. No improvement whatever last year, and present prospects do not appear to be good. The fishermen hold about two acres of land each. The spirit of emigration prevails amongst the fishermen and coast population here, who state that they will leave the country as soon as they have the means to do so; but if they were fully employed most of them would remain at home. [illegible]	16
410	1,814	12	In that part of the division extending from Dunboy Head to Butter Point, Reenaheavon, the general condition of boats, gear, &c. about same as last two years. The fishermen hold from one to two acres of land each. No sign of improvement in the fisheries last year, and prospects very poor. [illegible]	17
202	1,336	11	General state of fisheries, boats, and gear, good. The fishermen have small holdings of land—two or three acres each. No improvement in the fisheries within the last year, but prospects are good. Emigration still prevails, but if the fishermen were fully employed they would remain at home. [illegible]	18
57	298	–	The general condition of the fisheries about the same in this district during the last three years. The fishermen hold, on average, from four to six acres of land each. No improvement has taken place in the fisheries within the last year, and prospects same as past years. [illegible]	19
283	1,287	50	The general condition of the fisheries in this district much the same compared with last three years. The fishermen hold from one to seven acres of land each. There has been some improvement in trawling within the last year, more boats employed, and fair prospects. [illegible]	20

APPENDIX,

STATE of the REGISTRY of FISHING VESSELS on the COAST

No.	Name of Division.	Boundaries.	Registering Officer.	1st Class employed in 1870.			2nd Class employed in 1870.			3rd Class employed in 1870.		
				Vessels.	Men.	Boys	Vessels.	Men	Boys	Vessels.	Men.	Boys
21	Killybegs, .	Donegal quay to Lower Ferry, East,	Francis Osburn, Lieut., R.N.,	2	4	-	200	1,539	187	-	-	-
22	Dunfanaghy,	Gweebarra to Rathmelton, . .	E. C. Ball, Divisional Officer,	-	-	-	231	947	276	243	546	-
23	Carn, .	Buncrana to Magilligan Point, .	James D. Curtis, Commander, R.N.	5	16	-	255	1,170	21	114	576	6

No. 1—*continued.*

of IRELAND from 1st January, 1870, to 1st January, 1871.

Total employed in 1870.			Substance of Observations made by Inspecting Commanders of Coast Guards and other Registering Officers, up to the 1st January, 1870	No.
Vessels.	Men.	Boys		
			by trawl and otherwise, sold in local markets, with the exception of salmon, which are sent to distant places for sale. [illegible]	
389	1,542	137	The general condition of the fisheries of this district not improved within the last three years. [illegible]	21
473	1,492	370	No improvement in the state of the fisheries of this district for the last three years. [illegible]	22
374	1,782	37	The fisheries of this district continue in much the same condition during the last three years. [illegible]	23

APPENDIX,

STATE of the REGISTRY of FISHING VESSELS on the COAST

No.	Name of District.	Boundaries.	Registering Officer.	1st Class employed in 1870			2nd Class employed in 1874.			3rd Class employed in 1876.		
				Vessels.	Men.	Boys	Vessels	Men.	Boys.	Vessels	Men.	Boys
24	Ballycastle (Antrim).	Down Hill Railway Station to Jenning's Bridge.	A. W. J. Richardson, Commander, R.N.	–	–	–	148	485	4	15	49	1
25	Carrickfergus,	Jenning's Bridge, near Carron Point, to White Railings near Belfast.	William G. England, Commander, R.N.	–	–	–	53	141	–	101	246	–
26	Donaghadee,	Cultra, Fitty's Burn, to Clegiry, Newcastle Quay.	F. R. Hartwell, Commander, R.N.	17	118	1	199	648	23	33	80	–
27	Strangford,	Newcastle Quay, North, to Sheepland Head, South.	James Pyper, Staff Commander, R.N.	–	–	–	147	338	3	9	13	–
28	Newcastle,	Gun's Island, North, to River Fane, Kilkeel, South.	R. Mansel, Commander, R.N.	24	153	9	98	370	26	30	40	4

No. 1—*continued.*

of Ireland from 1st January, 1870, to 1st January, 1871.

Total employed in 1870. Vessels.	Men.	Boys.	Substance of Observations made by Inspecting Commanders of Coast Guards, and other Registering Officers, up to the 1st January, 1871.	No.
260	543	0	The general condition of the fisheries in this district is fair, and boats in good order. With the exception of those at Portrush most of the fishermen hold from four to twenty acres of land each, and are employed in farming when not fishing. No sign of improvement except in the boats last year, and prospects bad. The spirit of emigration does not prevail here, the fishermen remain at home. The last year's take of fish about the same as the quantity captured the preceding year. No oyster beds in this division. No curing establishment formed for curing fish—all sold fresh. An increase of each salmon fishery. Conflicts do not occur between the fishermen, they are orderly and industriously disposed, and are partially employed fishing. No trawling practised in this district, nor are trammel nets used. There are fourteen salmon nets averaging in size from fifty yards by eight to one hundred yards by sixteen yards. No herring nets. There are fourteen salmon boats of from one ton to one ton and a half, and 152 boats employed line fishing. The fish captured sold in local markets. Herrings, bream, horse-mackerel, and glassen, are taken by seine; cod, ling, and grey gurnet by line. Salmon fish in best condition in summer. Line fish in spring and fall. The quantity of fish frequenting this part of the coast nearly the same each of the last five years. Loans to fishermen here would not benefit the fishermen, security could not be procured for repayment of money advanced. The means of transit for fish to market for sale are good, and no complaints of high charges for conveyance of fish. No natural harbours in the division; artificial harbours at Portrush, Portstewart, and Cushendall. Portrush harbour can accommodate vessels up to 400 tons, but the others only coasting vessels of small tonnage. Registry of vessels correct here. A good means of obtaining accurate statistical information of the kinds and quantities of fish taken would be for men from the Customs or Coast-guard to attend and inspect the boats when they return from fishing.	24
153	387	-	No improvement in the general condition of the fisheries of this district as compared with the last three years, and boats and gear in much the same state also. Some fishermen in north part of division hold from one to five acres of land each. At Carrickfergus they hold little or nothing but their boats and gear. There has been no improvement in the fisheries last year, and prospects appear dull. The spirit of emigration does not exist here, but the younger men seem inclined to go to sea. The take of fish has been less, on the whole, last year than it was the preceding year. The oyster fisheries improving. There are natural banks at Grey point, Holywood, and Kilroot, which are improving in supply. No new beds discovered lately. No steps taken to stock private oyster beds. The quality of the oysters is good, and they sell at 5s. to 10s. the per hundred. About 60,000 or 80,000 sold within the year. No fish curing establishment in the district—fish sold in fresh state. There is an ice-house at Glenarm for salmon, belonging to Earl of Antrim. The fishermen pursuing different modes of capture do not quarrel or have conflicts amongst them, they are orderly disposed, the younger men employed at sea—the older ones do the fishing. Trawling exists in Belfast Lough, and a trammel was used last year at Blackhead, but no complaints arose [illegible] fishery. The general opinion is that trawling is injurious where spawn is. There are nine herring nets eight hundred yards long and nine yards deep, four seine nets thirty-five fathoms long and four and a half fathoms deep, one trammel net forty-five fathoms long and six feet deep with three and a half inch mesh. The trawling is supposed to be injurious to spawn in shallow water, and that fish deposit their spawn on soft bottom along Belfast Lough. There are eleven boats of about eighty tons employed trawling in water from four to five and a half fathoms deep. Size of mesh of trawl net one and three-quarter inches. One trawl boat, being useless from decay and old age, broken up last year, so that their number is one less than the preceding year. One hundred and forty-two boats of average tonnage of two tons employed using trammel, and line fishing, but of these only fourteen solely engaged fishing, the remainder used occasionally by farmers for fishing purposes along the coast. The fish caught all sold in local markets. Flat fish of different kinds captured by trawlers; pollock, mullet, and codling, by seine and trammel; cod and ling by line. Flat fish are best in summer, and worst in spring. Cod in best condition in winter, and worst in summer. Rather a decrease in the quantity of flat fish frequenting this part of the coast during the last five years. Loans would benefit the fishermen of Carrickfergus for repairs to boats, &c., but they could not give good security for repayment of the money. Transit for fish to market very good by railway, and no complaints of high charges for its conveyance. Glenarm and Carnlough are partly natural and partly artificial harbours, and can accommodate all kinds of fishing vessels, Larne Lough the same. Carrickfergus [illegible] Harbour accommodates all the trawlers. Scotch Quarter-pier used by long line and herring craft. A west wall required at Scotch Quarter-quay to shelter boats in S.W. winds, which would enable fishermen to get in or out in all weathers. Registry of boats perfect in this district, but it would be better if all the registrations of boats were obtained through the nearest Coast-guard Officer, as some get them direct from Collector of Customs, which causes confusion in the returns. Statistical information of kinds and quantities of fish taken might be accurately obtained by appointing a person solely for the purpose of visiting and reporting on it. It is a subject of dispute whether trawling injures spawn, but that mode of fishing should be confined to certain defined bounds.	25
219	666	36	The state of the fisheries, boats, gear, &c., in this district has not improved within the last three years. Most of the fishermen hold from one to six acres of land each. No signs of improvement in the fisheries last year, but present prospects fair. The spirit of emigration does not prevail amongst the fishermen here, they prefer stopping at home. According to general opinion, the take of fish was slightly better last year than the preceding one. There are two small natural oyster banks off Groomsport, which are not very productive, and are not improving in supply. No new oyster banks lately discovered, nor are there any private oyster beds in this division. The natural quality of the oysters is very good, and they are sold at from 4s. to 5s. per hundred, several thousands sold within the year. No curing establishment for fish known at any time to have existed here, the fish sold fresh, no attempt made to cure it. No ice-house in the division. No collisions occur between fishermen pursuing different modes of capture, they are orderly and industriously disposed, the able-bodied men are generally employed in fishing. Trawling is practised in Belfast Lough, but no contentions arise with other fishers. No trammel nets used in this locality. Trawling is not injurious to the fishing interests, if not carried on within the spawning limits. There are eight trawl boats of ten to nineteen tons each, worked in water from six to nine fathoms deep, having nets with four-inch mesh. Number of herring nets are about fifty-seven, and are each 1,230 fathoms long, 4 fathoms deep, with a one-inch mesh. Thirteen seine nets from forty to fifty fathoms long, and from one and a half to three fathoms deep, with one and a quarter to one and three-quarter inches mesh. The number of trawl boats the same these two years. Two hundred boats of from half a ton to three tons, employed in seine and line fishing. The fish taken by trawl sold in local markets, as are the fish captured by seine and line, except some which are sent to distant places. The fish captured generally in this district are—all kinds of flat fish, salmon, trout, cod, ling, conger, pollock, and whiting; the flat fish are in best condition from August to November, salmon and trout best from April to June, and ling, conger, pollock, and whiting are best from December to April. There was a decrease of all kinds of fish on this part of the coast during the last five years, but this last year it has been slightly improved in quantity. It is very doubtful whether the fishermen could procure security for repayment of loans of money to purchase boats, &c.; loans would not be beneficial to them. The means of transit for fish to market for sale are very good, improvements in that respect would not lead to employment of more men and boats, no complaints of high charges for conveyance of the fish to market. The harbours at Bangor, Groomsport, Donaghadee, Ballywalter, and Portaferry, can accommodate vessels up to fifteen tons, and they are all in good repair, requiring nothing on them. Registry of boats perfect here. Correct statistical information of the kinds and quantities of fish captured, might be obtained by appointing an inspector in each division for the purpose, keeping an account, and reporting on it periodically. With the exception of cod, the fishing here is so bad, that there is no suggestion to offer for its improvement.	26
150	341	5	The fishermen in this district in much the same condition these last three years. Some of the fishermen hold land, from one to ten acres each, and some a less quantity. No improvement in the fisheries within the last year, and prospects bad. The spirit of emigration does not prevail here amongst the fishermen. The take of fish has been less productive last year than it was the previous year. No oyster fishery in the district of any kind, neither public nor private beds. Trawling is most prejudicial to the general fishing interests, as that mode of fishing destroys the young fish, is unfair to the line fishers, and prevents many hundreds of men from a fair chance of gaining an honest living. Trawling is not practised in this locality. There are three deep-sea herring boats of from twelve to fifteen tons each, the remainder, seventy-five boats, are line fishers of from one to one and a half tons each. The fish captured sold where landed on shore. The registry of boats perfect in this district. The means of obtaining accurate statistical information of the kinds and quantities of fish taken might be secured by compelling the fishermen to keep or furnish accounts periodically, as required, to the nearest Coast-guard officer. The fish captured here are herrings, codling, whiting, and cod. Herrings are taken in best condition in June, July, and August, and are found in worst condition from September to March. Codling in best condition January to June, inclusive, and in worst condition July to September. Whiting best from January to March, inclusive; worst from April to September. Cod best from January to June, inclusive, worst from July to September. There has been a decrease of fish on this part of the coast during last five years. The fishermen would not be benefited by loans of money for purchase or repairs of boats. The means of transit for fish to markets for sale is good, but not availed of, as the consumption of fish in the immediate neighbourhood is quite equal to the supply. No complaints of high charges for the carriage of fish. No harbour in the district for fishing craft but Strangford Lough.	27
143	562	39	The fisheries, boats, gear, &c., in much the same condition during the last three years in this district. The fishermen hold from one to eight acres of land each. Some improvement in the take of herrings last year; but other fish more scarce than in preceding year, and prospects not good. Very little emigration of fishermen occurring here. Altogether the produce of fishing has been less last year than it was the previous year. No oyster fisheries in the district. Some oyster beds said to exist off Annalong. No curing establishment for fish, it is sold in the fresh state. No conflicts occur between the fishermen, they are orderly and industrious, excepting at Newcastle; the able-bodied men are generally employed fishing. No trawling carried on here, and its prohibition is injurious to the take of fish. Four hundred and eight herring nets in use, averaging 100 yards long, and sixteen yards deep, with mesh of one inch, one salmon, 180 yards long, ten feet deep, with one and three-quarter inches mesh. Trawling should be permitted, as it would increase the produce of fishing; but measures might be taken to prevent injury to spawn, by making spawning time a "close season" to trawlers. In some places in this division, where the fishermen are energetic, they desire to trawl. No trammel nets in use. One boat of one ton employed salmon fishing, 194 boats, 338 tons, engaged line fishing. Some of the fish taken sold in local markets, but larger quantities sent to distant places. Cod, ling, haddock, and whiting taken by line; in best condition from October to March. Flat fish in best condition from April to September; mackerel in best condition from August to October. The various kinds of fish here enumerated may be considered in bad condition during the months, respectively, wherein they are not stated to be in "best condition." There has been a decrease in all kinds of fish on this part of the coast during the last five years, excepting herrings. Loans might be of temporary advantage to the fishermen, but they could not procure security for repayment of the money. Transit for fish to market for sale quite sufficient, and no complaints of high charges for its carriage. Ardglass Harbour, which is partly natural and partly artificial, is capable of accommodating 400 boats of twenty tons each, but it is in bad repair; an outlay on it strongly recommended, the harbour being naturally good and advantageous, but the artificial part has fallen into bad repair. Killough Harbour which is also part natural and part artificial, can accommodate only fishing boats of twenty tons each, is in good repair. Newcastle Harbour, which is an artificial one, cannot accommodate anything larger than a whale boat in its present state, is thoroughly out of repair; an outlay recommended.	28

APPENDIX,

STATE of the REGISTRY of FISHING VESSELS on the COAST

No.	Name of Division.	Boundaries.	Registering Officer.	1st Class employed in 1870.			2nd Class employed in 1870.			3rd Class employed in 1870.		
				Vessels	Men	Boys	Vessels	Men	Boys	Vessels	Men	Boys
29	Carlingford, .	Ballaghan Point, South, to the River Fort, Kilkeel, North.	W. F. A. Harris, Lieut., R.N.,	14	94	12	142	587	6	147	459	–
30	Dundalk, .	Ballaghan Point, county Louth, to Maiden Tower, Drogheda.	G. D. Bell, Lieut., R.N., .	–	–	–	221	827	15	–	–	–
31	Malahide, .	Mouth of Boyne to Whip of the Waters, Baldoyle.	William Moriarty, Commander, R.N.	61	414	82	35	145	8	15	88	–

No. 1—*continued*.

of Ireland, from 1st January, 1870, to 1st January, 1871.

Total employed in 1870			Substance of Observations made by Inspecting Commanders of Coast Guards, and other Registering Officers, up to the 1st January, 1871	No.
Vessels	Men	Boys		
			mended; the expense of repairing it would be too great for any return. Annalong Harbour, which is part natural and part artificial, can accommodate sixty fishing boats of twenty tons each, but requires an outlay to afford suitable accommodation for them. Registry of boats in this division perfect. Accurate statistical information of the kinds and quantities of fish taken, could be obtained by appointing a qualified person for that purpose, and by imposing a fine on the master of every fishing boat who did not give the return of fish captured, before leaving the harbour. It is strongly recommended that the prohibition against trawling between St. John's Point and [illegible] off Cranfield Point, be withdrawn; these points include all the Bay of Dundrum, which is only fished by a few long line men in a miserable way, in small boats averaging one ton, and these are most of the winter incapable of taking the sea. If trawling were permitted a large supply of fish would be developed.	
808	1,140	18	The fisheries, boats, gear, &c., have rather improved in this district during the last three years. The greater number of the fishermen hold from three to ten acres of land each. Some little improvement last year in the fisheries, but prospects are not favourable. Emigration does not prevail here to a great extent amongst the fishermen. If fully employed they would remain at home. Fisheries more productive from fishing last year than the preceding year. The oyster fisheries are improving a little. The whole of Carlingford Lough may be taken as a natural oyster bed, and the supply increasing—but very little. Steps have been taken to stock [illegible] for private oyster beds. Although the size of the oysters is not large, the quality is very good, and they sell at 6s. to 7s. per hundred, 357,000 sold within the past year. No fish curing establishment in this district. No conflicts occur between the fishermen; they are orderly and industriously disposed, and when not fishing they ferry boats and work their land. No trawling practised in this district. The first-class vessels carry about 1,000 yards of herring nets each, the second class boats carry fifty yards each; size of mesh—one inch. There has been no increase in the quantity of herrings frequenting this part of the coast during the last five years. The fishermen would be benefited by loans for the purchase of boats, gear, &c., and they could procure security for the repayment of the money. Means of transit for fish to market for sale good. Improvement in that respect would not lead to increased employment of men and boats. No complaints of high charges for carriage of fish. Carlingford Lough is the harbour used by fishing craft here. The registry of boats perfect in this district. Accurate statistical information as to the quantities of the different kinds of fish captured, &c., might be obtained from the local buyers of fish.	29
221	697	15	No improvement in boats, gear, &c., in this district within the last three years. Some slight improvement in the fishing last year; and prospects good. The fishermen if fully employed would be likely not to emigrate, but remain at home. Some of them hold from half an acre to two acres of land each. Last year has been more productive in the take of herrings and salmon than the year preceding. No oyster fisheries in this locality. No fish curing establishment in the district, the fish sold in a fresh state. The fishermen are very quiet and orderly, and the able-bodied men are generally employed in fishing, having no contentions amongst them. No trawling allowed here. In fishing for herrings there are five men to each boat who have to provide a net each of from twenty-five to thirty fathoms in length and three and a half fathoms in depth. Herrings only taken by drift nets in the bay. The seine nets used for taking salmon are from forty to sixty fathoms long and five fathoms deep in centre, to three and a half fathoms in the ends. Trawling in a bay spoils line fishing, destroys spawn, destroys great quantities of young fish, and tends to frighten herrings, mackerel, &c., from coming into it. Admitting that in a bay where trawling is not allowed, and fish are well fed, the ground fish will seldom take bait, as in this bay (Dundalk), the only way to get turbot or sole would be by trawl; still, after many years' experience in the protection of fisheries, such is the conclusion come to [illegible]. There are 171 boats of from half a ton to a ton and a half employed in this division. The fish taken sold in local markets. Mackerel in best condition in July and August, herrings in September, cod and ling whiting in winter, salmon best in July and August. A slight increase in herring and salmon on this part of the coast last year, as compared with the five previous years. No doubt the fishermen would be benefited by loans to fishermen for purchase and repairs of boats, thereby advancing the fishery, and some of the men could procure security for repayment of the money so advanced. The fish are transmitted to market for sale by carts, or rail. It is mostly sold on the beach to regular buyers, no complaints of high rates charged for its carriage. [illegible] and Dundalk are natural and partly natural harbours. A small harbour has been constructed out of a quarry hole at Clogher Head, which might be made into a very good boat harbour, with small outlay, for fishing boats of from one to two tons, or for even larger boats. At present it is very badly constructed, and its enlargement and improvement would be a great boon to the fishermen using it. Registry of boats perfect in this division. By appointing and paying men to obtain and furnish statistical information as to the quantities of the different kinds of fish captured, &c., would be the best means of getting it accurately.	30
111	509	37	The fisheries slightly improved in this district during the last three years. Some few fishermen hold from a rood to an acre of land each. Some slight improvement in last year's fishing, prospects only as usual. No emigration of fishermen from this division. Last year less productive in the take of fish than the preceding year. No natural oyster banks in this district. A private oyster bed at Malahide, the property of Lord Talbot de Malahide, in fair condition, and improving in supply; their quality is good, and sell at 5s. per hundred—but little or none sold. No steps taken to stock any other oyster beds here. There is one curing establishment for fish at Rush, where some are cured, but the rest of the fish sold in a fresh state. No increase in this division. Conflicts do not occur between trawlers and other fishermen following different modes of capture, the men are steady and industriously disposed, and are generally employed fishing. Trawling exists here, but does not cause contentions. No opinion as to restraints on trawling. [illegible] only description of net in use in this locality. A train of nets is 700 fathoms long and ten fathoms deep. There are seven trawling vessels, averaging twenty-six tons each, which trawl in water from three to ten fathoms deep, meshes of nets vary from one inch to three and a half inches. The same number of small boats working the same last years. Forty-three boats, of from two to thirty tons, employed in line fishing. No other new trawl and nets in use here. The fish taken by trawling mostly sent to distant places for sale, that taken by line sent to Dublin market. Cod and plaice are captured by trawl and by line, these fish are in best condition in winter, and in worst condition in summer. Fish have decreased on this part of the coast during the last five years, especially haddock and ling. The fishermen would be greatly benefited by public loans, and fishing interests advanced thereby, but security for repayment of the money could not generally be procured. The means of transit for fish to market for sale is good and no complaints of high rates for its carriage. Balbriggan has an artificial pier and harbour, in fair repair, where vessels of 150 tons can enter. At Skerries pier and harbour also artificial, vessels of 200 tons can enter, but it is in bad repair, would be greatly improved. Rush has likewise an artificial pier and harbour, where vessels of from eighty to 100 tons could enter, this harbour requires cleaning. Registry of vessels perfect in this district.	31

APPENDIX No. 2.—ABSTRACT of RETURNS from COAST GUARD

Appendix, No. 3.

Howth Herring Fishery for Season 1870.

Abstract of Returns of Herring Fishery at Howth, between the 1st June, 1870, and 19th November, 1870, furnished by Chief Officer of Coast Guard at Howth.

Date, Week ending—	Average daily Number of Boats employed. Cornish.	Scotch.	Manx.	Irish.	Number of Mease of 630 fish each.	Average price per Mease of 630 fish.	Gross Receipts.	Number of days Employed.	Observations.
1870.						£ s. d.	£ s. d.		
June 4,	37	25	–	43	1,200	0 18 11¼	1,137 10 0	5	Mixed quality of fish.
" 11,	–	–	–	–	–	—	—	–	—
" 18,	–	–	–	–	–	—	—	–	—
" 25,	14	6	0	31	516	0 18 0	466 7 0	5	Very good quality.
July 2,	77	25	13	65	13,200	0 0 10¾	4,641 0 0	5	Do.
" 9,	84	34	9	56	3,160	0 18 3	2,843 0 0	5	Do , some mixed quality.
" 16,	73	28	1	45	3,980	0 17 6½	3,313 10 0	5	Good fish
" 23,	56	33	–	56	5,193	0 17 3½	4,465 0 0	5	Very bad fish—being "Black Gut."
" 30,	54	33	3	64	4,230	0 18 0¾	4,010 0 0	5	Some very bad fish, and some very good. The English buyers lost over £500 last week—one man bought £50 worth of fish and sent them to England, and a bill for £8 more came back. The fish were completely rotten by the time they got to market. They were what are called "Black Gut."
August 6,	73	80	10	67	3,400	1 1 11½	3,846 15 0	6	Good fish.
" 13,	37	17	1	32	2,084	0 9 10¾	800 0 0	6	Inferior fish.
" 20,	9	7	4	40	3,400	0 6 10	1,101 5 0	5	Some very good, and some mixed.
" 27,	5	6	–	56	1,895	0 17 2	1,463 10 0	5	Very good fish.
September 3,	5	6	–	35	1,570	1 0 8½	1,625 10 0	4	Do.
" 10,	1	5	–	11	1,170	0 14 7	854 10 0	5	Mixed fish, some good.
" 17,	4	2	7	27	2,180	0 11 7½	1,260 5 0	5	Do do.
" 24,	4	2	10	28	3,440	0 18 [illegible]	1,926 15 0	5	Do. do.
October 1,	5	1	25	38	1,812	0 18 5	1,404 15 0	5	Do. do.
" 8,	2	1	67	31	6,601	0 8 1½	2,736 10 0	4	Do.
" 15,	–	7	55	40	1,500	0 10 5	390 0 0	3	Good fish.
" 22,	–	1	19	8	102	1 4 0½	172 10 0	3	Do ; but [illegible].
" 29,	–	0	21	8	12	1 2 4½	14 11 0	3	Do
November 5,	–	–	20	35	780	0 11 11½	460 0 0	5	Indifferent fish.
" 12,	1	–	40	30	786	0 10 6¾	415 15 0	4	Mixed quality.
" 19,	–	–	60	26	290	0 14 [illegible]	100 0 0	3	Middling quality.
Totals,	–	–	–	–	61,063	—	49,876 19 0	103	
Average numbers and amounts per day for the 109 days worked,	26	13	17	34	578½	0 16 0½	446 12 0¾	–	

Appendix, No. 4.

Ardglass Harbour.

Abstract of Herring Fishery for Season 1870 (which commenced 4th June and ended on 15th October), showing number of Boats employed, and greatest number of Mease caught per Boat; also highest and average price per Mease in each month, and total quantity caught, and gross sum realized.

Month ending	Highest Number of Boats employed on any one Night, English, Irish, and Scotch.	Highest Number of Mease per Boat.	Total Number of Mease.	Highest and Average Price.	Total Amount realized.	Number of Days out.
				£ s. d.	£ s. d.	
June 30th,	258	64	6,830	1 6 0 0 11 8½	3,935 14 2	20
July 30th,	196	84	11,588	1 8 0 0 14 9¾	3,589 15 4½	19
August 31st,	149	75	6,770	1 5 0 0 13 2½	4,471 0 5	21
October 15th.	23	66	1,501	1 7 0 0 17 5	1,307 2 5	26
Total,			26,689		£15,306 12 4½	87

APPENDIX, No. 5.

APPENDIX, No. 5.

LIST of LICENCES GRANTED to Plant OYSTER BEDS up to 31st December, 1870.

Date of Licence.		Persons to whom Granted.	Locality of Beds	Area of Beds. A.	R.	P.
1846,	5th November,	W. H. Carter, esq.	Tramore Bay, county Mayo,	19	1	11
	7th December,	Luke Lyons, esq.	Mosroughrony, county Mayo,	17	0	0
1848,	9th June,	F. H. Downing,	Off Dauros Point, county Kerry,	3	2	28
1849,	24th February,	R. T. Evanson,	Dunmanus Bay, county Cork,	10	0	10
1851,	5th February,	John Mahony, esq.	Estuary of Kenmare River, county Kerry,	165	2	0
	5th February,	Rev. Denis Mahony,	Estuary of Kenmare River, county Kerry,	147	2	0
1852,	17th November,	Thomas White, esq.	Ballisodare Bay, county Sligo,	132	1	26
	17th November,	John C. Garvey, esq.	Clew Bay, county Mayo,	108	3	33
1853,	22nd September,	J. O. Woodhouse, esq.	Mulroy Bay, county Donegal,	63	0	26
1854,	1st July,	Burton Bindon, esq.	Carlingford Lough, county Louth,	81	3	10
	15th November,	Hon. David Plunket,	Killary Harbour, county Mayo,	288	0	0
	15th November,	J. K. Boswell, esq.	Ballyconnelly Bay, county Galway,	233	0	0
1855,	18th July,	John Richards, esq.	Blacksod Bay, county Mayo,	90	0	0
1856,	30th July,	Lord Charles P. P. Clinton,	Bear Haven, county Cork,	45	0	0
	21st August,	William Foreman, esq.	Ardbear Bay, county Galway,	96	2	0
1857,	7th August,	Thomas Eccles, esq.	Glengariff Harbour, county Cork,	0	1	0
1858,	13th February,	Rev. A. Magee,	Streamstown and Cleggan Bays, co. Galway,	377	0	0
	15th February,	A. C. Lambert, esq.	Killary Harbour, county Galway,	114	0	0
1860,	3rd February,	Rev. R. H. Wall,	Mannin and Ardbear Bays, county Galway,	348	0	0
	3rd February,	Knight of Kerry,	Valencia Harbour, county Kerry,	78	0	0
	3rd February,	Captain W. Houston,	Killery Harbour, county Mayo,	43	0	0
	13th February,	William M'Cormick, esq.	Achill Sound, county Mayo,	149	0	0
	11th May,	Edward Browne, esq.	Ballinakill Harbour, county Galway,	223	0	0
	4th October,	M. C. Cramer, esq.	Oyster Haven, county Cork,	20	0	0
	9th October,	Ebenezer Pike, esq.	Lough Mahon, Estuary of Lee, county Cork,	47	0	0
	14th November,	William Pike, esq.	Achill Sound, county Mayo,	1,670	0	0
1861,	10th January,	William Forbes, esq.	Mweenish Bay, county Galway,	225	0	0
1862,	14th February,	Robert W. C. Reeves, esq.	Clonderlaw Bay, county Clare,	112	0	0
	3rd March,	James Walker, esq.	Belfast Lough, Carrickfergus,	137	0	0
	6th March,	Edmund Power, esq.	Tramore Bay, county Waterford,	270	0	0
1863,	29th May,	George Clive, esq., M.P.	Achill Sound, county Mayo,	480	0	0
1864,	2nd February,	Lord Fortescue,	Tramore Bay, county Waterford,	63	0	0
	8th April,	Lord Wallscourt,	Galway Bay, county Galway,	1,770	0	0
	10th June,	Colonel C. M. Vandeleur, M.P.	Poulnasherry Bay, county Clare,	190	0	0
	10th June,	A. W. Wyndham, esq.	Newport Bay, county Mayo,	80	0	0
	30th September,	Captain George Austin,	Westport Bay, county Mayo,	194	0	0
	31st October,	John Kendall, esq.	Ardbear and Mannin Bays, county Galway,	236	0	0
	31st October,	Robert T. Atkins, esq.	Lough Hyne, county Cork,	25	0	0
	31st October,	R. B. L. Athy, esq.	Galway Bay, county Galway,	100	0	0
	31st October,	P. M. Lynch, esq.	Galway Bay, county Galway,	320	0	0
	11th November,	A. Boate, esq.	Dungarvan Harbour, county Waterford,	65	0	0
	11th November,	J. R. Dower, esq.	Dungarvan Harbour, county Waterford,	27	0	0
	31st December,	Captain W. F. Barry,	Glandore Harbour, county Cork,	60	0	0
	31st December,	C. P. Archer, esq.	Ballinakill Harbour, county Galway,	48	0	0
	31st December,	T. Young Prior, esq.	Ballinakill Harbour, county Galway,	90	0	0
	31st December,	P. Macauley, esq.	Ballinakill and Barnaderg Bays, co. Galway,	150	0	0
	31st December,	Colonel F. A. K. Gore,	Killala Bay, county Mayo,	375	0	0
1865,	13th April,	Marquess of Sligo,	Clew Bay, county Mayo,	190	0	0
	13th April,	Sir Robert Gore Booth,	Drumcliff Bay, county Sligo,	148	3	0
	20th April,	Right Hon. John Wynne,	Sligo Bay, county Sligo,	190	0	0
	12th May,	Lord Baron Ventry,	Dingle Harbour, county Kerry,	120	0	0
	2nd November,	Law Life Assurance Society,	Clew Bay, county Mayo,	118	0	0
	2nd November,	Marquess of Sligo,	Clew Bay, county Mayo,	26	0	0
	1st December,	Most Rev. Dr. M'Hale,	Shores of Achill Island, county Mayo,	125	0	0
	1st December,	Thomas M'Carthy Collins, esq.	Roaringwater Bay, county Cork,	75	0	0
	1st December,	Marquess of Sligo,	Clew Bay, county Mayo,	26	0	0
	1st December,	John Obins Woodhouse, esq.	Carlingford Lough, county Louth,	54	0	0
	1st December,	Captain Acheson,	Ballinakill Harbour, county Galway,	18	0	0
	1st December,	Richard J. Verschoyle, esq.	Ballisodare Bay, county Sligo,	54	0	0
	1st December,	Richard Mahony, esq.	Kenmare Estuary, county Kerry,	80	0	0
	1st December,	Mr. Robert M'Keown,	Killary Harbour,	61	0	0
1866,	20th April,	William Dargan, esq.	Wexford Harbour,	70	0	0
	20th April,	Marquess of Sligo,	Clew Bay, county Mayo,	270	0	0
	21st April,	Miss Anne Fowler,	Blacksod Bay, county Mayo,	11	0	0
	4th June,	John Obins Woodhouse, esq.	Carlingford Lough, county Louth,	42	0	0

APPENDIX, No. 5—*concluded.*

LIST of LICENCES GRANTED to Plant OYSTER BEDS up to 31st December, 1870.

Date of Licence.		Persons to whom Granted.	Locality of Beds.	Area of Beds. A.	R.	P.
1867,	15th June,	Sir Robert Gore Booth, bart.	Drumcliff Bay, county Sligo,	87	0	0
	10th July,	Horatio Hamilton Townsend, esq.	Skull Harbour, county Cork,	230	0	0
	10th July,	Thomas Sandes, esq.	River Shannon, county Kerry,	780	0	0
	10th July,	Mrs. Elizabeth Atkinson,	Blacksod Bay, county Kerry,	100	0	0
	10th July,	M. J. C. Longfield, esq.	Roaringwater Bay, county Cork,	310	0	0
	10th July,	Thomas Kirkwood, esq.	Salem Harbour, county Mayo,	17	0	0
	10th July,	Richard D. Kane, esq.	Howth Strand, county Dublin,	36	0	0
	10th July,	William & J. St. George, esqrs.	Galway Bay, county Galway,	810	0	0
	10th July,	Christopher T. Redington, esq	Galway Bay, county Galway,	650	0	0
	10th July,	Mrs. Elizabeth Bury,	Lough Mahon, county Cork,	70	0	0
	10th July,	Rev. Nicholas Martin,	Trawbreaga Bay, county Donegal,	90	0	0
	15th July,	John Smyth, esq.	Midleton River, county Cork,	10	2	0
	15th July,	Stephen E. Collis, esq.	River Shannon, county Kerry,	212	0	0
	15th July,	Thomas Hicks, esq.	Roaringwater Bay, county Cork,	45	0	0
	16th July,	Robert W. C. Reeves, esq.	River Shannon, county Clare,	30	0	0
	24th July,	Francis J. Graham, esq	Barnaderg Bay, county Galway,	90	0	0
1868,	31st January,	William Hart, esq.	Lough Swilly, county Donegal,	790	0	0
	11th February,	Richard Lyons, esq.	Midleton River, county Cork,	15	0	0
	11th February,	Charles Sandes, esq.	River Shannon, county Kerry,	56	0	0
	13th March,	Stephen Browne, esq.	Dunmanus Bay, county Cork,	9	0	0
	13th March,	Colonel Edward Cooper,	Ballisodare Bay, county Sligo,	190	0	0
1869,	13th February,	Henry Herbert,	Kenmare Bay,	20	0	0
	13th February,	Earl of Bantry,	Adrigole Harbour,	18	0	0
	13th February,	Earl of Bantry,	Glengariffe Harbour,	80	0	0
	4th March,	John P. Nolan,	Ard Bay,	290	0	0
	11th March,	Richard J. Mahony,	Kenmare Bay,	46	0	0
	11th March,	Thomas Kingston Sullivan,	Kenmare Bay,	195	0	0
	15th March,	John W. Payne,	Bantry Bay,	51	0	0
	14th June,	John W. Stratford,	Killala Bay,	31	0	0
	14th June,	Mrs. Catherine Browne,	Courtmacsherry Bay,	60	0	0
	14th June,	William Little,	Killala Bay,	190	0	0
	10th September,	Lord Clermont,	Carlingford Lough,	46	0	0
	10th September,	Henry W. Meredith,	Sligo Bay,	20	0	0
	10th September,	Owen Wynne,	Sligo Bay,	77	0	0
	10th September,	Owen Wynne,	Sligo Bay,	53	0	0
1870,	12th March,	R. J. Verschoyle,	Ballisodare Bay,	13	2	0
			Total,	16,948	3	24

APPENDIX

RESULT of INQUIRIES held by the SPECIAL COMMISSIONERS and the INSPECTORS of IRISH FISHERIES into

No.	Where Fixed Net situated.	Description of Fixed Net.	Name of Person maintaining and using Fixed Net.	Name of Owner of Fixed Net, or of Land to which Net attached.	Name of Townland in which Net attached.	Parish.
1	Barrow, otherwise Ross, otherwise Nore and Barrow Rivers conjoined.	Head Weir,	Thomas Murphy,	John H. Glascott,	Dunganstown,	Whitechurch,
2	Barrow River,	Ditto,	Arthur Kavanagh,	Arthur Kavanagh,	Drummin,	St. Mullin's
3	Barrow, otherwise Ross River, otherwise Nore and Barrow Rivers conjoined.	Ditto,	Joseph Hunt,	W. M. Glascott,	Mountaunge,	Whitechurch,
4	Ditto,	Ditto,	Walter Sweetman,	Walter Sweetman,	Annaghs,	Shanbogh,
5	Ditto,	Ditto,	Michael and D. Cody,	—	Carrickcloney,	Kilmakevoge,
6	Ditto,	Ditto,	James Doody,	—	Great Island,	Kilmokea,
7	Ditto,	Ditto,	Samuel Bennett,	—	Ditto,	Ditto,
8	Ditto,	Ditto,	Richard Cashen,	—	Shanbogh, Upper,	Shanbogh,
9	Ditto,	Ditto,	John Sherlock,	—	Great Island,	Kilmokea,
10	Ditto,	Ditto,	P. Shanahan,	—	Ditto,	Ditto,
11	Ditto,	Ditto,	George Kent,	—	Ditto,	Ditto,
12	Suir,	Ditto,	John Lynch,	N. Power,	Faithlegg,	Faithlegg,
13	Ditto,	Ditto,	Hugh Treacy,	Ditto,	Ditto,	Ditto,
14	Ditto,	Ditto,	John Walsh,	—	Cheekpoint,	Ditto,
15	Suir, Nore, and Barrow Rivers conjoined.	Ditto,	John Lynch,	—	Coolbunnia,	Ditto,
16	Ditto,	Stake Weir,	Michael Dobbyn,	Marquess of Waterford,	Crooke,	Crooke,
17	Ditto,	Ditto,	Eliza Coghlan,	J. J. D. Coghlan,	Dromina,	Ditto,
18	Nore,	Head Weir,	W. F. F. Tighe,	W. F. F. Tighe,	Inistioge,	Inistioge,
19	Barrow, otherwise Ross River, otherwise Nore and Barrow conjoined.	Ditto,	Patrick Byrne,	R. W. Nunn,	Camlin,	Old Ross,
20	Barrow,	Ditto,	W. F. F. Tighe,	W. F. F. Tighe,	Kilconnelly,	The Rower,
21	Ditto,	Ditto,	John Hayes,	D. Burtchaell,	Coolmalay,	Ditto,
22	Barrow, otherwise Ross River, otherwise Nore and Barrow conjoined.	Ditto,	John Ferrestal,	—	Carrickcloney,	Kilmakevoge,
23	Nore River,	Ditto,	John Hunt,	Mrs. and Miss Vicars,	Brownsford,	Dysartmoon,
24	Suir River,	Ditto,	Paul Anderson,	N. A. Power,	Gurteens,	Rathpatrick,
25	Ditto,	Ditto,	Cath. and P. Moroney,	N. Power,	Drumdowney, Upper,	Ditto,
26	Barrow, otherwise Ross River, otherwise Nore and Barrow conjoined.	Ditto,	Michael Irish,	Dr. J. Mackey,	Ballyverneen,	Ballygurrim,
27	Ditto,	Ditto,	Thomas Murphy,	Col. Chas. Kearney,	Kearney's Bay,	Kilcolumb,
28	Ditto,	Ditto,	Joseph Hunt,	Peter Strange,	Rochestown,	Ditto,
29	Ditto,	Ditto,	P. Hanabury,	Ditto,	Ditto,	Ditto,
30	Ditto,	Ditto,	J. Doyle,	J. Devereux,	Snowhill,	Ditto,
31	Ditto,	Ditto,	J. Bolger,	Ditto,	Ditto,	Ditto,
32	Ditto,	Ditto,	W. Walsh,	Mrs. Bolton,	Drumdowney, Upper,	Rathpatrick,
33	Ditto,	Ditto,	J. Sullivan,	P. Hannebury,	Ballinlaw,	Kilcolumb,
34	Ditto,	Ditto,	John Brien,	N. Power,	Drumdowney, Upper,	Rathpatrick,
35	Suir River,	Ditto,	David Bennett,	Ditto,	Ditto,	Ditto,
36	Barrow, otherwise Ross River, otherwise Nore and Barrow conjoined.	Ditto,	James Butler,	Samuel King,	Fisherstown,	Kilmokea,
37	Ditto,	Ditto,	Pierce Cox,	Ditto,	Ditto,	Ditto,
38	Ditto,	Ditto,	James Kavanagh,	—	Ditto,	Ditto,
39	Suir, Nore, and Barrow conjoined, otherwise Waterford Harbour.	Scotch or Stake Weir,	A. Ryan, or Hayes,	Lord Templemore,	Dunmanus,	St. James and Dunbrody
40	Ditto,	Ditto,	M. Doyle,	Ditto,	Cheekbarragh,	Ditto,
41	Ditto,	Ditto,	A. Stephens,	Ditto,	Ditto,	Ditto,
42	Suir,	Head Weir,	N. A. Power,	N. A. Power,	Gurteens,	Rathpatrick,
43	Shannon River,	Fly-Net,	Randle Borough,	Randle Borough,	Querrin,	Moyarta
44	Ditto,	Stake-Net,	S. M'Auliffe,	Ditto,	Shanganagh,	Ditto,
45	Ditto,	Ditto,	William Kennedy,	John Cox,	Clarefield,	Ditto,
46	Ditto,	Ditto,	D. M'Auliffe,	Francis Keane,	Scattery Island,	Kilrush,
47	Ditto,	Fly-Net,	Francis Connell,	Ditto,	Ditto,	Ditto,
48	Ditto,	Stake-Net,	S. M'Auliffe,	Benjamin Cox,	Clarefield,	Moyarta,
49	Ditto,	Ditto,	J. Connell and D. M'Auliffe,	Colonel Vandeleur,	Carrowncalla, S.,	Kilrush,
50	Ditto,	Ditto,	Francis Connell,	Francis Keane,	Scattery Island,	Ditto,
51	Ditto,	Fly-Net,	Ditto,	Ditto,	Ditto,	Ditto,
52	Ditto,	Ditto,	John Cummins,	Colonel Vandeleur,	Inishbiggar Hog Island,	Ditto,
53	Ditto,	Ditto,	James Connell,	Ditto,	Ballynote, West,	Ditto,
54	Ditto,	Ditto,	John Slattery,	Ditto,	Ballymacrinan,	Killimer,
55	Ditto,	Ditto,	S. M'Auliffe,	Ditto,	Lakyle, South,	Killofin,
56	Ditto,	Ditto,	Ditto,	Ditto,	Ditto,	Ditto,
57	Ditto,	Ditto,	S. M'Auliffe and T. M'Namara,	Ditto,	Mount Shannon, West,	Ditto,
58	Ditto,	Stake-Net,	Marcus Sheehy,	Ditto,	Mount Shannon West,	Ditto,
59	Ditto,	Fly-Net,	Denis M'Auliffe,	Ditto,	Clonkerry, West,	Ditto,
60	Ditto,	Stake-Net,	S. M'Auliffe,	Lord Leconfield,	Rusheal,	Kilfidane,
61	Ditto,	Ditto,	S. Cunningham,	Ditto,	Ditto,	Ditto,
62	Ditto,	Ditto,	James O'Neill,	William Ashe,	Shannakeahog,	Ditto,
63	Ditto,	Ditto,	John Griffin,	James Kelly,	Cahiracon,	Kildysart,
64	Ditto (Clonderalaw Bay),	Ditto,	Daniel Molony,	Lord Annaly,	Kilkerrin,	Killofin,
65	Ditto,	Ditto,	Ditto,	Ditto,	Ditto,	Ditto,
66	Ditto,	Ditto,	James Browne,	Ditto,	Lakyle, North,	Ditto,
67	Ditto,	Ditto,	D. Molony,	Ditto,	Balline,	Ditto,
68	Ditto,	Ditto,	Ditto,	Ditto,	Kilkerrin,	Ditto,
69	Ditto,	Fly-Net,	Thomas M'Mahon,	Richard Barclay,	Ballyartney	Ditto,

APPENDIX, No. 6.

No. 6.

the Legality or Illegality of Fixed Nets erected or used for catching Salmon in Ireland.

No.	Barony.	County.	Judgment of Commissioners.	Date of Judgment.	Whether Judgment of Commissioners Appealed against.	Result of Appeal in Court of Queen's Bench.
1	Shelburne, .	Wexford, .	To be abated, as being injurious to navigation, and erected without the title required by the 5th and 6th Vic., c. 106.	17 Oct. 1863,	Appeal, . . .	Appeal withdrawn.
2	St. Mullin's, .	Carlow, .	To be abated, not having been legally erected in 1862.	Ditto, .	No appeal.	—
3	Shelburne, .	Wexford, .	To be abated, as being injurious to navigation, and erected without the title required by the 5th and 6th Vic., c. 106.	Ditto, .	Appeal, . . .	Judgment affirmed.
4	Ida, . .	Kilkenny, .	Ditto, ...	19 Oct. 1863,	Ditto, . . .	Ditto.
5	Ditto, .	Ditto, .	Ditto, ...	Ditto, .	No appeal.	—
6	Shelburne, .	Wexford, .	Ditto, ...	Ditto, .	Ditto.	—
7	Ditto, .	Ditto, .	Ditto, ...	Ditto, .	Ditto.	—
8	Ida, . .	Kilkenny, .	To be abated, not having been legally erected in 1862,	Ditto, .	Ditto.	—
9	Shelburne, .	Wexford, .	To be abated, as being injurious to navigation, and erected without the title required by the 5th and 6th Vic., cap. 106.	Ditto, .	Ditto.	—
10	Ditto, .	Ditto, .	To be abated, not having been legally erected in 1862.	Ditto, .	Ditto.	—
11	Ditto, .	Ditto, .	To be abated, as being injurious to navigation,	20 Oct. 1863,	Appeal, . . .	Judgment affirmed.
12	Gaultiere, .	Waterford, .	Ditto, and erected without the title required by the 5th and 6th Vic., c. 106.	21 Oct. 1863,	No appeal.	—
13	Ditto, .	Ditto, .	Ditto, ...	Ditto, .	Ditto.	—
14	Ditto, .	Ditto, .	Ditto, ...	Ditto, .	Ditto.	—
15	Ditto, .	Ditto, .	Ditto, ...	Ditto, .	Ditto.	—
16	Ditto, .	Ditto, .	Ditto, ...	23 Oct. 1863,	Appeal, . . .	Judgment affirmed.
17	Ditto, .	Ditto, .	Ditto, ...	24 Oct. 1863,	Ditto, . . .	Ditto.
18	Gowran, .	Kilkenny, .	To be abated, as injurious to navigation,	26 Oct. 1863,	Ditto, . . .	Ditto.
19	Bantry, .	Wexford, .	Ditto, and erected without the title required by the 5th and 6th Vic., c. 106.	Ditto, .	Ditto, . . .	Ditto.
20	Ida, . .	Kilkenny, .	Ditto, ...	Ditto, .	No appeal.	—
21	Ditto, .	Ditto, .	Ditto, ...	Ditto, .	Ditto.	—
22	Ditto, .	Ditto, .	Ditto, ...	Ditto, .	Ditto.	—
23	Ditto, .	Ditto, .	Ditto, ...	27 Oct. 1863,	Ditto.	—
24	Ditto, .	Ditto, .	Ditto, ...	29 Oct. 1863,	Ditto.	—
25	Ditto, .	Ditto, .	Ditto, ...	10 Dec. 1863,	Ditto.	—
26	Ditto, .	Ditto, .	Ditto, ...	Ditto, .	Appeal, . . .	Appeal withdrawn.
27	Ditto, .	Ditto, .	Ditto, ...	11 Dec. 1863,	Ditto, . . .	Ditto.
28	Ditto, .	Ditto, .	Ditto, ...	Ditto, .	Ditto, . . .	Ditto.
29	Ditto, .	Ditto, .	Ditto, ...	Ditto, .	No appeal.	—
30	Ditto, .	Ditto, .	Ditto, ...	Ditto, .	Ditto.	—
31	Ditto, .	Ditto, .	Ditto, ...	Ditto, .	Appeal, . . .	Judgment affirmed.
32	Ditto, .	Ditto, .	Ditto, ...	Ditto, .	No appeal.	—
33	Ditto, .	Ditto, .	Ditto, ...	12 Dec. 1863,	Ditto.	—
34	Ditto, .	Ditto, .	Ditto, ...	Ditto, .	Ditto.	—
35	Ditto, .	Ditto, .	Ditto, ...	Ditto, .	Ditto.	—
36	Shelburne, .	Wexford, .	Ditto, ...	Ditto, .	Appeal, . . .	Appeal withdrawn.
37	Ditto, .	Ditto, .	Ditto, ...	Ditto, .	No appeal.	—
38	Ditto, .	Ditto, .	Ditto, ...	Ditto, .	Ditto.	—
39	Ditto, .	Ditto, .	To be abated, as being injurious to navigation, .	16 Dec. 1863,	Appeal, . . .	Judgment affirmed.
40	Ditto, .	Ditto, .	To be abated, as being erected in narrow channel,	4 April, 1863,	No appeal.	—
41	Ditto, .	Ditto, .	To be abated, as being injurious to navigation, and being illegally erected—extending beyond low-water mark.	23 Dec. 1863,	Appeal, . . .	Judgment affirmed.
42	Ida, . .	Kilkenny, .	To be abated, as injurious to navigation, and erected without the title required by the 5th and 6th Vic., c. 106.	Ditto, .	No appeal.	—
43	Moyarta, .	Clare, .	To be abated, as erected without the title required by the 5th and 6th Vic., c. 106.	1 Jan. 1864,	Ditto.	—
44	Ditto, .	Ditto, .	Ditto, ...	Ditto, .	Ditto.	—
45	Ditto, .	Ditto, .	Ditto, ...	Ditto, .	Ditto.	—
46	Ditto, .	Ditto, .	Ditto, ...	Ditto, .	Ditto.	—
47	Ditto, .	Ditto, .	Ditto, ...	Ditto, .	Ditto.	—
48	Ditto, .	Ditto, .	Ditto, ...	2 Jan. 1864,	Ditto.	—
49	Ditto, .	Ditto, .	Ditto, ...	Ditto, .	Appeal, . . .	Judgment affirmed.
50	Ditto, .	Ditto, .	Ditto, ...	Ditto, .	No appeal.	—
51	Ditto, .	Ditto, .	Ditto, ...	Ditto, .	Ditto.	—
52	Ditto, .	Ditto, .	Ditto, ...	Ditto, .	Ditto.	—
53	Ditto, .	Ditto, .	Ditto, ...	Ditto, .	Appeal, . . .	Judgment affirmed.
54	Clonderalaw,	Ditto, .	Ditto, ...	Ditto, .	Ditto, . . .	Ditto.
55	Ditto, .	Ditto, .	Ditto, ...	4 Jan. 1864,	No appeal.	—
56	Ditto, .	Ditto, .	Ditto, ...	Ditto, .	Ditto.	—
57	Ditto, .	Ditto, .	Ditto, ...	Ditto, .	Ditto.	—
58	Ditto, .	Ditto, .	Ditto, ...	Ditto, .	Appeal, . . .	Judgment reversed.
59	Ditto, .	Ditto, .	Ditto, ...	Ditto, .	No appeal.	—
60	Ditto, .	Ditto, .	Ditto, ...	Ditto, .	Ditto.	—
61	Ditto, .	Ditto, .	Ditto, ...	Ditto, .	Ditto.	—
62	Ditto, .	Ditto, .	Ditto, ...	Ditto, .	Ditto.	—
63	Ditto, .	Ditto, .	Ditto, ...	Ditto, .	Ditto.	—
64	Ditto, .	Ditto, .	Ditto, ...	7 Jan. 1864,	Appeal, . . .	Judgment reversed.
65	Ditto, .	Ditto, .	Ditto, ...	Ditto, .	Ditto, . . .	Ditto.
66	Ditto, .	Ditto, .	Ditto, ...	Ditto, .	Ditto, . . .	Judgment affirmed.
67	Ditto, .	Ditto, .	Ditto, and not having been legally erected in 1862.	5 Jan. 1864,	No appeal.	—
68	Ditto, .	Ditto, .	Ditto, ...	Ditto, .	Ditto.	—
69	Ditto, .	Ditto, .	Ditto, ...	7 Jan. 1864,	Ditto.	—

APPENDIX, No. 6.

RESULT of INQUIRIES held by the SPECIAL COMMISSIONERS and the INSPECTORS of IRISH FISHERIES into

No.	Where Fixed Net situated.	Description of Fixed Net.	Name of Person maintaining and using Fixed Net.	Name of Owner of Fixed Net, or of Land to which Net attached.	Name of Townland to which Net attached.	Parish.
70	River Barrow, otherwise Nore and Barrow conjoined.	Head Weir, .	Richard Hewitson, .	M. W. Knox, .	Kilmannock, . .	Kilmokea, .
71	River Suir, ...	Ditto, .	G. Giles, . .	G. Giles, . .	Kilmurry, . .	Rathpatrick, .
72	Rivers Suir, Nore, and Barrow conjoined, otherwise Waterford Harbour.	Stake Weir, .	James Ryan, . .	Lord Ely, . .	Duncannon, . .	St. James and Dunbrody.
73	Slade Bay, ...	Bag-Net, .	W. Dunn, . .	Ditto, . .	Slade, . .	Hook, .
74	Suir, Nore, and Barrow conjoined.	Head Weir, .	J. Hanlon and others,	Lord Templemore, .	Nook, . .	St. James and Dunbrody
75	Ditto, ...	Ditto, .	Anthony Wallis, .	Ditto, . .	Ballyhack, . .	Ditto, .
76	Ditto, ...	Stake-Net, .	Arthur N. O'Neill, .	Lord Carew, . .	Woodstown, Lower, .	Crooke, .
77	Ditto, ...	Ditto, .	Ditto, . .	Ditto, . .	Knockaveelish, .	Killea, .
78	Suir, King's Channel, . .	Ditto, .	Mary O'Neill, . .	Mary O'Neill, . .	Knockboy, .	Ballygunner, .
79	Ditto, ...	Ditto, .	Ditto, . .	Ditto, . .	Ditto, . .	Ditto, .
80	Suir, Nore, and Barrow conjoined.	Head Weir, .	John Hanlon & others,	Lord Templemore, .	Saltmills, . .	St. James and Dunbrody
81	Ditto, ...	Ditto, .	Ditto, . .	Ditto, . .	Ballyhack, . .	Ditto, .
82	Shannon, ...	Stake-Net, .	Stephen Cunningham,	Bryan O'Loghlen, .	Aillroe[illegible], .	Killdisart, .
83	Ditto, ...	Fly-Net, .	R. W. C. Reeves, .	R. W. C. Reeves, .	Poulnaduras, .	Killimer, .
84	Ditto, ...	Stake-Net, .	Ditto, . .	Ditto, . .	Burrane, Lower, .	Ditto, .
85	Ditto, ...	Ditto, .	Ditto, . .	Ditto, . .	Ditto, . .	Ditto, .
86	Ditto, ...	Ditto, .	Ditto, . .	Ditto, . .	Ditto, . .	Ditto, .
87	Ditto, ...	Ditto, .	Michael Colpoys, .	Colonel Hickman, .	Knock, . .	Kilmurry, .
88	Ditto, ...	Ditto, .	S. M'Cauliffe & John Brooks	Ditto, . .	Ditto, . .	Ditto, .
89	Ditto, ...	Ditto, .	Ellen Hodnett, .	Ditto, . .	Kilmore, . .	Ditto, .
90	Ditto, ...	Ditto, .	Ditto, . .	Ditto, . .	Ditto, . .	Ditto, .
91	Ditto, ...	Ditto, .	Ditto, . .	Ditto, . .	Ditto, . .	Ditto, .
92	Ditto, ...	Ditto, .	John Hourihan, .	Ditto, . .	Carrowlane, . .	Ditto, .
93	Ditto, ...	Ditto, .	S. Pegum, . .	Rev. T. Butler, .	Poulnadaree, .	Killimer, .
94	Ditto, ...	Ditto, .	Ditto, . .	Ditto, . .	Ditto, . .	Ditto, .
95	Ditto, ...	Ditto, .	Henry S. O'Brien, .	Henry S. O'Brien, .	Foredrine, . .	Kilrush, .
96	Ditto, ...	Ditto, .	S. M'Auliffe, .	T. R. Ross, .	Shewdesley, .	Kilfidin, .
97	Ditto, ...	Ditto, .	T. Naughton & others,	E. T. Massy, .	Ballycannane, .	Ballynacally, .
98	Ditto, ...	Ditto, .	M. Shaughnessy and others.	Lord Gillamore, .	Gortbrown, .	Askeaton, .
99	Ditto, ...	Ditto, .	S. M'Cauliffe, .	Colonel Hickman, .	Knock, . .	Kilmurry, .
100	Ditto, ...	Ditto, .	J. Downes, . .	Lord Monteagle, .	Leakys, . .	Robertstown, .
101	Ditto, ...	Ditto, .	Ditto, . .	Ditto, . .	Durnish, . .	Shanagolden, .
102	Ditto, ...	Ditto, .	Ditto, . .	Ditto, . .	Foynes Island, .	Robertstown, .
103	Ditto, ...	Ditto, .	Ditto, . .	Ditto, . .	Ditto, . .	Ditto, .
104	Ditto, ...	Ditto, .	Ditto, . .	Ditto, . .	Mount Trenchard, .	Loghill, .
105	Ditto, ...	Ditto, .	Ditto, . .	Ditto, . .	Ditto, . .	Ditto, .
106	Ditto, ...	Ditto, .	P. Sheehan, . .	Lord Clare, . .	Ballynash (Clare), .	Robertstown, .
107	Ditto, ...	Ditto, .	M. M'Namara, .	R. Bateson, . .	Loghill, . .	Loghill, .
108	Ditto, ...	Ditto, .	John Griffin, .	Thomas Royse, .	Carrowbanaboy, .	Ditto, .
109	Ditto, ...	Ditto, .	M. M'Namara, .	Earl of Clare, .	Ditto, . .	Ditto, .
110	Ditto, ...	Ditto, .	J. Browne, . .	G. Mauhlin, .	Killacolla, .	Kilfergus, .
111	Ditto, ...	Ditto, .	Margaret Fitzland and others	Knight of Glin, .	Caheragh, .	Ditto, .
112	Ditto, ...	Ditto, .	Ditto, . .	Ditto, . .	Glin Demesne, .	Ditto, .
113	Ditto, ...	Ditto, .	Ditto, . .	Ditto, . .	Farranmullen, .	Ditto, .
114	Ditto, ...	Ditto, .	J. Browne, . .	Elizabeth Standish,	Killacolla (Decker), .	Ditto, .
115	Ditto, ...	Fly-Net, .	W. B. Barrington, .	W. B. Barrington,	Ballyhoolahan, .	Loghill, .
116	Ditto, ...	Ditto, .	J. Browne, . .	Rev. R. Fitzgerald,	Ballylongford, .	Kilfergus, .
117	Ditto, ...	Stake-Net, .	P. J. Mayne, .	P. J. Mayne, .	East Aster, .	Aberaillin, .
118	Ditto, ...	Ditto, .	Ditto, . .	Ditto, . .	West Aster, .	Ditto, .
119	Ditto, ...	Ditto, .	J. Finn, . .	W. C. Hickey, .	Glenamaun, .	Ditto, .
120	Ditto, ...	Ditto, .	C. Sandes, . .	C. Sandes, .	Carrig Island, .	Ditto, .
121	Ditto, ...	Ditto, .	J. Finn, . .	R. Leslie, . .	Kilcolgan, Lower, .	Kilnaughtin, .
122	Ditto, ...	Ditto, .	Alicia Wren, .	Lord Listowel, .	Common and Sand Hills,	Kilconly, .
123	Ditto, ...	Fly-Net, .	Ditto, . .	Ditto, . .	Castlequarter, .	Ditto, .
124	Ditto, ...	Stake-Net, .	Ditto, . .	Leslie Wren, .	Kyletallon, .	Ditto, .
125	Ditto, ...	Ditto, .	W. Sandes, . .	T. Sandes, .	Carhoonakineely, .	Kilnaughtin, .
126	Ditto, ...	Ditto, .	Alicia Wren, .	Leslie Wren, .	Carrigane, .	Aberaillin, .
127	Sea off Coast of County Cork,	Bag-Net, .	C. Desmond, .	Samuel Hodder, .	Ringabella, .	Tracton, .
128	Ditto, ...	Fly-Net, .	W. Atkinson, .	Lord Ponsonby, .	Redbarn, .	Clonpriest, .
129	Ditto, ...	Ditto, .	N. T. Foley, .	Murdock Green, .	Summerfield, .	Youghal, .
130	Ditto, ...	Stake-Net, .	J. Bennyno, .	Ditto, . .	Ditto, . .	Ditto, .
131	Ditto, ...	Fly-Net, .	N. T. Foley, .	D. L. Lewis, .	Clayeastle, .	Ditto, .

APPENDIX, No. 6.

the Legality or Illegality of Fixed Nets erected or used for catching Salmon in Ireland—continued.

No.	Barony.	County.	Judgment of Commissioners.	Date of Judgment.	Whether Judgment of Commissioners Appealed against.	Result of Appeal in Court of Queen's Bench.
70	Shelburne,	Wexford,	To be abated, as injurious to navigation, and as erected without the title required by 5 & 6 Vic., c. 106.	10 Mar. 1864,	Appeal,	Sent back for further inquiry as to partial abatement.—See No. 272.
71	Ida,	Kilkenny,	Ditto,	14 Mar. 1864,	No appeal.	—
72	Shelburne,	Wexford,	To be abated, as erected without the title required by 5 & 6 Vic., c. 106.	15 Mar. 1864,	Appeal,	Withdrawn.
73	Ditto,	Ditto,	Ditto,	Ditto,	No appeal.	—
74	Ditto,	Ditto,	Legally erected,	16 Mar. 1864,	—	—
75	Ditto,	Ditto,	To be abated, as injurious to navigation,	Ditto,	Appeal,	Withdrawn.
76	Gaultiere,	Waterford,	To be abated, as erected without the title required by 5 & 6 Vic., c. 106	17 Mar. 1864,	Ditto.	Sent back for reconsideration.—See Nos. 261 to 264 inclusive.
77	Ditto,	Ditto,	Ditto,	Ditto,	Ditto,	
78	Ditto,	Ditto,	Ditto,	18 Mar. 1864,	Ditto,	
79	Ditto,	Ditto,	Ditto,	Ditto,	Ditto,	
80	Shelburne,	Wexford,	To be abated, Lord Templemore consenting,	Ditto,	No appeal	—
81	Ditto,	Ditto,	Ditto,	Ditto,	Ditto.	—
82	Clonderalaw,	Clare,	Legally erected,	26 Mar. 1864,	—	—
83	Ditto,	Ditto,	To be abated, not erected in 1862,	28 Mar. 1864,	No appeal.	—
84	Ditto,	Ditto,	To be abated, as erected without the title required by 5 & 6 Vic., c. 106; and extending beyond low-water mark. The latter question to be tried by Commissioners when appeal on title decided.	29 Mar. 1864,	Appeal,	Judgment reversed.
85	Ditto,	Ditto,	Ditto,	Ditto,	Ditto,	Sent back.—See No. 266.
86	Ditto,	Ditto,	To be abated, as erected without the title required by 5 & 6 Vic., c. 106 and as being injurious to navigation,	Ditto,	Ditto,	Judgment affirmed.
87	Ditto,	Ditto,	To be abated, not erected in 1862,	30 Mar. 1864,	Ditto,	Ditto.
88	Ditto,	Ditto,	Ditto,	Ditto,	No appeal.	—
89	Ditto,	Ditto,	To be abated, as injurious to navigation, and as erected without the title required by 5 & 6 Vic., c. 106	31 Mar. 1864,	Appeal,	Judgment affirmed.
90	Ditto,	Ditto,	To be abated, as erected without the title required by 5 & 6 Vic., c. 106.	Ditto,	Ditto,	Judgment reversed.
91	Ditto,	Ditto,	To be abated, not erected in 1862,	Ditto,	Ditto,	Judgment affirmed.
92	Ditto,	Ditto,	To be abated, as injurious to navigation, and as erected without the title required by 5 & 6 Vic., c. 106.	Ditto,	Ditto,	Ditto.
93	Ditto,	Ditto,	To be abated by consent of Mr. Butler,	2 April, 1864,	No appeal.	—
94	Ditto,	Ditto,	Ditto,	Ditto,	Ditto.	—
95	Bunratty, Lr.	Ditto,	To be abated, as being injurious to navigation, and to the public right of fishing.	4 April, 1864,	Appeal,	New trial granted upon point of form, see No. 250.
96	Clonderalaw,	Ditto,	To be abated, as erected without the title required by 5 & 6 Vic., c. 106.	Ditto,	No appeal.	—
97	Kenry,	Limerick,	Ditto,	Ditto,	Ditto.	—
98	Lower Connello.	Ditto,	Ditto,	Ditto,	Ditto.	—
99	Clonderalaw,	Clare,	Ditto,	Ditto,	Ditto.	—
100	Shanid,	Limerick,	To be abated, as injurious to navigation,	5 April, 1864,	Ditto.	—
101	Ditto,	Ditto,	To be abated, as erected without the title required by 5 & 6 Vic., c. 106, and injurious to public right of fishing.	6 April, 1864,	Appeal,	Judgment reversed.
102	Ditto,	Ditto,	To be abated, as erected without the title required by 5 & 6 Vic., c. 106.	Ditto,	Ditto,	Ditto.
103	Ditto,	Ditto,	Ditto,	Ditto,	Ditto,	Ditto.
104	Ditto,	Ditto,	Ditto,	Ditto,	Ditto,	Ditto.
105	Ditto,	Ditto,	To be abated by consent; not erected in 1862,	Ditto,	No appeal.	—
106	Ditto,	Ditto,	To be abated, as erected without the title required by 5 & 6 Vic., c. 106.	7 April, 1864,	Ditto.	—
107	Ditto,	Ditto,	Ditto,	Ditto,	Ditto.	—
108	Ditto,	Ditto,	Ditto,	Ditto,	Appeal,	Judgment reversed
109	Ditto,	Ditto,	To be abated, not having been erected in 1862,	Ditto,	No appeal	—
110	Ditto,	Ditto,	Legally erected,	Ditto,	Appeal,	Judgment affirmed.
111	Ditto,	Ditto,	To be abated, as erected without the title required by 5 & 6 Vic., c. 106.	Ditto,	Ditto,	Sent back.—See No. 265.
112	Ditto,	Ditto,	To be abated, injurious to navigation,	Ditto,	No appeal.	—
113	Ditto,	Ditto,	To be abated, as erected without the title required by 5 & 6 Vic., c. 106.	Ditto,	Ditto.	—
114	Ditto,	Ditto.	Ditto,	8 April, 1864,	Appeal,	Appeal withdrawn.
115	Ditto,	Ditto,	Legally erected,	Ditto,	No appeal.	—
116	Ditto,	Ditto,	To be abated, as erected without the title required by 5 & 6 Vic., c. 106, and not erected in 1862.	Ditto,	Ditto.	—
117	Iraghticonnor	Kerry,	To be abated: not legally erected in 1862, and injurious to the public right of fishing.	11 April, 1864,	Appeal,	Judgment affirmed.
118	Ditto,	Ditto,	Ditto,	Ditto,	Ditto,	Ditto.
119	Ditto,	Ditto,	To be abated, as erected without the title required by 5 & 6 Vic., c. 106.	Ditto,	Ditto,	Judgment reversed.
120	Ditto,	Ditto,	To be abated; not erected in 1862,	Ditto,	No appeal.	—
121	Ditto,	Ditto,	Ditto,	Ditto,	Ditto.	—
122	Ditto,	Ditto,	To be abated, as erected without the title required by 5 & 6 Vic., c. 106.	Ditto,	Ditto.	—
123	Ditto,	Ditto,	Ditto,	Ditto,	Ditto.	—
124	Ditto,	Ditto,	Ditto, and not erected in 1862,	22 April, 1864,	Appeal,	Judgment reversed.
125	Ditto,	Ditto,	Ditto,	Ditto,	Ditto,	Judgment affirmed.
126	Ditto,	Ditto,	To be abated, as injurious to public rights of fishing.	Ditto,	Ditto,	Judgment reversed; but public right of fishing preserved.
127	Kinalea,	Cork,	To be abated, as being within three miles of Carrigaline River mouth.	4 Aug. 1864,	Ditto,	Judgment reversed.
128	Imokilly,	Ditto,	To be abated, as erected without the title required by 5 & 6 Vic., c. 106.	8 Aug. 1864,	No appeal.	—
129	Ditto,	Ditto,	Ditto,	Ditto,	Ditto.	—
130	Ditto,	Ditto,	Ditto,	Ditto,	Ditto.	—
131	Ditto,	Ditto,	To be abated, as injurious to navigation,	Ditto,	Ditto.	—

Appendix, No. 6.

Result of Inquiries held by the Special Commissioners and the Inspectors of Irish Fisheries into

No.	Where Fixed Net situated.	Description of Fixed Net.	Name of Person maintaining and using Fixed Net.	Name of Owner of Fixed Net, or of Land to which Net attached.	Name of Townland to which Net attached.	Parish.
132	Sea off Coast of co. Cork,	Bag Net,	John Walsh,	Roger Davis,	Knockadoon,	Youghal,
133	Ditto,	Ditto,	D. Sullivan,	M. Longfield,	Ballycotton,	Kilmahon,
134	Ballycotton Bay, co. Cork,	Ditto,	J. Lawton,	J. Lawton,	Ditto,	Ditto,
135	River Blackwater,	Stake-Net,	R. Power,	Trustees of Mrs. Osborne,	Pillpark,	Clashmore,
136	Ditto,	Ditto,	P. Kennedy and others,	Lord Stuart de Decies,	Tinknock,	Ditto,
137	Ditto,	Ditto,	H. T. Dennehy,	Ditto,	Ardsallagh,	Ditto,
138	Ditto,	Ditto,	J. Rounayne,	Ditto,	Ditto,	Ditto,
139	Ditto,	Ditto,	Ditto,	Ditto,	Ditto,	Ditto,
140	Ditto,	Ditto,	M. B. Rounayne,	Ditto,	Ditto,	Ditto,
141	Ditto,	Ditto,	G. Crotty,	Ditto,	Coolbagh,	Ditto,
142	Ditto,	Head Weir,	G. Dalton,	Ditto,	Dromore,	Affane,
143	Ditto,	Stake-Net,	M. G. Adams,	Hon. C. W. M. Smyth,	Rincrew,	Templemichael,
144	Ditto,	Ditto,	Hon. C. W. M. Smyth,	Ditto,	Ballynatray,	Ditto,
145	Ditto,	Ditto,	E. M'Sweeny,	—	Templevrenchael,	Ditto,
146	Ditto,	Ditto,	S. Allen & N. T. Foley,	Samuel Allen,	D'Loughtane,	Kinsalebeg,
147	Ditto,	Ditto,	P. Shinay & J. Harley,	—	Newport, East,	Templemichael,
148	Ditto,	Ditto,	P. Deelan,	Lord Huntingdon,	Ballymaclash,	Clashmore,
149	Ditto,	Ditto,	M. Rounayne,	Ditto,	Ditto,	Ditto,
150	Ditto,	Ditto,	P. Mansfield,	J. Kiely,	Newport, East,	Kilcockan,
151	Ditto,	Ditto,	M. White & W. Murphy,	—	Strancally,	Ditto,
152	Ditto,	Ditto,	M. White,	—	Carriglea,	Ditto,
153	Ditto,	Ditto,	E. Collins,	Lord Stuart de Decies,	Tinnascart,	Aglish,
154	Ditto,	Ditto,	C. M'Sweeny,	—	Strad,	Templemichael,
155	Ditto,	Ditto,	John Neil and W. Hennessy,	Rev. G. Gumbleton,	Scart,	Kilcockan,
156	Ditto,	Ditto,	R. Drowne and Michl. M'Carthy,	C. Musgrave,	Glensassy, or Clonmore,	Aglish,
157	Ditto,	Ditto,	J. Fitzgerald,	C. O'Mahony,	Ballyphilip, East,	Kilcockan,
158	Ditto,	Ditto,	E. Healy,	J. Hargrave,	Dromore,	Aglish,
159	Ditto,	Ditto,	William Collins,	Ditto,	Ditto,	Ditto,
160	Ditto,	Ditto,	Maurice Hickey,	Ditto,	Ditto,	Ditto,
161	Ditto,	Head Weir,	C. Usher,	C. Usher,	Camphire,	Lismore,
162	Ditto,	Ditto,	J. Rice,	—	Killahaly, East,	Ditto,
163	Ditto,	Ditto,	Sir R. Musgrave,	Sir R. Musgrave,	Tourin Demesne,	Ditto,
164	Ditto,	Ditto,	Ditto,	Ditto,	Norrisland,	Ditto,
165	Bride,	Ditto,	M. Whelan,	C. Usher,	Camphire,	Ditto,
166	Ditto,	Ditto,	J. M'Grath,	Ditto,	O'Kyle,	Ditto,
167	Ditto,	Ditto,	P. Walsh,	C. Smith,	Shanglerough,	Kilwatermoy,
168	Ditto,	Ditto,	J. Cassell,	Duke of Devonshire,	Bridane, Lower,	Lismore,
169	Ditto,	Ditto,	R. P. Maxwell,	R. P. Maxwell,	Killanduney,	Kilwatermoy,
170	Ditto,	Ditto,	E. Evans,	R. Oliver,	Ballynaraha,	Lismore,
171	Ditto,	Ditto,	T. Hourigan,	Duke of Devonshire,	Kilnacarriga,	Ditto,
172	Ditto,	Ditto,	J. Barry,	Ditto,	Ballinvella,	Ditto,
173	Ditto,	Ditto,	R. P. Maxwell,	R. P. Maxwell,	Sapperton, North,	Kilwatermoy,
174	Ditto,	Ditto,	J. Morgan,	Duke of Devonshire,	Ballinvella,	Lismore,
175	Ditto,	Ditto,	J. Leahy,	Ditto,	Monatarva,	Ditto,
176	Ardmore Bay,	Bag-Net,	T. Geary,	H. O'Dell,	Duffcarrick,	Ardmore,
177	Ditto,	Ditto,	Ditto,	Ditto,	Dysert,	Ditto,
178	Castlemaine Harbour,	Stake Net,	H. W. Dodd & others,	The M'Gillycuddy,	Killeenagh,	Ballinvoher,
179	Ditto,	Ditto,	P. Ashe,	Reps. Lord Ventry,	Inch,	Ditto,
180	Ditto,	Ditto,	H. W. Dodd & others,	R. Mahony,	Douglas,	Killorglin,
181	Ditto,	Ditto,	Ditto,	Ditto,	Illaunsleak,	Ditto,
182	Ditto,	Ditto,	E. De Moleyns,	Reps. Lord Ventry,	Cromane, Lower,	Ditto,
183	Ditto,	Ditto,	Sir R. Blennerhassett,	Sir R. Blennerhassett,	Douglas,	Ditto,
184	Ballinskelligs Bay,	Bag-Net,	W. Hector,	E. Reeves,	Dungeagan,	Prior,
185	Kenmare River,	Ditto,	M. O'Sullivan,	H. B. Hartopp,	Rath,	Kilcrohane,
186	Sea off Coast of co. Louth,	Ditto,	T. A. Newcomen,	Smith Barry,	Glasspistol,	Clogher,
187	Ditto,	Ditto,	Arthur and Jane Newcomen,	Arthur Newcomen,	Callystown,	Ditto,
188	Ditto,	Ditto,	T. Kirk,	A. Godley,	Clogher,	Ditto,
189	Ditto,	Ditto,	Jane S. Newcomen,	Arthur Newcomen,	Callystown,	Ditto,
190	Ditto,	Ditto,	Ditto,	Ditto,	Ditto,	Ditto,
191	Ditto,	Ditto,	E. Jones,	Sir A. Bellingham,	Dunany,	Dunany,
192	Ditto,	Ditto,	John Jones,	Ditto,	Dunbanstown,	Ditto,
193	Ditto,	Ditto,	T. Kirk,	A. Godley,	Clogher,	Clogher,
194	Ditto,	Head Weir,	J. M'Keon,	Sir A. Bellingham,	Castlebellingham,	Gernonstown,
195	Sea off Coast of co. Antrim,	Bag-Net,	Charles Black,	Lord Antrim,	Portrush,	Dunluce,
196	Ditto,	Ditto,	Ditto,	Ditto,	Ditto,	Ditto,
197	Ditto,	Ditto,	Ditto,	Ditto,	Ditto,	Ditto,
198	Ditto,	Ditto,	Ditto,	Ditto,	Ditto,	Ditto,
199	Ditto,	Ditto,	Ditto,	Ditto,	Ditto,	Ditto,
200	Ditto,	Ditto,	Ditto,	Ditto,	Ditto,	Ditto,
201	Ditto,	Ditto,	Ditto,	Ditto,	Ditto,	Ditto,
202	Ditto,	Ditto,	John Rooney,	Ditto,	Tour,	Culfeightrin,
203	Ditto,	Ditto,	N. D. Crommelin,	Ditto,	Ballyteerim,	Ditto,
204	Ditto,	Ditto,	A. M'Keegan,	Ditto,	Glebe,	Layd,
205	Ditto,	Ditto,	Lord Antrim,	Ditto,	Carnlough,	Ardclinis,
206	Ditto,	Ditto,	Ditto,	Ditto,	Town parks, Glenarm,	Tickmacrevan,
207	Ditto,	Ditto,	J. M'Intosh,	H. H. M'Neile,	Redbay,	Layd,
208	Ditto,	Ditto,	A. M'Keegan,	Charles Black,	Moneyvart,	Ditto,

the Legality or Illegality of Fixed Nets erected or used for catching Salmon in Ireland—*continued.*

No.	Barony	County	Judgment of Commissioners.	Date of Judgment.	Whether Judgment of Commissioners Appealed against.	Result of Appeal in Court of Queen's Bench.
132	Imokilly, .	Cork, .	To be abated, being within three miles of mouth of Womanagh River.	11 Aug. 1864,	No appeal.	—
133	Ditto, .	Ditto, .	Postponed	—	—	—
134	Ditto,	Ditto, .	Legally erected, ...	30 June 1863,	No appeal.	—
135	Decies-without-Drum.	Waterford, .	To be abated, as injurious to navigation, . .	13 Aug 1864,	Ditto.	—
136	Ditto, .	Ditto, .	Ditto, by consent, ...	Ditto, .	Ditto.	—
137	Ditto, .	Ditto, .	Ditto, ditto, ...	Ditto, .	Ditto.	—
138	Ditto, .	Ditto, .	Ditto, ditto, ...	Ditto, .	Ditto.	—
139	Ditto, .	Ditto, .	Ditto, ditto, ...	Ditto, .	Ditto.	—
140	Ditto, .	Ditto, .	Ditto, ditto, ...	Ditto, .	Ditto.	—
141	Ditto, .	Ditto, .	Ditto, ditto, ...	Ditto, .	Ditto.	—
142	Decies-without-Drum.	Ditto, .	Ditto, ditto, ...	Ditto, .	Ditto.	—
143	Coshmore & Coshbride.	Ditto, .	Ditto, ditto, ...	15 Aug. 1864,	Ditto.	—
144	Ditto, .	Ditto, .	To be abated, as injurious to navigation, . .	15 Aug. 1864,	Ditto.	—
145	Ditto, .	Ditto, .	Ditto, ...	16 Aug 1864,	Ditto.	—
146	Decies-within-Drum	Ditto, .	To be abated, as erected without the title required by 5 & 6 Vic., c. 106.	Ditto, .	Ditto.	—
147	Coshmore & Coshbride.	Ditto, .	To be abated, as injurious to navigation, . .	Ditto, .	Ditto.	—
148	Decies-within-Drum.	Ditto, .	To be abated by consent of Lord Huntingdon, . .	Ditto, .	Ditto.	—
149	Ditto, .	Ditto, .	Ditto, ...	Ditto, .	Ditto.	—
150	Coshmore & Coshbride.	Ditto, .	To be abated, as injurious to navigation, . .	Ditto, .	Ditto.	—
151	Ditto, .	Ditto, .	Ditto, ...	Ditto, .	Ditto.	—
152	Ditto, .	Ditto, .	To be abated by consent, ...	Ditto, .	Ditto.	—
153	Decies-within-Drum.	Ditto, .	To be abated, as injurious to navigation, .	17 Aug. 1864,	Ditto.	—
154	Ditto, .	Ditto, .	To be abated, as erected without the title required by 5 & 6 Vic., c. 106.	Ditto, .	Appeal, ...	Sent back.—See 273.
155	Ditto, .	Ditto, .	To be abated so far as it extends beyond low water-mark; legally erected as regards the rest	Ditto, .	Ditto, . . .	Judgment affirmed.—See 275.
156	Decies-within-Drum.	Ditto, .	To be abated, as erected without the title required by 5 & 6 Vic., c. 106.	Ditto, .	No appeal.	—
157	Coshmore & Coshbride.	Ditto, .	Ditto, ...	Ditto, .	Ditto.	—
158	Decies-within-Drum.	Ditto, .	Ditto, ...	Ditto, .	Ditto.	—
159	Ditto, .	Ditto, .	Ditto, ...	Ditto, .	Appeal, ...	Sent back.—See 274
160	Ditto, .	Ditto, .	Ditto, ...	Ditto, .	No appeal.	—
161	Coshmore & Coshbride.	Ditto, .	To be abated not erected in 1862, . .	Ditto, .	Ditto.	—
162	Ditto, .	Ditto, .	To be abated, as injurious to navigation, . .	Ditto, .	Ditto.	—
163	Ditto, .	Ditto, .	Ditto, ...	Ditto, .	Ditto.	—
164	Ditto, .	Ditto, .	Ditto, ...	Ditto, .	Ditto.	—
165	Ditto, .	Ditto, .	Ditto, ...	Ditto, .	Ditto.	—
166	Ditto, .	Ditto, .	Ditto, ...	Ditto, .	Ditto.	—
167	Ditto, .	Ditto, .	Ditto, ...	Ditto, .	Ditto.	—
168	Ditto, .	Ditto, .	Ditto, ...	Ditto, .	Ditto.	—
169	Ditto, .	Ditto, .	Ditto, ...	Ditto, .	Ditto.	—
170	Ditto, .	Ditto, .	Ditto, ...	Ditto, .	Ditto.	—
171	Ditto, .	Ditto, .	Ditto, ...	Ditto, .	Ditto.	—
172	Ditto, .	Ditto, .	Ditto, ...	Ditto, .	Ditto.	—
173	Ditto, .	Ditto, .	Ditto, ...	Ditto, .	Ditto.	—
174	Ditto, .	Ditto, .	Ditto, ...	Ditto, .	Ditto.	—
175	Ditto, .	Ditto, .	Ditto, ...	Ditto, .	Ditto.	—
176	Decies-within-Drum.	Ditto, .	To be abated, as erected without the title required by 5 & 6 Vic., c. 106.	Ditto, .	Ditto.	—
177	Ditto, .	Ditto, .	Ditto, ...	Ditto, .	Ditto.	—
178	Corkaguiny,	Kerry, .	Ditto, ...	22 Aug 1864,	Ditto.	—
179	Ditto, .	Ditto, .	Ditto, ...	Ditto, .	Ditto.	—
180	Iveragh, .	Ditto, .	Ditto, ...	Ditto, .	Ditto.	—
181	Ditto, .	Ditto, .	Ditto, ...	Ditto, .	Ditto.	—
182	Ditto, .	Ditto, .	Ditto, ...	24 Aug 1864,	Appeal, ...	Appeal withdrawn.
183	Ditto, .	Ditto, .	To be abated, not erected in 1862, . .	Ditto, .	No appeal.	—
184	Ditto, .	Ditto, .	To be abated, within three miles of mouth of Inny River.	Ditto, .	Ditto.	—
185	Dunkerron, N.	Ditto, .	Legally erected, ...	Ditto, .	Ditto.	—
186	Ferrard, .	Louth, .	To be abated, as erected without the title required by 5 & 6 Vic., c. 106.	26 Aug. 1864,	Ditto.	—
187	Ditto, .	Ditto, .	Ditto, ...	Ditto, .	Ditto.	—
188	Ditto, .	Ditto, .	Ditto, ...	Ditto, .	Ditto.	—
189	Ditto, .	Ditto, .	Ditto, ...	Ditto, .	Ditto.	—
190	Ditto, .	Ditto, .	Ditto, ...	Ditto, .	Ditto.	—
191	Ditto, .	Ditto, .	Ditto, ...	Ditto, .	Ditto.	—
192	Ditto, .	Ditto, .	Legally erected, ...	Ditto, .	Ditto.	—
193	Ditto, .	Ditto, .	To be abated, as erected without the title required by 5 & 6 Vic., c. 106.	27 Aug 1864,	Ditto.	—
194	Ditto, .	Ditto, .	Legally erected, ...	Ditto, .	Ditto.	—
195	Lr. Dunluce,	Antrim, .	Ditto, ...	29 Aug 1864,	Ditto.	—
196	Ditto, .	Ditto, .	Ditto, ...	Ditto, .	Ditto.	—
197	Ditto, .	Ditto, .	Ditto, ...	Ditto, .	Ditto.	—
198	Ditto, .	Ditto, .	Ditto, ...	Ditto, .	Ditto.	—
199	Ditto, .	Ditto, .	Ditto, ...	Ditto, .	Ditto.	—
200	Ditto, .	Ditto, .	Ditto, ...	Ditto, .	Ditto.	—
201	Ditto, .	Ditto, .	To be abated; injurious to navigation, . .	Ditto, .	Ditto.	—
202	Cary, .	Ditto, .	Legally erected, ...	30 Aug 1864,	Ditto.	—
203	Ditto, .	Ditto, .	To be abated; within 3 miles of mouth of Cushendun River.	Ditto, .	Ditto.	—
204	Lr. Glenarm,	Ditto, .	Ditto, . . . ditto	Ditto, .	Ditto.	—
205	Ditto, .	Ditto, .	Ditto, ditto Glenarm River,	Ditto, .	Appeal, ...	Judgment reversed.
206	Ditto, .	Ditto, .	Ditto; in Estuary of Glenarm River, .	Ditto, .	Ditto, ...	Judgment affirmed.
207	Ditto, .	Ditto, .	Ditto; within 3 miles of mouths of Cushendall and Glenariffe Rivers.	Ditto, .	No appeal.	—
208	Ditto, .	Ditto, .	Ditto, ...	Ditto, .	Ditto.	—

APPENDIX, No. 6.

RESULT of INQUIRIES held by the SPECIAL COMMISSIONERS and the INSPECTORS of IRISH FISHERIES into

No.	Where Fixed Net situated	Description of Fixed Net.	Names of Persons maintaining and using Fixed Net.	Names of Owner of Fixed Net, or of Land to which Net attached	Name of Townland to which Net attached	Parish
209	Sea of coast of co. Antrim,	Bag-Net,	Thomas Tait,	A. Boyd,	Ballycastle,	Ramoan,
210	Ditto,	Ditto,	Ditto,	Ditto,	Ditto,	Ditto,
211	Ditto,	Ditto,	J. M'Gildowney,	J. M'Gildowney,	Clarepark,	Ditto,
212	Ditto,	Ditto,	A. M'Quillan,	J. K. Trimm,	Cregganboy,	Ditto,
213	Ditto,	Ditto,	S. Woodside,	Ditto,	Ditto,	Ditto,
214	Ditto,	Ditto,	H. Dobson,	G. S. Fullerton,	Carrick-a-rede Island,	Ballintoy,
215	Ditto,	Ditto,	H. Kelly,	Ditto,	Larrybane,	Ditto,
216	Ditto,	Ditto,	R. Stewart,	Sir E. M'Naghten,	Portbraddan,	Ditto,
217	Ditto,	Ditto,	Ditto,	J. K. Leslie,	Templastragh,	Ditto,
218	Ditto,	Ditto,	J. M'Allister,	E. M'Neile,	Currysheskin,	Ditto,
219	Ditto,	Ditto,	F. Mills,	J. C. Anderson,	Portcoon - Feigh Magaston,	Dunseverick,
220	Ditto,	Ditto,	Ditto,	Ditto,	Ditto,	Ditto,
221	Ditto,	Ditto,	W. Gregg,	Sir E. M'Naghten,	Ardihannon,	Billy,
222	Ditto,	Ditto,	Ditto,	Ditto,	Bushfoot,	Dunluce,
223	Sea off Coast of co. Londonderry,	Ditto,	H. O'Neill,	A. Shuldham and Hon. Mrs Campbell,	East Ballyquelagh,	Ballyaghran,
224	Ditto,	Ditto,	J. M'Keeman,	Sir H. H. Bruce,	Prochall,	Dunbeogh,
225	Sea off coast of co. Donegal,	Ditto,	C. M'Kinney,	Rev. S. Montgomery,	Glenagivney,	Lower Moville,
226	Ditto,	Ditto,	Ditto,	J. S. Nicholson,	Mossy Glen,	Ditto,
227	Ditto,	Ditto,	Ditto,	Anne Knox,	Ballymagaragh,	Ditto,
228	Ditto,	Ditto,	Ditto,	L. M'Clintock,	Ballyduirey,	Ditto,
229	Ditto,	Ditto,	B. Sheffry,	J. S. Nicholson,	Tremoronagh,	Culdaff,
230	Ditto,	Ditto,	A. Maddison,	R. C. Stewart,	Hare Head,	Clondahorky,
231	Sea off Coast of co. Londonderry,	Ditto,	R. Stewart,	Sir H. H. Bruce,	Ballymaclary,	Magilligan,
232	Ditto,	Ditto,	Ditto,	Ditto,	Douglas,	Ditto,
233	Lough Foyle,	Stake Net,	R. Allen,	Irish Society,	Gransha,	Glendermott,
234	Ditto,	Ditto,	Ditto,	Ditto,	Ditto,	Ditto,
235	Ditto,	Ditto,	Ditto,	Ditto,	Ditto,	Ditto,
236	Ditto,	Ditto,	Ditto,	Ditto,	Ballymacalloge,	Templemore,
237	Ditto,	Ditto,	Ditto,	Ditto,	Ditto,	Ditto,
238	Ditto,	Ditto,	Ditto,	Ditto,	Culmore,	Ditto,
239	Ditto,	Ditto,	Ditto,	Ditto,	Culmore Level,	Ditto,
240	Ditto,	Ditto,	Ditto,	Ditto,	Lower Clampsey,	Faughanvale,
241	Ditto,	Ditto,	Ditto,	Ditto,	Coolkeeragh,	Clondermott,
242	Ditto,	Ditto,	Ditto,	Ditto,	Ditto,	Ditto,
243	Ditto,	Ditto,	Ditto,	Ditto,	Culmore,	Culmore,
244	River Erne,	Ditto,	Allen Sheil,	Thomas Connolly,	Veemar,	Inishmacsaint,
245	Sea off Coast of co. Sligo,	Bag-Net,	William Petrie,	Ormsby Jones,	Streedagh,	Ahamlish,
246	Ditto,	Ditto,	William Little,	R. Orme,	Carrowkilbleck,	Kilglass,
247	Sea off Coast of co. Mayo,	Ditto,	M. Flynn,	Colonel Knox,	Castletown or Lackan,	Lackan,
248	Ditto,	Ditto,	William Little,	Rev. J. M'Naughten,	Ballinlena,	Kilcummin,
249	Ditto,	Ditto,	Ditto,	Rev. C. L. Thomas,	Ballyggary,	Ditto,
250	Shannon River,	Stake-Net,	H. S. O'Brien,	H. S. O'Brien,	Percifine,	Kilfintinan,
251	Bantry Bay, Glengarriffe Har.,	Bag-Net,	Lord Bantry,	Lord Bantry,	Mountcoumelder,	Kilcaskin,
252	Ditto,	Ditto,	Ditto,	Ditto,	Ditto,	Ditto,
253	Ditto,	Ditto,	Ditto,	Ditto,	Ditto,	Ditto,
254	Bantry Bay, Adrigole Harbour,	Ditto,	Ditto,	Ditto,	Adrigole,	Ditto,
255	Sea of co. Mayo,	Ditto,	Alexander Hector,	William Pike,	Achillbeg,	Achill,
256	Ditto,	Ditto,	Ditto,	Ditto,	Ditto,	Ditto,
257	Sea off Achill Island,	Ditto,	Ditto,	M. M. Blacker,	Keem Net,	Ditto,
258	Ditto,	Ditto,	Ditto,	C. Bryant,	Gupreadinun,	Achill,
259	Ditto,	Ditto,	Ditto,	Ditto,	West Net,	Ditto,
260	Ditto,	Ditto,	Ditto,	Trustees Achill Mission,	Keel,	Ditto,
261	Waterford Harbour,	Stake-Net,	A. N. O'Neill,	A. N. O'Neill,	Woodstown,	Crooke,
262	Ditto,	Ditto,	Ditto,	Ditto,	Knockaveelish,	Ditto,
263	River Suir, King's Channel,	Ditto,	A. N. O'Neill and Mary O'Neill,	A. N. O'Neill and Mary O'Neill,	Knockboy,	Ballygunner,
264	Ditto,	Ditto,	Ditto,	Ditto,	Ditto,	Ditto,
265	River Shannon,	Ditto,	Jn. Jameson & others,	Knight of Glin,	Cahiragh,	Killorgan,
266	Ditto,	Ditto,	R. W. C. Reeves,	R. W. C. Reeves,	Durrane, Lower,	Kilimurry,
267	Lower Bunratty,	Head Weir,	Thomas Studdert,	Thomas Studdert,	Bunratty,	Bunratty,
268	Sea off the Coast of co. Sligo,	Bag-Net,	William Peters,	Lady Palmerston and Hon. W. Cowper,	Mullaghmore,	Ahamlish,
269	Killala Bay,	Ditto,	William Little,	R. Orme,	Carrowkilbleck,	Kilglass,
270	Sea off Coast of co. Sligo,	Ditto,	William Petrie,	O. Jones,	Streedagh,	Ahamlish,
271	Sea off Coast of co. Londonderry,	Ditto,	Sir H. Bruce,	Sir H. Bruce,	Ballymaclary,	Magilligan,
272	Sea off co. Sligo,	Ditto,	Lady Palmerston and [illegible]	—	Mullaghmore,	Ahamlish,

APPENDIX. No. 6.

the Legality or Illegality of Fixed Nets erected or used for catching Salmon in Ireland—*continued.*

No.	Barony.	County.	Judgment of Commissioners.	Date of Judgment.	Whether Judgment of Commissioners Appealed against.	Result of Appeal to Court of Queen's Bench.
209	Cary,	Antrim,	To be abated, within 3 miles of Ballycastle River,	30 Aug 1864,	No appeal.	—
210	Ditto,	Ditto,	Ditto,	Ditto,	Ditto.	—
211	Ditto,	Ditto,	Ditto,	Ditto,	Ditto.	—
212	Ditto,	Ditto,	Ditto,	Ditto,	Ditto.	—
213	Ditto,	Ditto,	Ditto,	Ditto,	Ditto.	—
214	Ditto	Ditto,	Legally erected,	Ditto,	Ditto.	—
215	Ditto,	Ditto,	Ditto,	Ditto,	Ditto.	—
216	Ditto,	Ditto,	Ditto,	Ditto,	Ditto.	—
217	Ditto,	Ditto,	To be abated, as erected without the title required by 5 & 6 Vic., c. 106.	Ditto,	Ditto.	—
218	Ditto,	Ditto,	Ditto,	Ditto,	Ditto.	—
219	Ditto,	Ditto,	Legally erected,	Ditto,	Ditto.	—
220	Ditto,	Ditto,	Ditto,	Ditto,	Ditto.	—
221	Ditto,	Ditto,	To be abated; within Estuary of Bush River,	Ditto,	Appeal,	Judgment affirmed.
222	Lr. Dunluce,	Ditto,	Ditto,	Ditto,	Ditto,	Ditto.
223	Coleraine,	Londonderry,	Legally erected,	31 Aug 1864	No Appeal.	—
224	Ditto,	Ditto,	To be abated; within three miles of mouth of Bann River.	Ditto,	Ditto.	—
225	Inishowen,	Donegal,	To be abated, as erected without the title required by 5 & 6 Vic., c. 106.	3 Sept 1864,	Ditto.	—
226	Ditto,	Ditto,	Ditto,	Ditto,	Ditto.	—
227	Ditto,	Ditto,	Ditto,	Ditto,	Ditto.	—
228	Ditto,	Ditto,	Ditto,	Ditto,	Ditto.	—
229	Ditto,	Ditto,	Ditto,	Ditto,	Ditto.	—
230	Kilmacrenan,	Ditto,	Ditto,	Ditto,	Ditto.	—
231	Keenaght,	Londonderry,	Ditto,	6 Sept. 1864,	Appeal,	Sent back on motion before hearing of appeal, to enable the owner to make a case abandoned at first trial.—See No. 271.
232	Ditto,	Ditto,	To be abated; within Estuary of Foyle River,	Ditto,	No Appeal.	—
233	Tirkeeran,	Ditto,	Legally erected,	—	Ditto	—
234	Ditto,	Ditto,	Ditto,	—	Ditto.	—
235	Ditto,	Ditto,	Ditto,	—	Ditto.	—
236	City & Liberties,	Ditto,	To be abated; injurious to navigation,	—	Ditto.	—
237	Ditto,	Ditto,	Ditto,	—	Ditto.	—
238	Ditto,	Ditto,	Ditto,	—	Ditto	—
239	Ditto,	Ditto,	Ditto,	—	Ditto.	—
240	Tirkeeran,	Ditto,	Ditto,	—	Ditto.	—
241	Ditto,	Ditto,	Ditto,	—	Ditto.	—
242	Ditto,	Ditto,	Ditto,	—	Ditto.	—
243	Ditto,	Ditto,	Ditto,	—	Ditto.	—
244	Tyrhugh,	Donegal,	Legally erected,	8 Sept. 1864,	Ditto.	—
245	Carbury,	Sligo,	See No. 270.	—	—	—
246	Tireragh,	Ditto,	To be abated, as erected without the title required by 5 & 6 Vic., c. 106.	10 Sept. 1864,	Appeal,	Sent back in consequence of the evidence at first trial being defective.—See No. 269.
247	Tyrawley,	Mayo,	Ditto,	12 Sept. 1864,	No Appeal.	—
248	Ditto,	Ditto,	Ditto,	Ditto,	Appeal,	Judgment reversed.
249	Ditto,	Ditto,	Ditto,	Ditto,	Ditto,	Judgment affirmed.
250	Lr. Bunratty	Clare,	To be abated, as injurious to navigation and public rights of fishing, and as erected on the site of a weir previously condemned. Vide sec. 17 of 13 & 14 Vic., c. 88.	17 Sept. 1864,	Ditto,	Ditto.
251	Bere,	Cork,	To be abated; within Estuary of River,	8 May, 1867,	—	—
252	Ditto,	Ditto,	Ditto,	Ditto.	—	—
253	Ditto,	Ditto,	Ditto,	Ditto.	—	—
254	Ditto,	Ditto,	Abandoned,	Ditto	—	—
255	Burrishoole,	Mayo,	To be abated, as erected without the title required by 5 & 6 Vic., c. 106.	12 July, 1865,	No Appeal.	—
256	Ditto,	Ditto,	Ditto,	Ditto,	Ditto.	—
257	Ditto,	Ditto,	Postponed for further evidence,	Ditto,	Ditto.	—
258	Ditto,	Ditto,	To be abated, as erected without the title required by 5 & 6 Vic., c. 106.	Ditto.	Ditto.	—
259	Ditto,	Ditto,	Ditto,	Ditto,	Ditto.	—
260	Ditto,	Ditto,	Legally erected,	Ditto,	Ditto.	—
261	Gaultiere,	Waterford,	(See 73 to 78 inclusive.) Report made to Court of second trial.	No Judgment,	Set down on report,	Judgment reversed.
262	Ditto,	Ditto,		Ditto,	Ditto,	
263	Ditto,	Ditto,		Ditto,	Ditto,	
264	Ditto,	Ditto,		Ditto,	Ditto,	
265	Shanid,	Limerick,	Report made to Court,	Ditto,	Ditto,	Ditto.
266	Clonderalaw,	Clare,	Ditto,	Ditto,	Ditto,	Ditto.
267	Lr. Bunratty,	Ditto,	Legally erected,	10 Nov. 1866,	No appeal.	—
268	Carbury,	Sligo,	Ditto,	14 Nov 1866,	Ditto.	—
269	Tireragh,	Ditto,	Report made to Court,	—	Appeal pending	—
270	Carbury,	Ditto,	Legally erected,	14 Nov 1866,	No appeal.	—
271	Keenaght,	Londonderry,	Report made to Court,	20 Nov 1866,	Set down on report,	Judgment reversed.
272	Carbury,	Sligo,	Illegal. Within 3 miles of mouth of Duff River,	15 June, 1867,	Appeal,	Judgment affirmed.
273	Decies-without-Drum,	Waterford,	Report made to Court,	No Judgment,	Appeal,	Judgment reversed.
274	Ditto,	Ditto,	Ditto,	Ditto,	Ditto,	Appeal withdrawn.
275	Ditto,	Ditto,	Legal,	4 Jan. 1868,	No appeal.	—
276	Shelburne,	Wexford,	Report to Court—That it is injurious to navigation—26th February, 1868.	No Judgment,	Set down on report,	Judgment affirmed.
277	Inishowen,	Donegal,	Legal,	6 Mar. 1868,	No appeal.	—
278	Clonderalaw,	Clare,	To be abated,	13 Nov. 1868	Appeal,	Judgment reversed.
279	Ditto,	Ditto,	Ditto,	Ditto.	No Appeal.	—
280	Ditto,	Ditto,	Ditto,	Ditto.	Appeal,	Judgment reversed.
281	Ditto,	Ditto,	Ditto,	Ditto	Ditto,	Ditto.
282	Iraghticonnor,	Kerry,	—	17 Nov. 1868.	—	—
283	Ditto,	Ditto,	To be abated,	Ditto.	—	—
284	Ditto,	Ditto,	Given up by Mr. Nelligan. Not erected or used either as Bag or Stake Net in 1862.	Ditto.	—	—

Appendix, No. 6.

RESULT of INQUIRIES held by INSPECTORS

No.	Where Fixed Net situated.	Description of Fixed Net.	Name of Person maintaining and using Fixed Net.	Name of Owner of Fixed Net, or of Land in which Net attached	Name of Townland to which Net attached.	Parish.
285	Sea off Coast co. Antrim, .	Fixed Draft Net	Denis Black, . .	Denis Black, . .	Moneyvart, . .	Layd, . .
286	Ditto, ...	Ditto, . .	Archibald M'Keegan,	Earl of Antrim, .	Glebe, . .	Layd, . .
287	Sea off Coast co. Cork, . .	Stake-Net, .	Sampson French, .	Sampson French, .	Cushinney, . .	Templerobin, .
288	Coomhola River (estuary), .	Fixed Draft, .	R. Vickery, . .	Earl of Bantry, .	Drumkeal, . .	Kilmacomoge,
289	Ditto, ...	Ditto, . .	R. Warner, . .	Ditto, . .	Rossmacowen, . .	Ditto, . .
290	Ouvane River, . . .	Ditto, . .	William Sullivan, .	Ditto, .	Ditto, .	Ditto, . .
291	Sea off Coast co. Cork, . .	Ditto, . .	Michael Murphy, .	Ditto, . .	Reenabougna, . .	Kilmacoliga,
292	Dunmanus River (estuary), .	Ditto, . .	Ditto, . .	—	Gurteenroe and Newtown.	Ditto, . .
293	Shannon, ...	Stake-Net, .	Thomas Sandes, .	Thomas Sandes, .	Cooluanmeagh, .	Kilnaughtin, .
294	Sea off Coast co. Antrim, .	Fixed Draft Net	Sir H. H. Boyd, .	Sir H. H. Boyd, .	Towngradin, . .	Ramoan,
295	Ditto, ...	Ditto, . .	Archibald M'Keegan,	Earl of Antrim, .	Glebe, . . .	Layd, . .
296	Ditto, ...	Ditto, . .	John Finlay, . .	John Finlay, . .	Ballyteerum, . .	Culfeightrin, .
297	Ditto, ...	Ditto, . .	Henry H. M'Neill, .	H. H. M'Neill, .	Rectory, . .	Layd, . .
298	Ditto, ...	Ditto, . .	Edmund M'Neill, .	Edmund M'Neill, .	Carryshoolan, . .	Ballintoy, .
299	Ditto, ...	Ditto, . .	Denis Black, . .	Denis Black, . .	Moneyvart, . .	Layd, . .
300	Ditto, ...	Ditto, . .	John M'Gildowney, .	John M'Gildowney, .	Clare, . . .	Ramoan, .
301	Ditto, ...	—	Robert Stewart, .	James Leslie, . .	Templastragh, . .	Ballintoy, .
302	Ditto, ...	Fixed Draft Net	Sir H. H. Boyd, .	Sir Hugh Boyd, bart.,	Greggenboy, . .	Ditto, . .
303	Sea off Coast co. Londonderry,	Ditto, . .	John Cromie, . .	John Cromie, . .	North Mulinghemall, .	Ballyaghran,
304	Ditto, ...	—	Henry O'Neill, .	Arnold White and John P. Broughton.	East and West Tullaghmurray and Cranmurgh.	Ditto, .
305	Ditto, ...	Fixed Draft Net	Sir H. H. Bruce, bt.,	Sir H. Harvey Bruce, bart	Ballymaclary, . .	Tamlaghtard, .
306	Estuary of Inver River, . .	2 Ditto, . .	William Sinclair, .	William Sinclair, .	Inver Estuary, . .	Inver, . .
307	Eske River, ...	Fixed Draft Net	Earl of Arran, . .	Earl of Arran, . .	Eske River, . .	Donegal, and Inver
308	Sea off Coast co. Donegal, .	Ditto, . .	Marquis Conyngham,	Marquis Conyngham	Ballyederlan, . .	Killaghtee, .
309	Ditto, ...	Bag-Net, .	Ditto, . .	Ditto, . .	Ditto, . .	Ditto, . .
310	Estuary of Leannan River, .	2 Fixed Draft Nets	R. Kelly, . .	Sir Jas. Stewart, bt.,	Leannan River, .	Aughnish, .
311	Sea off Coast co. Donegal, .	Fixed Draft Net	W. B. Tredennick, .	W. B. Tredennick, .	Killultan, . .	Killaghtee, .
312	Ditto, ...	Ditto, . .	Ditto, . .	Ditto, . .	Ballyvorey, . .	Ditto, . .
313	Ditto, ...	Ditto, . .	S. Shell, . . .	S. Shell, . . .	Magheramar, . .	Inishkeeragh
314	Ditto, ...	Ditto, . .	Mrs. S. M'Donnell, .	Mrs. S. M'Donnell, .	Ballymaggart, . .	Killaghtee, .
315	Ditto, ...	Ditto, . .	A. Hamilton, . .	A. Hamilton, . .	Cashmore, . .	Kilbarron, .
316	Ditto, ...	Ditto, . .	Murray Stewart, .	Murray Stewart, .	Gortalia, . . .	Kilcar, . .
317	Ditto, ...	Ditto, . .	Ditto, . .	Ditto, . .	Mucross, . . .	Ditto, . .
318	Ditto, ...	Ditto, . .	Ebenezer Bustard, .	Ebenezer Bustard, .	Drumanoo, . .	Killybegs, .
319	Ditto, ...	Ditto, . .	James Hoskins, .	—	Ballybodonell, &c., .	Killaghtee, .
320	River Moy, ...	6 Ditto, . .	Mary Anne Little and Andrew Clarke.	Mary Anne Little and A. Clarke.	—	—
321	Ditto, ...	5 Ditto, . .	William Petrie, .	John Wingfield Stratford.	Scurmore, . .	Castleconnor, .
322	Sea off Coast of Sligo, . .	Fixed Draft Net	J. Conway, . .	Richard G. Brinkley,	Streedagh, . .	Ahamlish, .
323	River Owenmore . . .	3 Ditto, . .	William Petrie, .	—	—	—
324	Tullaghan Bay, . . .	7 Fixed Drafts,	Helen Little, . .	—	Tullaghan Bay, .	Kilmore, &c.

up to 31st December, 1870.

Appendix, No. 6.

No.	Barony	County	Judgment of Commissioners.	Date of Judgment.	Whether Judgment of Inspectors Appealed against	Result of Appeal in Court of Queen's Bench.
285	Lr. Glenarm,	Antrim,	See No. 299.	—	—	—
286	Ditto,	Ditto,	Postponed.—See No. 295.	—	—	—
287	Imokilly,	Cork,	Legal,	22 Sept. 1870.	—	—
288	Bantry,	Ditto,	To be abated, as erected without the Title required by 5 & 6 Vic., c. 106.	21 Feb. 1870.	—	—
289	Ditto,	Ditto,	Ditto,	Ditto.	—	—
290	Ditto,	Ditto,	Ditto,	Ditto.	—	—
291	Ditto,	Ditto,	Withdrawn,	Ditto.	—	—
292	Ditto,	Ditto,	Ditto,	Ditto.	—	—
293	Iraghticonnor,	Kerry,	Legal,	11 Mar. 1870	—	—
294	Cary,	Antrim,	Ditto.	3 May, 1870	—	—
295	Lr. Glenarm,	Ditto,	Ditto,	10 May, 1870.	—	—
296	Cary,	Ditto,	Ditto,	Ditto.	—	—
297	Lr. Glenarm,	Ditto,	Ditto,	Ditto.	—	—
298	Cary,	Ditto,	Ditto,	Ditto.	—	—
299	Lr. Glenarm,	Ditto,	Ditto,	Ditto.	—	—
300	Cary,	Ditto,	Ditto,	Ditto	—	—
301	Ditto,	Ditto,	Ditto,	Ditto.	—	—
302	Ditto,	Ditto,	Ditto,	Ditto.	—	—
303	N.E. Liberties of Coleraine.	Londonderry,	Ditto,	11 May, 1870.	—	—
304	Ditto,	Ditto,	Ditto,	Ditto.	—	—
305	Keenaght,	Ditto,	Ditto,	Ditto.	—	—
306	Banagh,	Donegal,	Ditto,	13 May, 1870.	—	—
307	Ditto,	Ditto,	Withdrawn,	Ditto.	—	—
308	Ditto,	Ditto,	Legal,	Ditto.	—	—
309	Ditto,	Ditto,	Illegal. Injurious to navigation,	Ditto.	—	—
310	Kilmacrenan,	Ditto,	Legal,	Ditto.	—	—
311	Banagh,	Ditto,	Withdrawn,	Ditto.	—	—
312	Ditto,	Ditto,	Ditto,	Ditto.	—	—
313	Tirhugh,	Ditto,	Illegal, as not having the title required by 5 & 6 Vic., c. 106.	Ditto.	—	—
314	Banagh,	Ditto,	Ditto,	Ditto.	—	—
315	Tirhugh,	Ditto,	Ditto,	Ditto.	—	—
316	Banagh,	Ditto,	Legal,	Ditto.	—	—
317	Ditto,	Ditto,	Ditto,	Ditto.	—	—
318	Ditto,	Ditto,	Ditto,	Ditto.	—	—
319	Ditto,	Ditto,	Illegal, as not having the title required by 5 & 6 Vic., c. 106.	Ditto.	—	—
320	—	Mayo and Sligo.	Legal,	17 May, 1870.	Appeal.	—
321	Tireragh,	Sligo,	Ditto,	18 May, 1870.	Ditto.	—
322	Ditto,	Ditto,	Withdrawn.	—	—	—
323	Erris,	—	Legal,	18 May, 1870.	—	—
324	Ditto,	Mayo,	Ditto,	Ditto.	—	—

APPENDIX, No. 7.

APPENDIX,

TABLE showing the CLOSE SEASONS for SALMON and TROUT in

No. and Name of District.	Boundary of District.	Tidal.
1. Dublin, . .	Skerries to Wicklow.	From Howth to Dalkey Island, between 31st July and 16th January. For remainder of District, between 31st Aug and 15th Feb
2. Wexford, . .	Wicklow to Kiln Bay, East of Bannow Bay.	Between 15th September and 9th April
3. Waterford, .	Kiln Bay to Helvick Head.	" 31st August and 16th February.
4. Lismore, . .	Helvick Head to Ballycottin.	" 31st August and 16th February.
5. Cork, . .	Ballycottin to Galley Head.	" 15th August and 16th February for Electoral Division A (between Ballycottin and Barry's Head). " 31st August and 1st March, for Electoral Division B (between Barry's Head and Galley Head).
6¹. Skibbereen, .	Galley Head to Mizen Head.	" 15th September and 1st April.
6². Bantry, . .	Mizen Head to Crow Head.	" Do. do.
6³. Kenmare, . .	Crow Head to Lamb Head.	" Do. do.
7. Killarney, . .	Lamb Head to Dunmore Head, including Blaskets.	" 31st July and 16th January, save Rivers Maine, Ferta, or Valentia, Inny, and Waterville, and their Tributaries. Maine, Ferta or Valentia, Inny, and Tributaries, 15th September to 1st May. Waterville and its Tributaries, 16th July and 1st January.
8. Limerick, . .	Dunmore to Hags Head.	Between 15th July and 1st February, save Rivers Cashen and Doonbeg Rivers between Kerry Head and Dunmore Head, 15th September and 1st April. For Rivers Cashen, Feale and Geale and their Tributaries, between 15th August and 1st May.
9. Galway, . .	Hags Head to Slyne Head.	Between 15th August and 16th February.
10¹. Ballinakill, .	Slyne Head to Pigeon Point.	" 31st August and 16th February.
10². Bangor, . .	Pigeon Point to Benwee Head.	" Do. do.
11. Ballina, . .	Benwee to Coonamore.	" 15th August and 16th March, save Palmerston and Easkey Rivers, between 31st August and 1st June.
12. Sligo, . .	Coonamore to Mullaghmore.	" 19th August and 4th February, save Sligo River, which is 31st July and 16th January.
13. Ballyshannon, .	Mullaghmore to Rossan.	" 19th August and 4th February.
14. Letterkenny, .	Rossan to Malin Head.	" 19th August and 4th Feb., and one mile above Tideway.
15¹. Londonderry, .	Malin to Downhill Boundary.	" 31st August and 15th April.
15². Coleraine, .	Downhill Boundary to Portrush.	" 19th August and 4th February.
16. Ballycastle, .	Portrush to Donaghadee	" Do. do.
17. Drogheda, .	Donaghadee to Skerries.	" 19th August and 12th February, from Skerries to Round Tower at Dromiskin, north of Castlebellingham; but between 15th August and 1st April, from Round Tower at Dromiskin to Donaghadee.

NOTE.—The 21st section of the 26th & 27th Vic., c. 114, requires there shall not be fewer than 168 days Close Season in each Fishery.
WEEKLY CLOSE SEASON.—By the 20th section of the 26th & 27th Vic., c. 114, no Salmon or Trout shall be fished for or taken in any way, except by Single Rod and Line, between six of the clock on Saturday morning and six of the clock on the succeeding Monday morning.

No. 7.

the different Districts in Ireland, up to 31st December, 1870.

Fresh Water.	Angling with Cross Lines.	Angling with Single Rod and Line.	Date of last change.	No. and Name of District.
From Howth to Dalkey Island, between 31st July and 1st Feb. From mouths of [illegible] between 31st Aug. & 1st March.	15th October and 2nd April. 25th September and 16th March.	1st Nov. to 1st Feb.	10th Dec. 1861.	1. Dublin.
Between 15th September and 9th April.	30th September and 16th March.	30th Sept. and 1st March.	15th Feb. 1870.	2. Wexford.
” 31st August and 16th February.	31st August and 10th February.	14th Sept. and 1st Feb.	4th Nov. 1870.	3. Waterford.
” 31st August and 16th February.	31st August and 16th February.	20th Sept. and 1st Feb.	10th Dec. 1870.	4. Lismore.
” 15th Sept. and 1st April, for Electoral Division C.	9th October and 27th March.	1st Nov. to 1st Feb.	20th June, 1863.	5. Cork.
Between 31st August and 1st April, for Electoral Division D.	15th October and 2nd April.		22nd June, 1869.	
Between 15th September and 1st April.	15th October and 2nd April.		7th Feb. 1856.	6[1]. Skibbereen.
” Do. do.	Do. do.		”	6[2]. Bantry.
” Do. do.	Do. do.		”	6[3]. Kenmare.
Same as Tidal.	Same as Netting.	20th Sept. and 1st Feb., save in Maine, Laune, Carra, and Tributaries. [illegible]	20th April, 1870.	7. Killarney.
Same as Tidal.	Same as Netting.	[illegible]		
Same as Tidal.	Same as Netting.	[illegible]		
Between 31st July and 1st February, save Rivers Cashen and Doonbeg and their Tributaries. Rivers between Kerry Head and Dunmore Head, 15th September and 1st April.	Same as Netting.	Between 20th Sept. and 1st Feb., save Cashen and Doonbeg Rivers. And for Rivers between Kerry Head and Dunmore Head, between 15th Sept. and 1st April.	16th Dec. 1870.	8. Limerick.
Between 15th August and 16th February.	20th September and 16th March.	1st Nov. to 1st Feb.	6th Jan. 1863.	9. Galway.
” 31st August and 1st March.	Do. do.		14th July, 1849.	10[1]. Ballinakill.
” Do. do.	Do. do.		”	10[2]. Bangor.
” 31st July and 1st February, save Palmerston and Easkey Rivers, between 31st August and 1st June.	Same as Netting.	Between 15th Sept. and 1st Feb.; Palmerston and Easkey Rivers, 30th Sept. and 1st June.	19th Dec., 1870.	11. Ballina.
” 19th August and 4th February, save Sligo River, which is 31st July and 16th January.	20th September and 16th March; and for Drumcliffe River and Glencar Lake, 15th October and 2nd April.	1st November to 1st February.	11th Dec. 1867. 2nd Sept. 1857. 22nd Aug. 1851.	12. Sligo.
” 19th August and 4th February.	Between 19th Aug. and 4th Feb. for Salmon; but between 20th Sept. and 1st March for Trout; and for River Inver and all Rivers running into the Sea between Rossan Point and Muckros Point, between 20th Sept. and 16th March, and for River Bundrowes and Lough Melvin, between 15th September and 3rd March.		27th Aug. 1856. 17th Apr., 1860. 24th Nov. 1860.	13. Ballyshannon.
” 19th August and 1st March.	20th September and 16th March.		2nd Sept. 1857.	14. Letterkenny.
” 31st August and 15th April.	20th September and 15th April.		27th Jan. 1862.	15[1]. Londonderry.
” 19th August and 1st March.	20th September and 16th March.†		18th Dec. 1856.	15[2]. Coleraine.
” Do. do.	20th September and 16th March.		15th Dec. 1858.	16. Ballycastle.
” 19th August and 12th Feb. from Skerries to Round Tower at Dromiskin, north of Castlebellingham; but between 19th Aug. and 1st April, from Round Tower at Dromiskin to Donaghadee.	20th September and 16th March.		20th Dec. 1867.	17. Drogheda.

* Close Season for Fixed Engines for the capture of Eels, between the 10th January and 1st July, save in the River Shannon, which is between the 31st January and 1st July, and in all other rivers in the *Limerick* District between 31st December and 1st July in year following.

† Pollan Fishing by Trammel Nets in Lough Neagh, 20th September and 1st March.

Appendix, Nos. 8 and 9.

Appendix,

Schedule of Licence Duties payable in each District

District.	1. Salmon Rods. £ s. d.	2. Cross Lines. £ s. d.	3. Snap Nets. £ s. d.	4. Draft Nets. £ s. d.	5. Drift Nets. £ s. d.	6. Trammel Nets for Pollen. £ s. d.	7. Pole Nets. £ s. d.
1. Dublin,	1 0 0	1 0 0	1 10 0	5 0 0	3 0 0	1 10 0	2 0 0
2. Wexford,	1 0 0	1 0 0	0 15 0	3 0 0	1 10 0	0 15 0	1 0 0
3. Waterford,	1 0 0	2 0 0	1 10 0	3 0 0	3 0 0	1 10 0	2 0 0
4. Lismore,	1 0 0	2 0 0	1 10 0	3 0 0	3 0 0	1 10 0	2 0 0
5. Cork,	1 0 0	2 0 0	1 10 0	3 0 0	3 0 0	1 10 0	2 0 0
6[1] Skibbereen,	1 0 0	1 0 0	0 15 0	3 0 0	3 0 0	0 15 0	1 0 0
6[2] Bantry,	1 0 0	1 0 0	0 15 0	3 0 0	3 0 0	0 15 0	1 0 0
6[3] Kenmare,	1 0 0	1 0 0	0 15 0	1 10 0	1 10 0	0 15 0	1 0 0
7. Killarney,	1 0 0	2 0 0	1 0 0	3 0 0	3 0 0	0 15 0	1 0 0
8. Limerick,	1 0 0	2 0 0	1 10 0	3 0 0	3 0 0	1 10 0	2 0 0
9. Galway,	1 0 0	2 0 0	1 10 0	3 0 0	3 0 0	1 10 0	2 0 0
10[1] Ballynakill,	1 0 0	2 0 0	1 10 0	3 0 0	3 0 0	1 10 0	2 0 0
10[2] Bangor,	1 0 0	2 0 0	1 10 0	3 0 0	3 0 0	1 10 0	2 0 0
11. Ballina,	1 0 0	2 0 0	1 10 0	3 0 0	3 0 0	1 10 0	2 0 0
12. Sligo,	1 0 0	2 0 0	1 10 0	3 0 0	3 0 0	1 10 0	2 0 0
13. Ballyshannon,	1 0 0	2 0 0	1 10 0	3 0 0	3 0 0	1 10 0	2 0 0
14. Letterkenny,	1 0 0	2 0 0	1 10 0	3 0 0	3 0 0	1 10 0	2 0 0
15[1]. Londonderry,	1 0 0	2 0 0	1 10 0	3 0 0	3 0 0	1 10 0	2 0 0
15[2]. Coleraine,	1 0 0	2 0 0	0 15 0	3 0 0	1 10 0	1 [illegible] 0	2 0 0
16. Ballycastle,	1 0 0	2 0 0	1 10 0	3 0 0	3 0 0	1 10 0	2 0 0
17. Drogheda,	1 0 0	2 0 0	1 10 0	3 0 0	3 0 0	0 15 0	2 0 0

Appendix,

Schedule of Licence Duties received by the Boards of

District.	1 Salmon Rods.	2 Cross Lines.	3. Snap Nets.	4. Draft Nets.	5. Drift Nets.	6. Trammel Nets or Draft Nets for Pollen.	7. Pole Nets.	Bag Nets.	8. Fly Nets.	10 Stake Nets.	11. Head Weirs.	12 Box, Crib, &c.	13 Gap, Eye, &c.	14. Sweepers.	15. Coghills.	16. Loop Nets.	1868. Amount of Licence Duty. £ s. d.	1869. Per-centage on Poor Law Valuation. £ s. d.	1868. Total Amount received. £ s. d.	1868. Average No. employed.
1. Dublin,	222	2	–	13	–	–	–	–	–	–	–	–	–	–	–	–	150 10 0	—	150 10 0	318
2. Wexford,	106	–	–	35	–	1	–	–	–	–	–	–	–	–	–	–	103 15 0	—	103 15 0	220
3. Waterford,	222	22	209	16	60	–	–	–	–	4	8	6	28	–	–	–	610 2 4	—	619 2 4	1,083
4. Lismore,	516	16	64	–	31	–	–	1	–	3	–	–	–	–	–	–	447 0 0	20 0 0	467 0 0	604
5. Cork,	301	8	–	42	–	–	–	1	–	–	–	–	–	–	–	–	358 0 0	—	368 0 0	604
6[1]. Skibbereen,	24	–	–	11	–	–	–	–	–	–	–	–	–	–	–	–	28 10 0	—	28 10 0	96
6[2] Bantry,	14	–	–	7	8	–	–	–	–	–	–	–	–	–	–	–	27 0 0	—	27 0 0	72
6[3] Kenmare,	32	–	–	9	–	–	–	2	–	–	–	–	–	4	–	–	51 0 0	—	51 0 6	102
7. Killarney,	124	5	–	66	–	–	–	–	–	–	–	2	–	–	–	–	273 0 0	—	273 0 0	605
8. Limerick,	441	30	34	90	80	–	26	–	–	16	1	16	147	–	–	–	1,668 0 0	8 15 0	1,670 15 0	1,048
9. Galway,	98	8	–	16	–	2	–	–	–	–	–	6	–	–	21	–	288 0 0	34 0 0	300 0 0	211
10[1] Ballynakill,	37	–	–	16	–	–	5	–	–	–	–	–	–	–	–	–	84 0 0	—	84 0 0	180
10[2]. Bangor,	26	–	–	20	–	–	–	–	–	–	–	–	–	–	–	–	80 0 0	—	80 0 0	170
11. Ballina,	7	–	–	36	7	–	–	–	–	–	–	6	12	–	–	–	244 0 0	—	244 0 0	215
12. Sligo,	11	–	–	36	–	–	–	2	–	–	–	–	1	–	–	–	80 0 0	—	80 0 0	117
13. Ballyshannon,	63	1	–	34	–	–	4	–	–	1	–	4	–	–	86	–	327 0 0	19 0 1	346 0 0	375
14. Letterkenny,	84	1	–	15	–	–	–	–	–	–	–	2	–	–	–	6	106 0 0	—	100 0 0	111
15[1] Londonderry,	87	6	–	38	–	–	2	4	–	5	–	–	–	–	–	–	238 0 [illegible]	109 3 [illegible]	346 3 6	338
15[2] Coleraine,	66	1	1	2	–	76	–	5	–	–	–	4	40	–	81	–	406 5 0	51 0 0	517 5 0	780
16. Ballycastle,	29	–	–	12	–	–	–	12	–	–	–	–	–	–	–	–	173 0 0	—	173 0 0	164
17. Drogheda,	137	6	6	46	–	–	–	5	–	–	1	6	97	–	–	–	263 5 0	—	263 5 0	364
Total,	2,581	115	270	608	151	78	27	24	–	3	6	46	282	5	87	6	6,444 3 4	256 18 0	6,700 [illegible] 4	8,626

The estimate of the average number of

Salmon Rods,	1 man.	Draft Nets,	5 men.	Pole Nets,	3 men.
Cross Lines,	2 men.	Drift Nets,	5 do.	Bag Nets,	4 do.
Snap Nets,	4 do.	Trammel Nets,	3 do.	Fly Nets,	4 do.

* Increase in Licence Duty in

No. 8.

on Engines used for Fishing for Salmon, January, 1871.

8. Bag Nets.	9. Fly Nets.	10. Stake Nets.	11. Head Weirs.	12. Box, Crib, &c.	13. Gap, Eye, &c.	14. [illegible]	15. Coghills.	16. Loop Nets.
£ s. d.	£ s. d.	£ s. d.	£ s. d.	£ s. d.	£ s. d.	£ s. d.	£ s. d.	£ s. d.
					1 0 0	—	—	—
					0 10 0	—	—	—
					0 12 4	—	—	—
					1 0 0	—	—	—
					1 0 0	—	—	—
					0 10 0	—	—	—
					0 10 0	—	—	—
					0 10 0	3 0 0	1 10 0	—
					0 10 0	—	—	—
					1 0 0	—	—	—
10 0 0	20 0 0	20 0 0	3 0 0	10 0 0	1 0 0	—	—	—
					1 0 0	—	—	—
					1 0 0	—	—	—
					1 0 0	—	—	—
					1 0 0	—	—	—
					1 0 0	—	—	—
					0 10 0	—	—	1 0 0
					1 0 0	—	—	—
					1 0 0	—	—	—
					1 0 0	—	—	—
					1 0 0	—	—	—

No. 9.

CONSERVATORS for the Years 1869 and 1870.

District.	Number and Description of Licenses sold in 1870.																1870. Amount of License Duty.	1870. Percentage on Poor Law Valuation.	1870. Total Amount received.	1870. Average No. employed.	Increase or Decrease between 1869 and 1870			
	1. Salmon Rods.	2. Cross Lines.	3. [illegible] Nets.	4. Draft Nets.	5. Drift Nets.	6. Trammel Nets for Pollen.	7. Pole Nets.	8. Bag Nets.	9. Fly Nets.	10. Stake Nets.	11. Head Weirs.	12. Box, Crib, &c.	13. Gap, Eye, &c.	14. [illegible]	15. Coghills.	16. Loop Nets.					Increase in Amount.	Decrease in Amount.	Increase in Number employed.	Decrease in Number employed.
																	£ s. d.	£ s. d.	£ s. d.		£ s. d.	£ s. d.		
1	316	1	–	17	–	–	–	–	–	–	–	–	–	–	–	–	156 0 0	—	156 0 0	314	—	1 10 0	–	1
2	117	–	–	84	–	1	–	–	–	–	–	–	–	–	–	–	167 0 0	—	167 0 0	442	3 10 0	—	5	–
3	298	28	21	34	60	–	–	–	–	–	6	1	4	13	–	–	961 13 4	—	646 16 4	1,716	43 18 0	—	84	–
4	346	12	88	4	65	–	2	1	–	2	–	2	–	–	–	–	654 10 0	19 10 0	685 0 0	694	78 0 0	—	–	–
5	539	6	–	38	–	–	–	1	–	–	–	–	–	–	–	–	390 10 0	—	398 10 0	778	41 10 0	—	87	–
6a	17	–	–	19	–	–	–	–	–	–	–	–	–	–	–	–	28 0 0	—	28 0 0	80	—	0 10 0	–	1
6b	13	–	–	16	4	–	–	–	–	–	–	–	–	–	–	–	55 10 0	—	55 10 0	71	8 10 0	—		–
6c	31	–	–	6	–	–	–	1	–	–	–	–	–	1	–	–	56 10 0	—	58 10 0	128	7 10 0	—	16	–
7	144	6	–	68	–	–	–	–	–	–	–	2	–	–	–	–	190 0 0	—	209 0 0	58[illegible]	23 0 0	—	60	–
8	833	38	34	117	121	–	20	–	–	22	1	10	162	–	–	–	1,838 10 0	21 0 0	1,860 10 0	3,206	272 10 0	—	818	–
9	73	6	–	18	–	2	–	–	–	–	–	6	23	–	–	–	216 0 0	27 0 0	243 0 0	231	—	29 0 0	10	–
10a	30	–	–	16	–	–	1	–	–	–	–	–	–	–	–	–	85 0 0	—	85 0 0	184	1 0 0	—	4	–
10b	80	–	–	28	–	–	–	1	–	–	–	–	–	–	–	–	90 0 0	—	90 0 0	144	4 0 0	—	–	1
11	60	1	–	28	8	–	–	2	–	–	–	7	15	–	–	–	270 0 0	—	279 0 0	317	36 0 0	—	60	–
12	49	–	–	18	–	–	–	2	–	–	–	–	6	–	–	–	93 10 0	—	95 10 0	186	16 18 0	—	62	–
13	106	6	–	84	1	–	6	–	–	1	–	4	–	–	31	–	332 0 0	10 0 0	351 0 0	362	8 0 0	—	6	–
14	58	1	–	18	–	–	–	–	–	–	–	3	–	–	–	11	120 0 0	—	120 0 0	146	14 0 0	—	84	–
15a	166	8	–	36	11	–	2	4	–	2	–	–	–	–	–	–	353 10 0	88 0 0	441 10 0	442	58 7 0	—	101	–
15b	96	1	1	102	–	72	–	2	–	–	–	4	–	–	62	–	633 15 0	183 0 0	826 15 0	702	189 10 0	—	–	–
16	31	–	–	12	–	–	–	14	–	–	–	–	–	–	–	–	181 10 0	—	161 18 0	180	16 10 0	—	8	–
17	106	6	3	86	–	–	–	1	–	–	1	3	84	–	–	–	346 10 0	—	346 10 0	486	56 0 0	—	36	–
	2767	[illegible]	[illegible]	896	375	78	28	26	–	60	3	45	391	9	66	11	7,233 0 0	378 10 0	7,611 13 4	10,436	388 7 0	31 0 0	888	1

[illegible] men employed is made up as follows—

Stake Nets, . . 4 men. Head weirs, . . 1 man. Box, crib, &c. (every 2) 3 men. | Gap, Eye, &c. . 1 man. [illegible], . 6 do. | Coghills, . . . 1 man. Loop or Pooke Nets, . 1 do.

1870 over 1869—£311 7s. 0d.

APPENDIX, No. 16.—AMOUNT of LICENSE DUTY received for the different Fishing Engines for the Year 18[illegible], in each District.

Districts.	Single Rods.	Cross Lines.	Snap Nets.	Draft Nets.	Drift Nets.	Trammel Nets, or Drain Nets for Pollan.	Pole Nets.	Bag Nets.	Fly Nets.	Stake Nets.	Head Weirs.	Box, Cribs, &c.	Gaps, Eyes, &c.	Scoops.	Coghills.	Loop Nets.
	£ s. d.	£ s. d.	£ s. d.	£ s. d.	£ s. d.	£ s. d.	£ s. d.	£ s. d.	£ s. d.	£ s. d.	£ s. d.	£ s. d.	£ s. d.	£ s. d.	£ s. d.	£ s. d.
Dublin,	180 0 0	5 0 0	–	91 0 0	–	–	–	–	–	–	–	–	–	–	–	–
Wexford,	45 10 0	–	–	[illegible] 0 0	–	5 10 0	–	–	–	–	–	–	–	–	–	–
Waterford,	140 0 0	20 0 0	620 0 0	10 0 0	100 0 0	–	–	–	–	408 0 0	9 0 0	40 0 0	5 10 0	–	–	–
Lismore,	120 10 0	20 0 0	45 0 0	12 0 0	303 0 0	–	4 0 0	10 0 0	–	99 0 0	–	20 0 0	–	–	–	–
Cork,	380 10 0	15 0 0	–	120 0 0		–	–	10 0 0	–	–	–	–	–	–	–	–
Skibbereen,	9 10 0	–	–	10 10 0	–	–	–	–	–	–	–	–	–	–	–	–
Bantry,	7 10 0	–	–	20 0 0	5 0 0	–	–	–	–	–	–	–	–	–	–	–
Kenmare,	15 10 0	–	–	15 0 0	–	–	–	10 0 0	–	–	–	–	–	21 0 0	–	–
Killarney,	75 0 0	10 0 0	–	204 0 0	–	–	–	–	–	–	–	30 0 0	–	–	–	–
Limerick,	281 10 0	75 0 0	61 0 0	120 0 0	2000 0 0	–	40 0 0	–	–	906 0 0	6 0 0	100 0 0	115 0 0	–	–	–
Galway,	75 0 0	15 0 0	–	80 0 0	–	5 0 0	–	–	–	–	–	60 0 0	20 0 0	–	–	–
Ballynakill,	20 0 0	–	–	40 0 0	–	–	5 0 0	–	–	–	–	–	–	–	–	–
Bangor,	20 0 0	–	–	60 0 0	–	–	–	19 0 0		–	–	–	–	–	–	–
Ballina,	90 0 0	5 0 0	–	84 0 0	84 0 0	–	–	20 0 0	–	–	–	90 0 0	10 0 0	–	–	–
Sligo,	24 10 0	–	–	45 0 0	–	–	–	20 0 0	–	–	–	–	5 0 0	–	–	–
Ballyshannon,	154 0 0	30 0 0	–	180 0 0	6 0 0	–	6 0 0	–	–	20 0 0	–	46 0 0	–	–	30 0 0	–
Letterkenny,	90 0 0	1 0 0	–	90 0 0	–	–	–	–	–	–	–	30 0 0	–	–	–	21 0 0
Londonderry,	64 10 0	15 0 0	–	114 0 0	66 0 0	–	6 0 0	44 0 0	–	20 0 0	–	–	–	–	–	–
Coleraine,	40 0 0	5 0 0	5 10 0	200 0 0	–	75 0 0	–	22 0 0	–	–	–	40 0 0	–	–	20 0 0	–
Ballycastle,	10 10 0	–	–	80 0 0	–	–	–	140 0 0	–	–	–	–	–	–	–	–
Drogheda,	60 0 0	12 0 0	4 10 0	277 0 0	–	–	–	30 0 0	–	–	5 0 0	20 0 0	44 0 0	–	–	–
Total	1,[illegible] 0 0	[illegible] 0 0	[illegible] 0 0	1,[illegible] 10 0	[illegible] 0 0	85 10 0	60 0 0	[illegible] 0 0	–	[illegible] 0 0	15 0 0	480 0 0	[illegible] 10 0	21 0 0	60 0 0	[illegible] 0 0

APPENDIX, No. 11.

LIST of RIVERS, the MOUTHS of which have been defined, one hundred and thirty-six in number.

Section 22 of 5 & 6 Vic., c. 106, enacts "That where the breadth of the mouth or entrance into the sea of any river, the inland "portion of which is frequented by Salmon, is less than half a mile, statute measure, at low water of spring tides, it shall "not be lawful for any person whatsoever (save and except the proprietor of a several fishery within the limits thereof) to "place or erect any stake weir or fixed net within one statute mile, seaward, coastwards, or inwards, from or on either "side of the mouth or entrance of any such river into the sea."

Section 44 of 13 & 14 Vic., c. 88, enacts "That it shall not be lawful for any person, save and except the owner of a several "fishery within the limits thereof, at any time to shoot, draw, or use any net for taking Salmon at the mouth of any river, "where the breadth of such mouth between the banks thereof shall not exceed a quarter of a mile statute measure; and "that it shall not be lawful for any person, save such owner as aforesaid, within such limits as aforesaid, to shoot, draw, "or use any net for taking Salmon within half a mile seaward, or half a mile inwards, or along the coast from the mouth "of any river."

Section 3 of 26 & 27 Vic., c. 114, enacts "That no bag net shall be placed or allowed to continue in any river, or the estuary "of any river, as such river or estuary has been defined by the Commissioners of Fisheries, or shall be defined by the "Commissioners under this Act, or within a distance of less than three statute miles from the mouth of any river, as "defined."

District.	Name of River.	District.	Name of River.
Dublin,	Liffey.	Ballinakill,	Dawros.
	Dodder.		Derrycharmane.
	Bray.		Ballinaboy.
	Varty.	Bangor,	Glenamoy.
Wexford,	Slaney.		Owenmore.
	Owenavarragh or Courtown.		Owenduff.
	Inch.		Owengarve.
	Urrin.		Burrishoole.
	B[illegible].		Newport.
Waterford,	Suir, Nore, and Barrow.		Owenwee or Belclare.
	Barrow.		Bunowen or Louisburgh.
Lismore,	Blackwater.	Ballina,	Easky.
	Womanagh.		Moy.
Cork,	Tramore or Douglas.		Cloonaghmore or Palmerstown.*
	Lee.		Ballinglen or Ballycastle.
	Owenacurra or Midleton.	Sligo,	Drumcliff.
	Owenboy or Carrigaline.		Sligo.
	Argideen.		Ballisodare.
	Bandon.		Dunmoran.
Skibbereen,	Roury.	Ballyshannon,	Glen or Teelin.
	Ilen.		Ballyhalee or Kilcar.
Bantry,	Leamawaddra.		Eany-water or Inver.
	Glengarriff.		Eske.
	Coomhola or Snave.		Erne.
	Ouvane or Ballylickey.		Drowes or Bundrowes.
	Mealagh or Dunnamark.		Duff or Bunduff.
	Adrigole.		Oily.
Kenmare,*	Roughty.		Fintragh.
	Sheen.		Bungosteen or Loughhead.
	Finnehy.	Letterkenny,	Crana or Buncrana.
	Blackwater (Kerry).		Mill.
	Cloonee.		Leannan or Rathmelton.
	Owenreagh.		Swilly.
	Croansaght.		Owencarrow.
	Sneem.		Gweebarra.
Killarney,	Currane.		Owenea.
	Inny.		Owentocker.
	Carragh.		Bracky.
	Laune.		Lackagh.
	Maine.		Ray.
	Ferta or Valencia.		Tullaghobegly.
	Rosbehy.		Glenna.
Limerick,	Shannon.		Clady.
	Cashen.		Owenwee.
	Deel or Askeaton.	Londonderry,	Foyle.
	Fergus.		Roe.
	Maigue.		Culdaff.
	Bunratty.	Coleraine,	Bann.
	Doonbeg.	Ballycastle,	Glenarm.
	Feenagh.		Glenariffe (Red Bay).
	Glenomra.		Dall or Cushendall.
	Sound.		Glendun or Cushendun.
	Owenamore.		Margy or Ballycastle.
	Clohane.		Bush or Bushmills.*
Galway,	Corrib.	Drogheda,	Boyne.
	Furbogh.		Glyde and Dee, or Annagassan.
	Spiddle.		Fane.
	Screeb.		Castletown or Dundalk.
	Ballynahinch.		Piedmont.
	Cashla.		Quoile.
	Invermore.		Dundrum.
	Owengowla.		Shimna or Tollymore.
	Crumlin.		Annalong.
Ballinakill,	Carrowniskey.		Kilkeel.
	Bundorragha.		White Water.
	Erriff.		Causeway Water.
	Culfin.		

* Rivers marked thus have been redefined by the Inspectors of Irish Fisheries.

APPENDIX, No. 12

APPENDIX, No. 12

BY-LAWS, ORDERS, &c., made by the INSPECTORS of IRISH FISHERIES.

District.	Places affected.	Nature of By-law, Order, &c.	Date.
Cork, ...	Bandon River and Tributaries.	Prohibiting the use of all nets (except landing nets, as auxiliary to angling with rod and line), for the capture of salmon or trout, for three years, in any part of, above a line drawn across the said river, at right angles with the river's course, from the northern point of the quay, at the mouth of the creek, between the townlands of Rockhouse and [illegible], to a point on the opposite shore, in the townland of Ahern.	2nd November, 1869.
Belfast Lough, . .	Lough of Belfast, . .	Repealing by-law prohibiting trawling. .	27th November, 1869.
Lough Swilly,	Lough Swilly, . . .	Repealing by-law prohibiting trawling, .	3rd December, 1869.
Ballycastle, . .	Bush River, ...	Repealing the definition of the mouth and estuary of, .	28th February, 1870.
Sligo, .	Sligo River, . . .	Prohibiting snatching, . . .	1st March, 1870.
Killarney, . . .	Fishing weir in Waterville River.	Regulating the width between the bars or rails of the inscales, and of the heck, or the up-stream rails of the boxes or cribs in said weir.	7th March, 1870.
Bantry, . . .	Tidal portions of rivers, .	Permitting use of nets with meshes of $1\frac{1}{2}$ inches from knot to knot.	7th March, 1870.
Kenmare River, .	Kenmare River, . .	Repealing by-law prohibiting trawling in Kenmare, .	19th March, 1870.
Ballina, . . .	River Moy, . . .	Permitting use of nets with meshes of $1\frac{1}{2}$ inches from knot to knot.	31st May, 1870.
Ditto, . . .	Cloonaghmore or Palmerstown River.	Re-defining the mouth and estuary of, . .	16th June, 1870.
Waterford, . .	River Corock (above Wellington Bridge).	Permitting use of nets with meshes of 1 inch from knot to knot.	7th July, 1870.
Coleraine, . . .	The whole District, . .	Prohibiting snatching, . . .	17th October, 1870.
Wexford, . . .	Derrywater and River Derry,	Permitting the use of nets with meshes of 1 inch from knot to knot.	20th October, 1870.
Ditto, . . .	Potter River, . . .	Ditto, .	20th October, 1870.
Lismore, . . .	River Blackwater, . .	Limiting the length of drift nets to 220 yards, . .	2nd November, 1870.
Donegal Bay, . .	Donegal Bay, . . .	Repealing by-law prohibiting trawling; save so far as it relates to Inver Bay.	15th November, 1870.
Limerick, . .	Fergus River, . . .	Prohibiting the use of drift nets, . .	16th December, 1870.

Appendix, No. 13.

Abstract of By-Laws, Orders, &c., in force on 1st January, 1871, relating to the Fisheries of Ireland.

Place affected by By-Law, and Date thereof.	Nature of By-Law.
	TRAWLING.
Belfast Lough, (27th Nov., 1869.)	Prohibiting the use of Trawl Nets in that part of the Lough of Belfast comprised within a straight line drawn from the Castle of Carrickfergus, in the County of the Town of Carrickfergus, to Rockport, in the County of Down, between the hours of Six o'clock in the evening and Six o'clock in the morning, during the months of December, January, and February.
Dublin Bay, (10th Oct., 1842.)	Prohibiting Trawling inside lines drawn from the Bailey Light-house at Howth, to the Easternmost point of the rocks called the "Muglins," thence by a straight line to the Southern point of Dalkey Island, thence by a straight line across Dalkey Sound, in the direction of the signal station on Killiney Hill.
East Coast, (14th Feb., 1851.)	Prohibiting Trawling within a line drawn from the Nose of Howth, to the Eastern point of St. Patrick's Island (Skerries), thence to Clogher Head, thence to Dunany Point, thence to Cranfield Point, in the County Down.
Dundrum Bay, &c., (3rd Dec., 1851.)	Prohibiting Trawling from Ballymurter Rock, off Craigalil Point, to St. John's Point, both in the County Down.
Donegal Bay, (16th Feb., 1857.)	Prohibiting Trawling within a straight line from the Bunn Rock, to a place called Doorin Point.
Belfast Lough, (27th Nov., 1869.)	Prohibiting the use of Trawl Nets in that part of the Lough of Belfast within a straight line drawn from the Castle of Carrickfergus to Rockport, in the County of Down, between the hours of six o'clock in the evening and six o'clock in the morning, during the months of December, January, and February.
Galway Bay, (22nd March, 1848, and 6th Jan., 1854.)	Prohibiting Trawling within a line from Barna Pier to Glenimagh Castle. Also when large shoals of Herrings shall have set in in the Bay, and while Boats are engaged in Drifting for Herrings or Mackerel, and when Boats shall commence Fishing for Herrings or Mackerel, then Trawl Boats shall keep at a distance of three miles from them.
Brandon Bay, (23rd Aug., 1869.)	Prohibiting Trawling within a line drawn from Brandon Point to Coosanea.
Bantry Bay, (17th March, 1855.)	Prohibiting Trawling within a straight line from Crowdy Point to Carrigskye Rock, and from thence to Reenavanny Point, on the North Shore of Whiddy Island.
	Prohibiting Trawling between sunset and sunrise.
Glandore Harbour, (11th Sept., 1861.)	Prohibiting Trawling between the 1st day of May and the 1st day of October in each year, within that part of the Harbour of Glandore lying to the northward of a straight line from the Telegraph or Signal Tower at "Foilnashark," or "Fileenahawk," on the north-eastern point of the entrance to the Harbour, and Sheela Point, on the western shore.
Waterford Harbour, (2nd March, 1863, and 18th June, 1866.)	Prohibiting Trawling by Boats exceeding five tons measurement, within a line drawn from Creden Head to Temple Church.
Wexford Coast, (20th April, 1869.)	Prohibiting Trawling in all places where there are Boats engaged in Herring or Mackerel Drift Net Fishing; and that Trawl Boats shall keep at a distance of at least three miles from all boats fishing for Herrings or Mackerel, with Drift Nets. And whenever Herring or Mackerel Boats shall commence Drift Net Fishing in any place, on or off the Coast of Wexford, the Trawl Boats shall depart therefrom, and keep at least three miles distant from the Drift Net Herring or Mackerel Boats.
	TRAMMEL NETS.
Dungarvan Bay, (4th July, 1848.)	Prohibiting the use of Trammel and every other Fixed or Moored Net (except Bag or other Nets for the taking of Salmon) in Dungarvan Bay, within the limit formed as follows, namely, the space lying between a line passing due East and West, through the Northernmost
Dungarvan Bay—*continued.*	point of Helvick Head, and a line passing due East and West through the Southernmost point of Ballynacourty Head, in the Co. Waterford; but to the North and East of the line through Ballynacourty Head, and to the South and West of the line through Helvick Head, such Trammel or Moored Nets may be set, and remain set in the water from Three o'Clock, p.m., of one day, until Nine o'Clock, a.m., in the following day, during January, March, October, November, and December in each Year; and from Five o'Clock, p.m., of one day, to Seven o'Clock, a.m., in the following day, during May, June, July, August, and September. Also prohibiting such Nets athwart or within [illegible] yards of any boat, which at the time of setting such net shall be moored, and the Crew thereof engaged in Line Fishing; and to every team of such Trammel or Moored Nets shall be attached at least one floating buoy or board, upon which shall be painted in legible characters not less than one inch in length, in white upon a black ground, the Letter of the District, and the name of the Owner to which such Net belongs.
Inver Bay, (24th Sept., 1860.)	Prohibiting the use of Trammel Nets within or to the North east of a line drawn from the Mouth of the Bunlagby River to Doorin Point.
Kenmare River Estuary, (31st Dec., 1864.)	Within the Estuary of the Kenmare River, in the County of Kerry, and eastward of a line drawn from the western point of Lamb's Head to the western point of Coal's Head, the use of Trammel and other Moored Nets for the capture of Sea Fish is authorized and permitted, from the hour of Three o'Clock in the Afternoon of any one day to the hour of Nine o'Clock in the Morning of the day next following, during the months of October, November, December, January, February, and March, in each year; and from the hour of Five o'Clock in the Afternoon of any one day to the hour of Seven o'Clock in the Morning of the day following, during the months of April, May, June July, August, and September.
	OYSTERS.
Wexford Coast, (8th April, 1863.)	First.—All persons engaged in fishing for or taking Oysters off the said Wexford Coast, south of Raven Point, shall cull all such Oysters as may be taken or caught, and shall not remove from any Fishing Ground or Oyster Bed any Oyster of less dimensions than three inches, at the greatest diameter thereof, and shall immediately throw back into the Sea all Oysters of less dimensions than aforesaid, as well as all gravel and fragments of shells as shall be raised or taken while engaged in such fishing; and no person shall take from any Oyster Bed, Bank, Strand, or Shore, off said Wexford Coast, south of Raven Point, any Oyster of less dimensions than three inches, at the greatest diameter thereof; and any person offending in any respect against this By-Law, Rule, or Regulation shall, for each offence, forfeit and pay a sum of Two Pounds.
	Second.—All persons are hereby prohibited from throwing into the Sea, on any Oyster Bed, or Oyster Fishing Ground off the said Wexford Coast, the ballast of any boat, or any other matter or thing injurious or detrimental to the Oyster Fishery; and all persons acting contrary hereto shall, for each offence, forfeit and pay a sum of Two Pounds.
Cork Harbour, (28th Oct., 1858.)	First.—That between the 1st May and 1st September, no boat shall have on board any dredge or other implement for taking Oysters.
	Second.—Every fisherman shall, on the fishing ground, cull all Oysters, and shall not remove any Oyster of less dimensions than two and a-half inches at the greatest diameter thereof; and shall throw back into the Sea all gravel and fragments of shells as he shall raise while engaged in such fishing.
	Third.—All persons are prohibited from throwing into the Sea, on any Oyster Bed or Oyster Fishing Ground, the ballast of any boat, or any other matter or thing injurious to the Oyster Fishery.

Appendix, No. 13. — Abstract of By-Laws, Orders, &c.

Appendix, No. 13—*continued.*

Abstract of By-Laws, Orders, &c., in force on 1st January, 1871, relating to the Fisheries of Ireland.

Place affected by By-Law, and Date thereof.	Nature of By-Law.
Cork Harbour—*con.*	Fourth.—No person shall, between Sunset and Sunrise, dredge for, take, or catch any Oysters within the Harbour of Cork.
Tralee Bay, (28th Sept., 1869.)	First.—That between the 1st day of April and the 1st day of November in any year, being the Close Season for Oysters in the said Bay of Tralee, no boat, in the said Bay of Tralee, shall have on board any dredge or other implement for the taking of Oysters; and if, between the periods aforesaid, there shall be on board any boat any such dredge or other implement for the taking of Oysters, the master or owner of such boat shall, for each such offence, forfeit and pay a sum of Five Pounds.
	Second.—All persons engaged in fishing for or taking Oysters in said Bay of Tralee, shall cull all such Oysters as may be taken or caught; and shall not remove from any fishing ground or Oyster Bed any Oyster of less dimensions than two inches and one-half, at the greatest diameter thereof, and shall immediately throw back into the Sea all Oysters of less dimensions than aforesaid, as well as all gravel and fragments of shells as shall be raised or taken while engaged in such fishing; and no person shall take from any rock, strand, or shore of said Bay of Tralee, any Oysters of less dimensions than two inches and one-half, at the greatest diameter thereof; and any person offending in any respect against this By-Law, Rule, or Regulation shall, for each offence, forfeit and pay a sum of Two Pounds.
	Third.—All persons are hereby prohibited from throwing into the Sea, on any Oyster Bed, or Oyster Fishing Ground in the said Bay of Tralee, the ballast of any boat, or any other matter or thing injurious or detrimental to the Oyster Fishery, and all persons acting contrary hereto shall, for each offence, forfeit and pay a sum of Two Pounds.
Achill Sound, Clew Bay, & Blacksod Bay. (14th Dec., 1869.)	First.—That between the 1st day of April and the 1st day of October in any year, being the Close Season for Oysters in said Clew Bay, Achill Sound, and Blacksod Bay, no boat, in the said Clew Bay, Achill Sound, and Blacksod Bay, shall have on board any dredge or other implement for the taking of Oysters; and if, between the periods aforesaid, there shall be on board any boat any such dredge or other implement for the taking of Oysters, the master or owner of such boat shall for each such offence, forfeit and pay a sum of Five Pounds.
	Second.—All persons engaged in fishing for or taking Oysters in said Clew Bay, Achill Sound, and Blacksod Bay, shall cull all such Oysters as may be taken or caught; and shall not remove from any Fishing Ground or Oyster Bed any Oyster of less dimensions than two inches and one-half, at the greatest diameter thereof, and shall immediately throw back into the Sea all Oysters of less dimensions than aforesaid, as well as all gravel and fragments of shells as shall be raised or taken while engaged in such fishing; and no person shall take from any rock, strand, bed, or shore of said Clew Bay, Achill Sound, and Blacksod Bay, any Oyster of less dimensions than two inches and one-half, at the greatest diameter thereof; and any person offending in any respect against this By-Law, Rule, or Regulation shall, for each offence, forfeit and pay a sum of Two Pounds.
	Third.—All persons are hereby prohibited from throwing into the Sea, on any Oyster Bed, or Oyster Fishing Ground in said Clew Bay, Achill Sound, and Blacksod Bay, the ballast of any boat, or any other matter or thing injurious or detrimental to the Oyster Fishery; and all persons acting contrary hereto shall, for each offence, forfeit and pay a sum of Two Pounds.
	Fourth.—No person shall, between sunset and sunrise, dredge for, take, or catch, any Oysters within said Clew Bay, Achill Sound, and Blacksod Bay; and every person acting contrary hereto shall, for each offence, forfeit and pay a sum of Five Pounds.
Clew Bay, County Mayo. (1st April, 1865.)	That, for the sole purpose of replenishing and supplying licensed Oyster beds and other Oyster beds, the exclusive property of any person or
Clew Bay, County Mayo—*continued.*	persons within Clew Bay alone, in the County of Mayo, and for no other purpose whatever, it may be lawful for any person to dredge for and take Oysters from any natural public bed in the said Clew Bay lying below the level of the lowest water of spring tides, between the 1st and 15th April and the 20th June and 1st October in each year, such periods being respectively included within the Close Time at present fixed for the Oyster fisheries within the said Clew Bay: Provided always, that if any Oysters dredged or taken during such part of the Close Season shall be brought to shore, or sold or offered for sale, or be found in the possession of any person on land, or be used for any other purpose than the replenishing or supplying any such licensed or other bed as aforesaid, every person so offending shall forfeit all such Oysters, and be subject and liable to the same penalties and forfeitures as by said first-recited Act (5 and 6 Vic.) prescribed in cases of offences against the provisions of the said first-recited Act for the observance of the Close Season in respect of Oysters.
Carlingford Lough (17th April, 1869.)	First.—That between the 1st day of March and 1st day of November in any year, it shall not be lawful for any person to dredge for, take, catch, or destroy any Oysters or Oyster Brood within the said Lough of Carlingford, or off or from any of the shores or rocks of said Lough, and any person offending against this By-law shall, for each such offence, forfeit and pay a sum of Five Pounds.
	Second.—That between the 1st day of March and the 1st day of November in any year no boat, in the said Lough of Carlingford, shall have on board any dredge or other implement for the taking of Oysters; and if, between the periods aforesaid, there shall be on board any boat any such dredge or other implement for the taking of Oysters, the master or owner of such boat shall, for each such offence, forfeit and pay a sum of Five Pounds.
	Third.—All persons engaged in fishing for or taking Oysters in said Lough of Carlingford, shall cull all such Oysters as may be taken or caught; and shall not remove from any Fishing Ground or Oyster Bed any Oyster of less dimensions than two inches and one-half, at the greatest diameter thereof, and shall immediately throw back into the Sea all Oysters of less dimensions than aforesaid, as well as all gravel and fragments of shells as shall be raised or taken while engaged in such fishing; and no person shall take from any rock, strand, or shore of said Lough of Carlingford, any Oyster of less dimensions than two inches and one-half, at the greatest diameter thereof, and any person offending in any respect against this By-Law, Rule, or Regulation shall, for each offence, forfeit and pay a sum of Two Pounds.
	Fourth.—All persons are hereby prohibited from throwing into the Sea, on any Oyster Bed, or Oyster Fishing Ground in the said Lough of Carlingford, the ballast of any boat, or any other matter or thing injurious or detrimental to the Oyster Fishery; and all persons acting contrary hereto shall, for each offence, forfeit and pay a sum of Two Pounds.
Galway Bay. (18th March, 1868.)	First.—All persons engaged in fishing for or taking Oysters in Galway Bay shall, on the Fishing Ground, cull all such Oysters as may be taken or caught, and shall not remove from any Fishing Ground or Oyster Bed any Oyster of less dimensions than two inches and one-half at the greatest diameter thereof, and shall immediately throw back into the Sea all Oysters of less dimensions than aforesaid, and all such gravel and fragments of shells as shall be raised or taken while engaged in such fishing; and any person offending in any respect against this By-Law, Rule, or Regulation shall, for each offence, forfeit and pay a sum of Two Pounds.
	Second.—All persons are hereby prohibited from throwing into the Sea on any Oyster Bed or Oyster Fishing Ground the ballast of any boat, or any other matter or thing injurious or detrimental to the Oyster Fishery; and all persons acting contrary hereto shall, for each such offence, forfeit and pay a sum of Two Pounds.

APPENDIX, No. 18—*continued.*

ABSTRACT of BY-LAWS, ORDERS, &c., in force on 1st January, 1871, relating to the FISHERIES of IRELAND.

Place affected by By-Law, and Date thereof.	Nature of By-Law.
Galway Bay—*con.*	Third.—No person shall, between Sunset and Sunrise, dredge for, take, or catch any Oysters within said Bay, or any of the Estuaries of the Rivers flowing into the same; and every person acting contrary hereto shall, for each offence, forfeit and pay a sum of Five Pounds.
	Fourth.—That between Nine o'clock in the Evening of any day and Six o'clock in the Morning of the following day, no boat shall have on board any dredge or other implement for the taking of Oysters; and if, between the hours aforesaid, there shall be on board any boat any such dredge or other implement for the taking of Oysters, the Master or Owner of such boat shall, for each such offence, forfeit and pay a sum of Five Pounds.
South-east Coast of Ireland, from Wicklow Head to Carnsore Point. (1st Sept., 1868.)	That the Close Time, during which it shall not be lawful to dredge for, take, catch, or destroy any Oysters or Oyster Brood, on or off the South-east coast of Ireland, between Wicklow Head and Carnsore Point, shall be between the 30th April and the 1st September in each year.
Coasts of Dublin, Wicklow and Wexford. (23rd April, 1869.) Approved by Her Majesty in Council, 28th April, 1869.	Prohibiting between the 30th April and 1st September in each year the dredging for, taking, catching, or destroying any Oyster or Oyster Brood on or off any part of the East and South-East Coast of Ireland, within the distance of Twenty Miles measured from a straight line drawn from the Eastern point of Lambay Island, in the County Dublin to Carnsore Point, in the County Wexford, outside the exclusive Fishery Limits of the British Islands.
	SALMON AND TROUT.
Teelin Estuary, (24th Feb., 1860.)	Prohibiting the use of Nets for the capture of Fish of any kind, with meshes of less than one inch from knot to knot (to be measured along the side of the square, or four inches to be measured all round each such mesh, such measurements being taken in the clear when the Net is wet), on that part of the coast of the County of Donegal inside, or to the North-east and North of lines drawn from Rossan Point to Teelin Head, and from Teelin Head to Carrigan Head, and from Carrigan Head to Muckros Point, all in the Barony of Bannagh, and County of Donegal.
River Liffey, (19th Jan., 1865.)	Prohibiting the catching, or attempting to catch, Salmon with any Net of greater length than 500 yards, in that part of the River Liffey which is situated between the Weir known as the Island Bridge Weir and a line drawn due North from Poolbeg Lighthouse.
River Slaney, Co. Wexford (25th March, 1854, and 4th March, 1862.)	Prohibiting, during the Close Season for Salmon, the use of Nets of any kind whatsoever, between Ferrycarrig Bridge and the Town of Enniscorthy.
	Prohibiting, during the Open Season for Salmon, the use of Nets with meshes of less size than one and three-quarter inches from knot to knot, between Ferrycarrig Bridge and the Town of Enniscorthy.
Bessborough Demesne, Co. Kilkenny (5th May, 1866.)	Permitting the use of Nets for the capture of Fish with Meshes of one inch from knot to knot (to be measured along the side of the square, or four inches to be measured all round each such Mesh, such measurements being taken in the clear, when the Net is wet,) within the Waters in, and Rivers running through the Demesne of Bessborough, in the County of Kilkenny: Provided that no Net having a less Mesh than one inch and three-quarters from knot to knot, shall be used in the said Rivers during the Months of April, May, and June.
Cork District, (11th Sept., 1868.)	Prohibiting the catching or attempting to catch Salmon or Trout in any Tidal Water in the Cork District with a Spear, Lyster, Otter, Strokehaul, Draw Dcow, or Gaff, except when the latter instrument may be used solely as auxiliary to angling with Rod and Line, or for the purpose of removing Fish from any legal Weir or Box by the Owner or Occupier thereof.
Cork District—*con.*	Prohibiting the catching or attempting to catch Salmon or Trout in any Tidal or Fresh Water in the Cork District with any kind of Fish-hook, covered in part or in whole with any matter or thing, or uncovered.
River Lee, Co. of the City of Cork. (7th January, 1863.)	Prohibiting, during the Close Season for Salmon the use of Draft Nets, or any other Net or Nets used as a Draft Net, having a foot-rope and leads or weights affixed thereto, within the following limits, viz.:—in that part of the River Lee, situate between Patrick's Bridge, in the City of Cork, and a line drawn across the said River Lee, from Blackrock Castle, on the south, to the Western extremity of the Townland of Dunkettle, on the North.
Argideen River, (25th Feb., 1869.)	Prohibiting the use of Nets of any kind whatsoever in the tidal part of the river known as the Argideen River, in the County of Cork, situated between the junction of the Owenbeagh or Blind River with the said Argideen River and the Bridge of Timoleague, all in the Barony of the East Division of East Carbery, and County of Cork.
Bandon River, (4th Dec., 1865.)	Prohibiting for three years the use of Nets (except Landing Nets as auxiliary to angling with rod and line) in any part of the Bandon River or its tributaries, above a line drawn from the northern point of the quay, at the mouth of the creek, between the townlands of Rockhouse and Kilnacooney, to a point on the opposite shore in the townland of Abern.
Bandon River, (2nd Nov., 1869.)	Extending for a further period of three years the By-Law (bearing date 4th December, 1865), and prohibiting the use of all Nets, except Landing Nets as auxiliary to angling with Rod and Line for the capture of Salmon or Trout, in any part of the Bandon River or its Tributaries, above a line drawn across said River at right angles with the River's course from the northern point of the quay at the mouth of the Creek between the Townlands of Rock House and Kilnacooney to a point on the opposite shore in the Townland of Abern.
River Shannon, (5th Feb., 1856.)	Prohibiting Net Fishing in that part of the River Shannon between Wellesley Bridge and the Railway Bridge, between 1st June and 12th February.
River Shannon, (22nd Nov., 1863.)	First.—Prohibiting, between the 20th day of July and 1st day of November in each year, the use of Draft Nets, or any other Net or Nets used as a Draft Net, having a foot-rope and leads or weights affixed thereto, within the following limits, viz.:—in that part of the River Shannon situate between the Fishing Weir known as the Lax Weir, and a line drawn due North and South across the said River Shannon at the Western extremity of Georges Island.
	Second.—Prohibiting Draft Nets for the capture of Fish of any kind, of a mesh less than one and three-quarter inches from knot to knot, to be measured along the side of the square, or seven inches to be measured all round each such mesh, such measurements being taken in the clear when the Net is wet, in the tidal parts of the River Shannon, or in the tidal parts of any of the Rivers flowing into the said River Shannon.
Rivers Shannon and Maigue (8th June, 1857.)	Prohibiting the Shooting of Fish in that part of River Shannon between Portumna Bridge and Shannon Bridge, and also in River Maigue.
River Shannon. (8th May, 1858.)	Prohibiting the Fishing for Salmon or Trout by any means whatsoever, within a space of Twenty Yards from the Weir Wall of Termonbarry, on the River Shannon.
Lough Ree, River Shannon. (27th August, 1859.)	Permitting the use of Nets in Lough Ree, having a mesh of five inches in the round, measured when the Net is wet.
River Fergus, (25th June, 1863.)	Prohibiting the Fishing for Salmon or Trout by any means whatsoever, within a space of Twenty Yards from the Weir Wall of Ennis, on the River Fergus.
River Maigue, (17th Oct., 1854.)	Prohibiting the use of Draft Nets between Ferry Drawbridge and the old Bridge of Adare.

Appendix, No. 13.—*continued.*

Appendix, No. 13.

Abstract of By-Laws, Orders, &c.

Abstract of By-Laws, Orders, &c., in force on 1st January, 1871, relating to the Fisheries of Ireland.

Place affected by By-Law, and Date thereof.	Nature of By-Law.
Killarney District, (8th Feb., 1863.)	Prohibiting the catching, or attempting to catch, Salmon in any tidal water with a Spear, Lyster, Otter, Strokehaul, Drag-Draw, or Gaff, except when the latter instrument may be used solely as auxiliary to angling with rod and line, or for the purpose of removing fish from any legal Weir or Box by the owner or occupier thereof.
Castlemaine Estuary, (27th Oct., 1868.)	Prohibiting, during the Salmon Close Season, the use of Draft Nets having a foot-rope and leads or weights affixed thereto, in the Estuary of Castlemaine inside the Bar of Inch.
Lough Neagh, (22nd April, 1848, and 24th Feb., 1860.)	Permitting Pollen to be taken by Trammel or Set Nets composed of Thread or Yarn of a fine texture, not less than ten hanks to the pound weight, doubled and twisted with a mesh of not less than one inch from knot to knot, from the 1st of March to the 20th September.
Lough Neagh, (28th Feb 1867.)	Prohibiting the use of Draft Nets for the capture of Pollen.
Galway River, Lough Corrib, &c. (24th July, 1846.)	Prohibiting the use of the Instrument, commonly called Strokehaul or Snatch, or any other such instrument, in River Galway, Loughs Corrib or Mask, or their Tributaries.
Galway District, (11th Sept., 1868.)	Prohibiting the snatching or attempt to snatch Salmon in any Tidal or Fresh Water in the Galway District with any kind of Fish-hook, covered in part or in whole with any matter or thing, or uncovered.
Clare and Clare-Galway or Turloughmore Rivers, Co. Galway. (22nd Dec., 1862.)	Prohibiting the use of Nets of any kind whatsoever in any part of the Rivers known as the Clare and the Clare-Galway or Turloughmore Rivers, in the County of Galway, above the junction of the said Rivers with Lough Corrib, in the County of Galway.
Owenmore River, Co. Mayo. (8th May, 1866.)	Prohibiting the removal of gravel or sand from any part of the bed of the Owenmore River, in the County of Mayo, where the spawning of Salmon or Trout may take place.
Owenduff or Ballycroy, Owenmore and Munhin Rivers. (11th Sept., 1868.)	Permitting the use of Nets with Meshes of one and a-half inches from knot to knot (to be measured along the side of the square, or six inches to be measured all round each such Mesh, such measurements being taken in the clear, when the Net is wet,) within so much of the said Rivers Owenduff or Ballycroy, Owenmore and Munhin, as lies above the mouth as defined, during so much of the Months of June, July, and August, as do now or at any time may form part of the Open Season for the capture of Salmon or Trout, with Nets, in the said Rivers.
Sligo River, (1st March, 1870.)	Prohibiting the snatching or attempting to snatch Salmon in Sligo River, with any kind of Fish-hook covered in part or in whole, or uncovered.
Caragh or Waterville River—Waterville Weir. (7th March, 1870.)	Permitting the space between the Bars or Rails of the Inscales, and of the Heck or upstream side of the Boxes or Cribs of the Waterville Weir to be one and a quarter inches apart.
Bush River, (28th Feb., 1870.)	Repealing Definition of Bush River Estuary as fixed by the late Special Commissioners on 8th February, 1864.
Rivers in Bantry District. (7th March, 1870.)	Permitting use of Nets of a Mesh of one and a quarter inches from knot to knot (to be measured along the side of the square, or five inches to be measured all round each such Mesh, each measurement being taken in the clear when the Net is wet), in the tidal waters of the Bantry District, which comprises the whole of the sea along the coast between Mizen Head in the County Cork and Crow Head in the same County, and around any Islands or Rocks situate off same, with the whole of the Tideways along said Coast and Rivers, and the whole of the tidal portions of the several Rivers and their Tributaries flowing into said Coast.
Ballina District, (31st May, 1870.)	Permitting the use of Nets with Meshes of one and a quarter inches from knot to knot (to be measured along the side of the square, or five inches to be measured all round each such Mesh, such measurements being taken in the clear, when the Net is wet).
Waterford District, Cormoch River. (7th July, 1870.)	Permitting use of Nets with Meshes of one inch from knot to knot (to be measured along the side of the square, or four inches to be measured all round such Mesh, such measurements being taken in the clear when the Net is wet).
Coleraine District, (17th Oct., 1870.)	Prohibiting snatching or attempting to snatch Salmon in any of the tidal or fresh waters of District.
Wexford District, Derry Water, and River Derry. (26th Oct., 1870.)	Permitting use of Nets for the capture of fish having Meshes of one inch from knot to knot (to be measured along the side of the square, or four inches, to be measured all round each such Mesh, such measurements being taken in the clear when the Net is wet), in the rivers and streams following, that is to say, in the Derry Water, from its source near Killaveny to Annacurragh Bridge, with the stream flowing into same from Moyne Church through Ballingate, and the Tomnaskela River, and in the Aghowle, Shillelagh, and Derry River, from the bounds of the County Carlow, flowing past Tinahely by Shillelagh to the bounds of the County Wexford, with the small streams flowing into that portion of the said river, all said rivers and streams being in the County Wicklow, for and during the months of May, June, July, and August, in each year.
Wexford District, Potter River (20th Oct., 1870.)	Permitting use of Nets for the capture of Fish with Meshes of one inch from knot to knot (to be measured along the side of the square, or four inches to be measured all round each such Mesh, such measurements being taken in the clear, when the Net is wet), in the tidal portion of the Potter River, situated below Brittas Bridge in the County of Wicklow.
Lismore District, River Blackwater. (2nd Nov., 1870.)	Prohibiting the catching or attempting to catch Salmon, with any Drift Net of greater length than 220 yards in the tidal portion of the River Blackwater, situated in the Counties of Waterford and Cork.
Fergus River, (16th Dec., 1870.)	Prohibiting the use of Drift Nets in the Tidal parts of River Fergus, County Clare.

APPENDIX, No. 14.

RIVERS, the TIDAL and FRESH WATER BOUNDARIES of which have been defined.

River.	Boundary.	Date.
Suir,	A line drawn across river at and opposite to the most up-stream part of the Coolnamuck Weir,	16th March, 1864.
Nore,	The Inistioge Bridge,	16th March, 1864.
Barrow,	The lowest Weir or Dam used for navigation purposes, near St. Mullins, in county Carlow,	16th March, 1864
Shannon,	The Weir or Dam known as the Cartally Mill Weir,	9th April, 1864.
Fergus,	The Bridge commonly known as the New Bridge, immediately below the Club House, at Ennis,	9th April, 1864.
Liffey,	The Weir or Dam on said river known as the Island Bridge Weir,	12th August, 1864.
Maigue,	The Bridge across river immediately outside and seaward of the Adare Demesne,	13th August, 1864.
Lee,	The Weir or Dam at the Water Works of Cork, known as the Water Works Weir,	16th August, 1864.
Bandon,	The Bridge at Innishannon, known as the Innishannon Bridge,	19th January, 1865.
Carragh,	The Carragh Bridge, being the bridge immediately seaward of the Salmon Weir,	19th January, 1865.
Laune,	The shallow at the head of the Pool, commonly called the Cat Pool,	25th July, 1865.
Maine,	A straight line drawn across river at right angles with its course at the boundary between the townlands of Coolklieve and Ballyfinnane,	25th July, 1865.
Moy,	The foot of the falls immediately below the Weirs at Ballina,	26th July, 1865.
Inah,	Adare Bridge,	1st February, 1866.
Slaney,	Enniscorthy Bridge,	1st February, 1866.
Boyne,	Eastern Point of Grove Island at Oldbridge,	9th April, 1868.
Eask,	Foot Bridge above Donegal Bridge,	17th July, 1868.
Shimna,	The Castle Bridge near Newcastle,	24th August, 1869.
Deel or Askeaton,	Askeaton Bridge,	29th November, 1876.

APPENDIX, No. 15.

LIST of STONE WEIRS in Ireland used for SALMON FISHING, with their Breadth, and the size of the Queen's Gap or share maintained therein respectively.

NAME OF			Breadth of Stream.	Size of Queen's Gap provided in pursuance of 26 & 27 Vic., c. 114.	OBSERVATIONS.
Fishery District.	River.	Weir.	Ft. In.	Ft. In.	
Ballinakill,	Bundorragha,	Bundorragha,	about 60 0	10 0	Not used.
	Aas or Erriff,	Aasleagh,	" 69 0	No gap,	Ditto.
Bangor,	Owenmore,	Gaulamore,	" 429 0	No gap,	Ditto.
	Munhin,	Munhim,	" 84 0	No gap,	Ditto.
	Newport,	Newport,	153 4		Gap 15 feet 10 inches.
Ballina,	Moy,	Ballina,	341 6	No gap,	Do. 34 feet 2 inches.
	Ditto,	Foxford,	296 10	11 6	Do. 29 feet 7 inches, weir not used.
Sligo,	Sligo,		432 0	No gap,	Not used.
Ballyshannon,	Bundrowes,	Bundrowes,	68 4	No gap,	Gap 6 feet 10 inches.
	Inver,		about 106 0	No gap,	Not used.
	Ditto,	Eske,	" 83 0	No gap,	Ditto.
Coleraine,	Bann,	The Cutts of Coleraine,	455 0	19 0	A holding mill-dam. Pass, 30 feet in breadth, opened.
Ballycastle,	Bush,		220 0	No gap,	Gap 12 feet 0 inches.
Drogheda,	Boyne,	Oldbridge,	240 0	25 0	Do. 24 feet.
	Ditto,	Rossnaree,	300 0	13 and 24	Do 30 feet.
	Ditto,	Newgrange,	234 0	No gap,	Do. 111 feet.
Letterkenny,	Leannan,	Rathmelton,	149 0	No gap,	Two Gaps of 6 feet each.
	Lackagh,	Lackagh,	311 0	No gap,	Not used. Gap to be 30 feet.
	Owenea,	Owenea,	145 0	No gap,	Gap 14½ feet.
Londonderry,	Finn,	Killygordon,	about 146 0	No gap,	Do. 30 feet.
	Buncrana,	Buncrana,	180 0	No gap,	Do. 18 feet
Waterford,	Nore,	Inistioge,	173 0	47 0	Do 68 feet.
	Ditto,	Rockview,	98 0	47 0	Do. 72 feet.
	Ditto,	Jerpoint,	80 0	49 0	Do 66 feet.
	Ditto,	Dysart,	93 0	44 0	Do. 47 feet.
	Suir,	Coolnamuck,	175 0	45 0	Do. 47 feet
	Tay,	Woodhouse,	55 0	No gap,	Do. 6 feet.
Lismore,	Blackwater,	Lismore Weir,	315 0	No gap,	Do. 31 feet 6 inches.
Cork,	Lee,	The North Lee Fishery Weir or "Hayes' Weir,"	400 0	No gap,	A fishing mill-dam. Not fished.
	Ditto,	The weir above Wellington Bridge,	780 0	No gap,	Ditto.
	Ditto,	"The Upper Gill Abbey Weir,"	378 0	No gap,	Ditto.
	Ditto,	"The Sugar House Weir,"	114 0	No gap,	Gap 11 feet 5 inches.
Killarney,	Carta,	Carra,	160 0	No gap,	Gap opened 16 feet.
	Waterville or Currane,	Waterville,	under 40 0	No gap,	Extension of weekly close season from noon on Friday to noon on Monday ordered instead of gap, stream being under 40 feet—26 & 27 Vic., c. 114, s. 11.
Limerick,	Shannon,	Lax Weir,	340 0	21 0	Gap 50 feet.
Galway,	Galway,	Galway Salmon Weirs,	206 10	16 0	Do. 20 feet 7 inches.
	Owenmore or Great River,	Ballinahinch Trout and Salmon Weirs,	226 0	No gap,	Do 22 feet.
	Spiddal,	Spiddal Salmon Weir,	varies greatly, 183 0 to 12 0	No gap,	Do. 12 feet.
	Furbough,	The Furbough Salmon Weir,	14 0	No gap,	Do. 3 feet.

Certificates granted up to 31st December, 1870, for Fixed Engines for fishing for Salmon or Trout.

No.	Place.	Name of Person to whom Certificate granted	Date of Certificate	District in which Net situated	Description of Fixed Net	Particulars of Same, &c.	Observations.
[illegible]	[illegible]	[illegible]	[illegible]	[illegible]	[illegible]	[illegible]	[illegible]

APPENDIX, No. 17.—ABSTRACT of

Substance of Queries issued to Boards of Conservators.	Replies received from Boards of Conservators. 1. Dublin
1. What is the general state of the Salmon Fisheries in this District?	1. Improving.
2. Has the take of salmon throughout the district been more or less productive in 1870 than in 1869, and to what is attributed the increase or diminution?	2. About the same.
3. What was the average price obtained for salmon last year by the captors? (This has no reference to price obtained by the dealers in salmon.) What was the highest price given for salmon last season? What was the lowest price?	3. 1s. to 1s. 6d. per lb. 2s. 6d. per lb. [illegible]d. per lb.
4. What proportion of the entire capture in your district is exported, and what proportion purchased for home consumption?	4. Very little, if any, exported.
5. What has been the amount of protection rendered during the several close season of 1870, as compared with preceding season of 1869?	5. About the same.
6. Has the quantity of breeding fish observed in the rivers in your district been greater or less as compared with preceding year, 1869?	6. Greater.
7. About what period do the salmon commence to spawn in the several rivers in your district? What are the greatest spawning months? and when is spawning over? and generally where are the most important spawning grounds situated?	7. November. November and December. Spawning is generally over about Christmas-day. The most important spawning-grounds are from Ballymore-Eustace to Kilcullen.
8. At what period of the year, in each river in your district, are the first clean fish taken? When do the grilse begin to run? When are the spent fish well out of the river? and when does the great bulk of the fry go to sea?	8. January. June. January. January and May.
9. During the descent of the fry to the sea, is angling prohibited by any of the proprietors of fisheries, or is it carried on during these months, and does much destruction of fry take place?	9. Angling, under pretence of trout, perch, and pike fishing, is practised throughout the year uninterfered with by the proprietors, and considerable quantities of fry are taken or destroyed.
10. At what period of the year do the fish begin to be discoloured, or to get heavy in spawn, and what is the general opinion as to the proper season for angling in your District?	10. The salmon begin to be discoloured in the River Liffey in October, but in the River Vartry not until November. The general opinion is that so long as angling in salmon rivers can be carried on under pretence of pike and perch fishing, by-laws having reference solely to salmon, effect very little good.
11. Have you reason to suppose that many spent fish have been destroyed hitherto in the month of February, and foul fish in the month of October by anglers?	11. No.
12. Are you aware of any change having taken place in regard to the period of the season when the salmon in your district is in best order, whether earlier or later than heretofore? If so, state particulars.	12. No.
13. Are there any pollutions or poisonous matter entering the rivers in your district? If so, state the particular cases.	13. Yes, the Gas and Chemical Works on the North and South Quays of the tideway of the River Liffey constantly discharge great quantities of poisonous matter through their conduits.
14. Have offences against the Fishery Laws increased or diminished?	14. Yes, fishing for salmon without license with rods in the rivers and with draft-nets on the sea coast under pretence of fishing for other fish than salmon, is greatly on the increase.
15. Give a list of the mill-weirs or dams, or other obstructions, in each river in your district, and specify where ladders or fish passes have been built, when, and by whom?	—
16. State where fish passes would be practicable and advantageous?	16. Fish-passes would be practicable on almost every weir mentioned, but their advantage is rather doubtful unless there was a sufficient staff of water-bailiffs to prevent their being used as fish traps. A fish-pass over Poulaphouca would give to the River Liffey thirty miles additional spawning-grounds; however as this cascade is 150 feet high, and is at the head of a long steep incline, it would probably cost £1,000 to construct it.
17. Give a list of all the fish ladders or passes built in your district, whether under the provisions of the Fishery Acts, or by the Board of Works or private individuals, and specify each locality.	17. The River Liffey Angling Association, between the years 1854 and 1857, under the direction of the Messrs Cane, had fish-passes constructed on the weirs of Island-bridge, Newbridge, Leixlip, Temple Mills, and the cascade called the Salmon Leap, all situate on the River Liffey.
18. Have gratings been attached to mill-leads, or other artificial channels, in conformity with the Act 32 Vic., cap. 9, and if so, specify the particular cases?	18. None.
19. State the instances in which the provision has been partially carried out, specifying whether at the head or tail race?	19. None.
20. State the instances and nature of precautions adopted at mills to prevent the destruction of fish, other than that prescribed by the late Act?	20. None.
21. State where and by whom fixed engines were used in 1870?	21. None.
22. State any instances where head and tail gratings, either or both, would be advantageous (specifying which), if erected?	22. The Conservators are of opinion that unless they had sufficient funds to engage a large staff of water-bailiffs to sentinel such gratings, their construction would be most detrimental to the salmon and trout fisheries, as from the rapid rise and fall of the rivers in this district, the gratings contemplated would lead to the destruction of the fish, either by detaining them after the subsidence of the water (where they would, if not removed by a caretaker into deep water, become the prey of otters and rats), but more particularly in remote situations, the gratings in question would prove gigantic fish-traps unless closely watched. However, as the Royal Hospital pumping mill is in the tideway, and its tail-race very much under public view, a grating to prevent salmon ascending it would be of great benefit to the River Liffey.
23. Can you give a list of the prosecutions instituted by the Conservators during the year 1870?	—
24. Are there any new modes of fishing for salmon adopted in your district? If so, describe them, and where used.	24. None.
25. Number of water-bailiffs employed by Conservators?	25. Four.
26. Number employed in district by private individuals?	26. Four.
27. For what length of time employed?	27. For the year.
28. Rate of wages paid by the Conservators?	28. From £[illegible] to £[illegible] per annum.
29. Are there any suggestions or general observations with which the Conservators may be disposed to favour the inspectors, with reference to the Salmon Fisheries in your district?	29. The Conservators are of opinion that the licensing of rods and nets should be extended to all such modes of fishing when used in salmon waters.

STATEMENTS from Boards of Conservators.

Replies received from Boards of Conservators.	
1. WEXFORD.	2. WATERFORD.
1. Good; there is a prospect of further improvement.	1. Very much improved, and has so improved steadily since 1862.
2. Much the same.	2. A steady increase has been observable each year since 1864. We have no doubt but that this favourable state of things is entirely attributable to the removal of the fixed engines in the tidal waters, and the zealous and close attention paid to the preservation of fish in the fresh waters, by the Conservators and proprietors in the district.
3. 6d., 1s. 6d. and 8s. 2s. 6d.	3. Cannot say exactly, but about 1s. I believe 8s. 6d. I believe 6d.
4. Generally for home supply.	4. About three-fourths exported. I may say none for home market, as it is impossible to get salmon in the neighbourhood to purchase, even at the highest London prices, owing entirely to the dealers having all fish engaged as they are caught.
5. The same.	5. For the last three years the funds at the disposal of the Conservators, have been totally inadequate to the requirements of the preservation, and where it not for the small assistance rendered by the "Suir Preservation Society," some three or four months of last year would have passed without a single water-bailiff being employed. The "Suir Preservation Society" at one time expended annually a sum of over £[illegible] in addition to that at the command of the Conservators. The money at the disposal of this Society being obtained by voluntary subscriptions, cannot be depended upon, and is now reduced to a very small sum annually. This year it is impossible to give any aid.
6. Greater.	6. By every one that I have spoken to on this subject, the very great increase has been remarked.
7. The months of November and December. December and January. The months of February and March. The Douglas, the Glashen, the Boro, and the Slaney, in the upper waters, the Boro and Urrin in the lower waters.	7. About the first week in November; but this entirely depends upon the state of the weather. December and January. Not till about the first week in March. This year (1871) some very large fish were in the pits as late as on the 20th March, and some very large fish (three) were taken by the rod and line, and, when on the bank, the spawn and milt flowed out on the grass. Three of these fish taken weighed, respectively, 2[illegible]lbs., 2[illegible]lbs., and 2[illegible]lbs. The main river from Ardfinnan upwards and all the tributaries.
8. March. —— April. March, April, and May.	8. Clean fish may be taken any month of the year in a less or more degree, and are so taken by the poacher when he gets his opportunity. About July. At this date, the 11th of April, there are numbers in the river, the dry weather for the past three weeks has been greatly the cause of this. The end of this month and May.
9. It is not. A great destruction of fry takes place.	9. No prohibition has been put upon the taking of the fry, and great injury has occurred thereby. This matter should be strongly taken in hands by the Inspectors.
10. October. From the 1st March to the 1st November.	10. Fish that have succeeded in getting to the upper waters before the end of May, become discoloured from June, and are the early spawners in November. Angling should on no river (on this river) begin before the 1st of March, even at that time great injury is done by the killing of kelts or spents, and angling should close about the middle of August or 1st of September.
11. Yes.	11. This year the most cruel destruction of spent fish has taken place, during the months of February and March. It has been most disheartening to those who have worked for years to find their labour thrown away by the apparent legalizing the destruction of these fish by the opening of the season on the 1st February for rods, and the 15th February for nets. After our preserving them through the winter three months, to open a flood of legalized destroyers, i.e., rod-fishers is more than the most disinterested philosophy could stand. Since the closing of the Autumn months it is expected there will be no complaints of the destruction of foul fish such as we had last year.
12. No.	12. No, as the matter entirely depends upon the weather.
13. None.	13. None has been reported to me.
14. Increased.	14. Increased considerably, particularly in the neighbourhood of Clonmel, where it appears that every man's hand seems to be raised against the law, and this feeling is strongly encouraged by the views and opinions adopted at Petty Sessions.
15. At St. John's mill, by Mr. A. Davis, partially.	15. On the Suir, Coolnamuck fishing-weir, Clonmel mill-weirs, Ardfinnan mill-weir, Cahir mill-weir, Athassel mill-weir, Golden mill-weir, Templemore eel-weir, Holycross eel-weir, on the Aherlow; Mr Bishop's mill-weir. Ladders or fish-passes have been erected at Cahir and Athassel mill weirs in 1870, by voluntary subscription.
16. At the head weir, above Mr A. Davis's mill, St. John's.	16. At Clonmel, and should be erected without loss of time. I beg to state on this matter, that in the year 1869 a fund was raised by voluntary subscription, amounting to £50, for the purpose of erecting a fish-pass at Fr[illegible] weir, at Clonmel, which sum was handed over to the Board of Works, who took upon themselves to build the pass. The works were completed, but they were carried away by the first flood, and we got no satisfaction for our £50 from that day to this. We consider that this matter should be brought under the consideration of the Commissioners of the Board of Works, for the purpose of obtaining such assistance as would enable us effectively to erect fish-passes there.
17. Mr. A. Davis's, St. John's mill, partially.	17. Two at Cahir under the Fishery Act. One, as before stated, was built by the Board of Works in 1858 or 1869.
18. Mr Rowe's, Castleboro, mills; Mr Bolger's, Milltown, Ferns mills. Messrs. Davis's, Fairfield mills.	18. Only at Galbally weir—Mr Bishop's.
19. Messrs. Davis's, Kilcarbery, tail-race partially, but not satisfactorily.	19. In the foregoing case, at the head race; but this is very imperfectly done.
20. None.	20. None.
21. None.	21. See Appendix.
22. Messrs. Davis's, Kilcarbery, flour mills tail-race.	22. Certainly, at all weirs, particularly at Clonmel weirs.
	23. This query can only be answered by reference to Petty Sessions books, or by clerk of sessions.
24. None.	24. None.
25. Inspector and four water-bailiffs during the open season. Inspector and twelve bailiffs during the close season.	25. Up to 1st of February there were in the D division six permanent men, and during the winter there were for three months under-bailiffs.
26. None.	26. None.
27. None.	27. Permanent men all the year; under-bailiffs three months.
28. Inspector of water-bailiffs 15s. per week during the year. Bailiffs during the close season 8s. per week. During open season 8s. weekly for one bailiff. Two bailiffs at 7s. 6d., and one bailiff at 9s. 6d. weekly for close season.	28. Head men £3 per month; under-bailiffs £1 1[illegible]s. per month.
29. That all rod-fishers for trout should pay a licence-duty of 5s.	29. That the right of appeal from a dismiss before magistrates to Quarter Sessions should be made more simple and defined, that a greater amount of surveillance should be exercised by the Inspectors in the different cases of prosecutions, the manner they are carried out, and the results accruing therefrom. That great attention should be paid to the Bill proposed to be brought before Parliament by Mr Heron. Many sections of the present Acts could well be done away with, and the Acts generally made more simple and concise.

APPENDIX, No. 17.—ABSTRACT of

Substance of Queries issued to Boards of Conservators.	Replies received from Boards of Conservators. 4. Lismore.
1. What is the general state of the Salmon Fisheries in this District?	1. Very inferior in upper waters, large take of fish in tidal portion.
2. Has the take of salmon throughout the district been more or less productive in 1870 than in 1869, and to what is attributed the increase or diminution?	2. Much less in upper waters from the dry season and excessive use of drift nets in the tideway, where the take of fish has far exceeded previous years.
3. What was the average price obtained for salmon last year by the captors? (This has no reference to price obtained by the dealers in salmon.) What was the highest price given for salmon last season? What was the lowest price?	3. 1s. 1d. 1s. 3d. 8d.
4. What proportion of the entire capture in your district is exported, and what proportion purchased for home consumption?	4. Greater part exported.
5. What has been the amount of protection rendered during the present close season of 1870, as compared with preceding season of 1869?	5. Two water-bailiffs less than last year employed, but the amount of protection far exceeded last year, the men being better paid and the Constabulary rendering the whole amount of the penalties imposed by them rendered very valuable assistance.
6. Has the quantity of breeding fish observed in the rivers in your district been greater or less as compared with preceding year, 1869?	6. Much less.
7. About what period do the salmon commence to spawn in the several rivers in your district? What are the greatest spawning months? and when is spawning over? and generally where are the most important spawning grounds situated?	7. Earlier than usual, about the 10th of October. November and December. Have not seen or heard of a fish in spawning-beds above Fermoy since December 30th. Fish spawn earlier in the upper parts of the river than near the tideway. The Blackwater and its tributaries above Fermoy. The Funshion and the Bride.
8. At what period of the year, in each river in your district, are the first clean fish taken? When do the grilse begin to run? When are the spent fish well out of the rivers? and when does the great bulk of the fry go to sea?	8. In February. About the 20th of May. March 15th. In April.
9. During the descent of the fry to the sea, is angling prohibited by any of the proprietors of fisheries, or is it carried on during these months, and does much destruction of fry take place?	9. Not prohibited. Great destruction.
10. At what period of the year do the fish begin to be discoloured, or to get heavy in spawn, and what is the general opinion as to the proper season for angling in your district?	10. End of September. From February 1st to September 30th, as at present, 1871.
11. Have you reason to suppose that many spent fish have been destroyed hitherto in the month of February, and full fish in the month of October by anglers?	11. Anglers are beginning to understand that it is for the interest of the fishery to return spent fish to the river, and the regulations now in force make it difficult to dispose of the latter class of them. A great number are destroyed. The latter class of spent fish, called [illegible], are publicly exposed for sale. Large numbers of full fish were taken from the middle to the end of October.
12. Are you aware of any change having taken place in regard to the period of the season when the salmon in your district is in best order, whether earlier or later than heretofore? If so, state particulars.	12. Spring fish are earlier in the river, and fall fish earlier.
13. Are there any pollutions or poisonous matter entering the rivers in your district? If so, state the particular cases.	13. None that I know of.
14. Have offences against the Fishery Laws increased or diminished?	14. Diminished in the upper waters, except at the mill-weirs, largely increased in the tidal waters.
15. Give a list of the mill-weirs, or dams, or other obstructions in each river in your district, and specify where ladders or fish passes have been built, when, and by whom?	15. List already furnished at Glendalane and Fermoy.
16. State where fish passes would be practicable and advantageous?	16. A new fish pass is very much required at Glendalane, in the Blackwater; it is almost impossible for fish to get over this weir. Mr. Hickey's weir, at Castletownroche, is quite impassable to fish. The owner of this weir has entered into an arrangement to contribute to a pass in this weir, which could be made at very little expense, and it would open about fourteen miles of river suitable for spawning-beds. Mr. Bowles' mill-weir on the Bride, at Allow, also requires a pass.
17. Give a list of all the fish ladders or passes built in your district, whether under the provisions of the Fishery Acts, or by the Board of Works or private individuals, and specify each locality.	17. One at Glendalane years ago; this pass is quite useless now, the lower end having given way. This pass was made under the provisions of the Fishery Acts, by the Conservators. One at Fermoy, under the Fishery Acts, half the cost paid by Board of Conservators, the remainder by Mr. Furlong, owner of mill-weir.
18. Have gratings been attached to mill-leads, or other artificial channels, in conformity with the 32 Vic., cap. 9, and, if so, specify the particular cases?	18. Yes, in the Bride; in the Allow; at Kanturk, Dr. Barry's mill; in the Blackwater, at Mr. Stawell's mills, Gortroe, and Mr. Hallinan's, Glendalane. Mr. Webb, at Quartertown on the Clyda, had the gratings made, but did not erect them this year.
19. State the instances in which the provision has been partially carried out, specifying whether at the head or tail races?	19. No gratings have been put on the head races of any of the mills.
20. State the instances and nature of precautions adopted at mills to prevent the destruction of fish, other than that prescribed by the late Act?	20. None.
21. State where and by whom fixed engines were used in 1870?	21. See Appendix.
22. State any instances where head and tail gratings, either or both, would be advantageous (specifying which), if erected?	22. At Fermoy, mills tail gratings particularly, there are three tail-races to this mill, and from the way the water runs into the river from them, nearly two-thirds of the fish in low water run into them. At Quartertown, on the Clyda, a tail grating is very much required when the fish are ascending to spawn, and a head grating at the extreme end of head race when the fish are returning.
23. Can you give a list of the prosecutions instituted by the Conservators during the year 1870?	—
24. Are there any new modes of fishing for salmon adopted in your district? If so, describe them, and where used.	24. No new legal modes.
25. Number of water-bailiffs employed by Conservators?	25. Sixty-one.
26. Number employed in district by private individuals?	26. One by N. T. Foley, esq., and R. Cliffe, esq.
27. For what length of time employed?	27. Twelve the whole year; the remainder from two to four months.
28. Rate of wages paid by the Conservators?	28. Head bailiffs 15s. per week and their train fare; extras 6s. per week.
29. Are there any suggestions or general observations with which the Conservators may be disposed to favour the Inspectors, with reference to the Salmon Fisheries in your district?	29. Additional licence duty on nets; that all boats fishing in the tideway should be numbered in large figures on each side of the bows; that the constant system of refunding fines by the Government tends largely to promote poaching. The Board are of opinion that the late change of close season in the tideway will be highly prejudicial to the fishery.

STATEMENTS from Boards of Conservators.

Replies received from Boards of Conservators.		
8. Cork.	8a. Skibbereen.	8b Bantry.
1. I should say improving.	1. Last season was an average season for nets, but unusually bad for angling	1 Very good
2 More fish taken in 1869. The weather was much against fishing in 1870	2 The take by nets has been less productive in 1870 than in 1869. The diminution has been caused by the dry weather	2 There was a considerable increase in the take of salmon in the year 1870 over that in 1869.
3 From 2s. to 1s. About 1s. 3d. 9d	3. 6d. 7d. 6½d.	3 6½d. per lb 9d to 4d. per lb. 6½d. per lb
4 Nearly all exported.	4 Nine-tenths exported; one-tenth consumed in the locality.	4 Nearly all sent to Cork.
5 There was a considerable increase in the bailiffs as the funds allowed us to do more than in 1869 An Anglers' Club was formed early last winter, and the sum of £148 extra subscribed for the better protection of the river, which was fearfully poached in 1868 and 1869	5 One-half as to bailiffs. The police protection, which is very valuable, continues the same	5. About the same as last year.
6. Much greater on account of the exertions used by the Cork Anglers' Club who greatly assisted the Conservators.	6 Up to the close of the open season there has been very few breeding fish in the river, but a considerable run took place at a later period—in November and December	6. Less than 1869.
7 The latter end of October, November, and December, and half of January. The upper tributaries of the River Lee.	7 The chief spawning months are November, December, and January. About five miles above the town of Skibbereen.	7. About the 1st of November November and December are the greatest. Over about the end of December.
8. Not many spring salmon killed in February Month of June. Middle of March. Latter end of April.	8. In the Ilen, the middle of June; but very few until August. The fry run down in April and May. The spent fish are down by the first of April.	8. About the end of May. 1st of February. In the month of April.
9. In no case, and much injury is done.	9. No; but it is not believed that much fry is destroyed.	9. Angling is not prohibited by the proprietors in this district, or carried on to any extent during the descent of the fry to the sea.
10 End of September. 20th February to 20th September open for angling No netting should commence until the 1st March This is my own idea, but I know it is not that of many members of the Board.	10 The colour of the fish depends on the length of time they are in the river The general opinion is that the present season is the proper one.	10. In October Angling may be carried on up to 20th October
11 A great many. Not very many.	11 No spent fish are destroyed by anglers of the district. A few full fish are taken in October.	11. Spent fish are never taken. Some full fish are taken in October.
12 None whatever.	12. No change.	12. None.
13 Hardly any, but several pools in the River Lee have been poisoned by poachers.	13. None.	13. None.
14. Considerably increased.	14 The convictions have diminished, but it is believed that night poaching in the upper waters prevails as much as ever.	14. Diminished.
—	15 The Lurriga mill-dam. A fish ladder was erected many years ago, but being useless a diagonal pass was put up about four years ago by the Conservators.	15. None
—	—	16 At Dunamark falls
17. A useless one, built in the works at the Waterworks weir—not on the weir at all, where it should be. The present pass at Carrigrohane weir is almost useless. A fair pass at the Ballincollig Powder Mills weir	17 One fish-pass over the Lurriga mill-dam by the Conservators.	17. None.
18. In very few cases.	18. There is one at the head of Lurriga mill.	18. At Carrigboy.
19. Waterworks weir mill and Fenville mill at Macroom	19 Already answered.	—
20 Cork Waterworks and Carrigaline Turbines.	—	—
21. See Appendix.	21. None.	—
22 A grating much required at the head of Carrigrohane millrace. Ditto at Ballincollig Powder mills. Ditto at Carrigaline mill-race	22. At the foot of the Lurriga mill tail-race.	—
—	23. None.	—
24. None.	24 None.	24. None.
25. Fifteen to eighteen.	25. One.	25 Three.
26. One at Carrigaline river by Captain Hodder; one on the Sullane by Sir George Colthurst, bart.	26. One bailiff last year; none at present.	26. Two by the Earl of Bantry.
27 About three months.	27. Six months.	27. 20th July to 16th January.
28 8s. and 14s.	28. 9s. a week.	28. 3s. per week.
29. A proper fish-pass at the Waterworks weir in Cork, as well as other places before mentioned. Gratings at the head of mill-races. Irrigating drains more attended to.	29 The Conservators do not wish to make any suggestions beyond the matters that have been already discussed before the Commissioners at Skibbereen.	29. None.

APPENDIX, No. 17.—ABSTRACT OF

Substance of Queries issued to Boards of Conservators.	Replies received from Boards of Conservators.	
	6[a]. KENMARE.	7. KILLARNEY.
1. What is the general state of the Salmon Fisheries in this district?	1. Very good.	1. Inferior as compared with last season. This no doubt is caused by continual freshes.
2. Has the take of salmon throughout the district been more or less productive in 1870 than in 1869, and to what is attributed the increase or diminution?	2. None.	2. More.
3. What was the average price obtained for salmon last year by the captors? (This has no reference to price obtained by the dealers in salmon.) What was the highest price given for salmon last season? What was the lowest price?	3. 6d. per lb. 4d. per lb. 6d. per lb.	3. Two shillings per lb. in spring, and 7d. per lb. in summer.
4. What proportion of the entire capture in your district is exported, and what proportion purchased for home consumption?	4. About one-hundredth part for home consumption.	4. Nearly all exported.
5. What has been the amount of protection rendered during the present close season of 1870, as compared with preceding season of 1869?	5. About the same.	5. About the same.
6. Has the quantity of breeding fish observed in the rivers in your district been greater or less as compared with preceding year, 1869?	6. Much greater.	6. Greater.
7. About what period do the salmon commence to spawn in the several rivers in your district? What are the greatest spawning months? and when is spawning over? and generally where are the most important spawning grounds situated?	7. From the 22nd of November to the 10th of January.	7. Salmon commence to spawn in the upper waters the first week in November, and end about the first of February. The Flesk and Gaddagh are the best spawning rivers.
8. At what period of the year, in each river in your district, are the first clean fish taken? When do the grilse begin to run? When are the spent fish well out of the river? and when does the great bulk of the fry go to sea?	8. Early in May. About the 1st of July. In the end of February. In April.	8. January 1st. About the 15th of May. About the middle of May. In April.
9. During the descent of the fry to the sea, is angling prohibited by any of the proprietors of fisheries, or is it carried on during these months, and does much destruction of fry take place?	9. It is not prohibited, and a good deal of fry is lost.	9. No. Yes. Very little destruction.
10. At what period of the year do the fish begin to be discoloured, or to get heavy in spawn, and what is the general opinion as to the proper season for angling in your district?	10. About the 1st of November.	10. About October. Angling should cease on the 1st October, and commence on February 1st.
11. Have you reason to suppose that many spent fish have been destroyed hitherto in the month of February, and full fish in the month of October by anglers?	11. Not many in either season.	11. No; not many spent fish destroyed in February, but a good many full fish have been destroyed in October.
12. Are you aware of any change having taken place in regard to the period of the season when the salmon in your district is in best order, whether earlier or later than heretofore? If so, state particulars.	12. About the same.	12. No.
13. Are there any pollutions or poisonous matter entering the rivers in your district? If so, state the particular cases.	13. None.	13. With the exception of the Brown Flesk, which flows into the main.
14. Have offences against the Fishery Laws increased or diminished?	14. Diminished.	14. About the same.
15. Give a list of the mill-weirs, or dams, or other obstructions in each river in your district; and specify where ladders or fish passes have been built, when, and by whom?	15. Only one mill on the Finiha; one ladder on Clonee; one ladder on Sheen; one ladder on Sneem River; all made by Mr Trench.	15. The Flesk, near Killarney. No ladders or fish-passes have been made.
16. State where fish passes would be practicable and advantageous?	16. One on Finiha mill-dam.	16. The Flesk Mills, near Killarney.
17. Give a list of all the fish ladders or passes built in your district, whether under the provisions of the Fishery Acts, or by the Board of Works or private individuals, and specify each locality.	17. Three built by private individuals—Clonee, Sheen, and Sneem.	17. None.
18. Have gratings been attached to mill-leads, or other artificial channels, in conformity with the 32 Vic., cap. 9; and, if so, specify the particular cases?	18. One grating on the Finiha in the tail race, none at the head.	18. None.
19. State the instances in which the provision has been partially carried out, specifying whether at the head or tail race?	19. In the Finiha in the tail race.	19. Cuinacoilum tail race.
20. State the instances and nature of precautions adopted at mills to prevent the destruction of fish, other than that prescribed by the late Act?	20. None.	20. None.
21. State where and by whom fixed engines were used in 1870?	21. Mr Morty O'Sullivan, Westcove, one bag-net.	21. James Butler, stone weir, Waterville.
22. State any instances where head and tail gratings, either or both, would be advantageous (specifying which) if erected?	22. In the Finiha a head-grating would be of great use as the fry comes on the mill-wheel, and foul fish also returning to the sea.	22. None.
23. Can you give a list of the prosecutions instituted by the Conservators during the year 1870?	23. None.	23. No.
24. Are there any new modes of fishing for salmon adopted in your district? If so, describe them, and where used.	24. None.	24. None.
25. Number of water-bailiffs employed by Conservators?	25. Eleven.	25. About sixty-six.
26. Number employed in district by private individuals?	26. Eighteen private bailiffs.	26. Very few.
27. For what length of time employed?	27. During spawning season.	27. From twelve to three months.
28. Rate of wages paid by the Conservators?	28. From 15s. per quarter to £1 5s.	28. From £6 to £2.
29. Are there any suggestions or general observations with which the Conservators may be disposed to favour the Inspectors, with reference to the Salmon Fisheries in your District?	29. None.	29. None.

STATEMENTS from Boards of Conservators.

Replies received from Boards of Conservators.		
8. LIMERICK.	9. GALWAY.	10. BALLINAKILL.
1. Very good.	1. Very good.	1. Not improving.
2. Considerably more productive in the tide-way, but less so in the fresh water, owing to the complete absence of floods during the spring and summer.	2. Somewhat less, owing to the very low water in summer. The fish were in abundance, but could not get up for want of water.	2. Less productive.
3. About 1s. 3d. 2s. 6d. 6d.	3. The general average was from 10d. to 1s per lb. The highest price in spring was 2s 6d., and the lowest in summer was 8d.	3. 9½d. per lb. 7d. 6d.
4. The greater portion is exported. Very little is purchased for home consumption.	4. Nine-tenths exported to England.	4. Nine-tenths for exportation; one-tenth for home.
5. The amount paid in wages to water-bailiffs in 1879 was £1,686 3s 10d.; in 1863, £2,120 14s. 8d.	5. Greater, by twenty extra bailiffs employed.	5. Not so good.
6. Greater.	6. Far greater. In fact about the best spawning season ever known.	6. A good stock, but not so much as in [illegible].
7. They generally commence about the middle of December. December and January are the chief spawning months. Spawning is over at the end of January. The most important are at Castleconnell, Killaloe, and in the rivers Maigue, Mulcaire, Nenagh, and Ballinasloe.	7. In November. The principal months are generally December and January. Fully as many fish spawned in January, which is unusual, and the spawning season extended into February this year.	7. About 20th November. December. Over about 9th January; white trout the latter end of October.
8. In the month of February, but they could be taken in December and January. In the month of June. At the end of April. In April and May.	8. In February, as soon as the season opens. In May. About 20th April. In April and May.	8. March. June. April. March and April.
9. Angling is not prohibited; but much destruction of fry does not take place.	9. No destruction of fry occurs here from angling as all trout-fishing is prohibited while the fry are descending.	9. No prohibition; but little angling so early.
10. About August. From 1st February to end of September.	10. Towards the middle of August. The general opinion here is that angling should cease at the old time—the 20th September.	10. September. Not later than 1st October.
11. I cannot speak positively as to the spent fish, but great numbers of full fish have been taken in October by anglers.	11. Not now, but were before the grating clause became law. Considerable numbers of full fish caught by anglers in various parts of this district in October.	11. Not many. Some full fish killed in October.
12. No.	12. No. About the same now as before.	12. None.
13. No.	13. Great injury has been done by allowing flax-water to flow into the rivers at and about Ballyhaunis last August and September.	13. None.
14. They are decreasing.	14. Rather diminished on the whole, but there is one place, on the upper portion of the Abbey river, where lawless bands of men, with blackened faces, and dressed in women's clothes, have turned out by night. Some strong measures must be adopted to stop such practices.	14. Diminished.
15. I cannot do this correctly at present.	—	15. Louisburgh Tuck Mill, the dam, &c. Belclare Mills, on the Belclare river.
16. Chiefly at Annacotty in the Mulcaire river, and Ballyartella in the Nenagh river.	16. None required.	—
17. I cannot do so at present correctly.	17. At Galway, Abbey, Knock, [illegible], Milltown, Ballinrobe, Cong—all by Board of Works, except the last, which was constructed by the late Thomas Ashworth, Esq.	—
18. No effective gratings have as yet been attached.	18. Gratings have been put on all the important mill-races at Galway, and many other of the outlying districts, at periods when fish go to and return from their spawning beds.	18. The gratings are not good.
19. Tail races at Annacotty and Ballyartella, but they were defective in both instances.	19. Galway, Oughterard, Abbey, Abbert, and Newtown, also at Grange and [illegible].	—
20. None, except by placing water-bailiffs at mills.	20. Gratings and Nettings.	—
—	21. See Appendix.	—
22. Annacotty in the Mulcaire river, and Ballyartella in the Nenagh river.	22. The principal ones are those where they have been erected.	—
—	23. Not at this moment.	—
24. No.	24. None.	—
25. Ninety-five during the open season, 130 during the close season.	25. Twenty-six.	25. Thirty.
26. None.	26. I am certain there are over 300.	26. Twelve.
—	27. Some by the year, but the great body are for the close season only.	27. Four all the year, the remainder for close season.
28. From 5s. a week to £1.	28. From £3 to £30.	28. One £18, the others from £3 to £1 10s.
29. No.	29. None at present.	—

APPENDIX, No. 17.—ABSTRACT of

Substance of Queries issued to Boards of Conservators.	Replies received from Boards of Conservators. 10. Bangor.	11. Ballina.
1. What is the general state of the Salmon Fisheries in this district?	1. Favourable.	1. Favourable.
2. Has the take of salmon throughout the district been more or less productive in 1870 than in 1869, and to what is attributed the increase or diminution?	2. Not quite so productive as in 1869. There may be natural causes; but killing the breed fish so late in the season by angling is very injurious.	2. The season of 1870 has not been nearly so good as that of the preceding year 1869, which to a certain extent was attributable to the dry weather in the latter end of July and August.
3. What was the average price obtained for salmon last year by the captors? (This has no reference to price obtained by the dealers in salmon.) What was the highest price given for salmon last season? What was the lowest price?	3. About 8d. per lb. In this district could not say. About 1s. 4d. per lb. in the beginning of season. Lowest price 6½d.	3. Cannot say. 2s. 6d.
4. What proportion of the entire capture in your district is exported, and what proportion purchased for home consumption?	4. All.	4. Cannot say.
5. What has been the amount of protection rendered during the present close season of 1870, as compared with preceding season of 1869?	5. The amount in Conservators' hands this year for protection is rather better than in 1869, in consequence, chiefly, of fines imposed in prosecutions by coast-guards for lifting small oysters.	5. £163 10s. in 1869. £271 10s. in 1870.
6. Has the quantity of breeding fish observed in the rivers in your district been greater or less as compared with preceding year, 1869?	6. Much less than in 1869.	6. Much greater.
7. About what period do the salmon commence to spawn in the several rivers in your district? What are the greatest spawning months? and when is spawning over? and generally where are the most important spawning grounds situated?	7. The spawning season is greatly influenced by the weather. December in general is the chief spawning month, and is over early in January.	7. 1st November. November and December are the principal spawning months. Owinduff, Crossmolina, Foxford, Curry, Tubbercurry, and Balaghy, are the most important spawning districts.
8. At what period of the year, in each river in your district, are the first clean fish taken? When do the grilse begin to run? When are the spent fish well out of the river? and when does the great bulk of the fry go to sea?	8. It is scarcely worth fishing in any of the rivers till May, when the first clean fish are taken, but they run up to Lake Carrowmore in December, and are there caught on the 1st of March. Grilse begin to run about the middle of June. About the end of January. April and May.	8. Moy, February; Easky, June; Rathfran and Ballymully, August. End of April. Middle of April. April and May.
9. During the descent of the fry to the sea, is angling prohibited by any of the proprietors of fisheries, or is it carried on during these months, and does much destruction of fry take place?	9. Where the lessees of the net-fishing of the rivers have an interest in the upper waters, angling during the descent of fry is prohibited by them, but where angling is carried on great destruction of fry takes place.	9. Angling for trout is prohibited by a recent by-law of the Inspectors of Fisheries on the Rivers Rathfran and Easky during the time the fry are descending to the sea, but not on the Moy where a good deal of destruction is done to them at that time.
10. At what period of the year do the fish begin to be discoloured, or to get heavy in spawn, and what is the general opinion as to the proper season for angling in your district?	10. Towards the end of September, and after that no angling should be allowed in the district.	10. Fish begin to get discoloured in August. The proper season for angling is as now fixed by the by-law of the Inspectors of Fisheries, viz., 1st February to 15th September on the Moy, and 1st to [illegible] October on the Rathfran and Easky.
11. Have you reason to suppose that many spent fish have been destroyed hitherto in the month of February, and full fish in the month of October by anglers?	11. Not many in the month of February, but in October great quantities of full ripe fish are usually destroyed.	11. Believe so.
12. Are you aware of any change having taken place in regard to the period of the season when the salmon in your district is in best order, whether earlier or later than heretofore? If so, state particulars.	12. Not aware of any change.	12. No.
13. Are there any pollutions, or poisonous matter, entering the rivers in your district? If so, state the particular cases.	13. None.	13. None.
14. Have offences against the Fishery Laws increased or diminished?	14. The strict preservation carried on tend to decrease them.	14. Diminished.
15. Give a list of the mill-weirs, or dams, or other obstructions in each river in your district, and specify where ladders or fish-passes have been built, when, and by whom?	15. None causing obstruction.	15. Beg to refer you to separate list sent last year. The only fish-pass in this district is upon the River Moy, near Foxford, put up by the Board of Works about the year 1848.
16. State where fish-passes would be practicable and advantageous?	16. None required in the district.	16. Upon three mills on the Cloonagh River, and upon one mill on the Palmerstown River.
17. Give a list of all the fish-ladders or passes built in your district, whether under the provisions of the Fishery Acts, or by the Board of Works or private individuals; and specify each locality?	17. None.	17. See query No. 15.
18. Have gratings been attached to mill-leads, or other artificial channels, in conformity with the 32 Vic., cap. 9; and, if so, specify the particular cases?	18. A mill on the Newport River is the only one in the district, and the lead to that is supplied with a grating according to law.	18. On the greater portion of the mills in the district.
19. State the instances in which the provision has been partially carried out, specifying whether at the head or tail race?	19. Newport mill. There is a grating at head and tail race.	—
20. State the instances and nature of precautions adopted at mills to prevent the destruction of fish, other than that prescribed by the late Act?	20. See above.	20. Am not aware of any.
21. State where and by whom fixed engines were used in 1870?	21. See Appendix.	21. See Appendix.
22. State any instances where head and tail gratings, either or both, would be advantageous (specifying which) if erected?	—	—
23. Can you give a list of the prosecutions instituted by the Conservators during the year 1870?	23. Lessees of fisheries in the district prosecute generally and not the Conservators.	23. Nil.
24. Are there any new modes of fishing for salmon adopted in your district? If so, describe them, and where used.	24. No new methods.	24. Drafting in the upper waters of the Moy.
25. Number of water-bailiffs employed by Conservators?	25. About Ninety.	25. Fifty.
26. Number employed in district by private individuals?	26. All are Conservators' water-keepers.	26. About 200.
27. For what length of time employed?	27. Generally six months.	27. November, December, and January for the protection of the salmon. April and May for the protection of the fry.
28. Rate of wages paid by the Conservators?	28. Conservators' funds contribute a very small sum to each man; but wages from lessees, with the Conservators' contribution, are from £1½ to £3, according to duty.	28. £1 to £10.
29. Are there any suggestions or general observations with which the Conservators may be disposed to favour the Inspectors, with reference to the Salmon Fisheries in your District?	29. The Conservators suggest the necessity of shortening the angling season, and the unanimous opinion of the Board of this district is, that it should cease on the 20th September each year.	—

STATEMENTS from Boards of Conservators.

Replies received from Boards of Conservators		
12. Sligo.	13. Ballyshannon.	14. Letterkenny.
1. Favourable.	1. In a fair state.	1. As a general rule improving.
2. Improvement in consequence of good protection.	2. Not so productive in 1870 as in 1869. Can assign no cause.	2. In some districts the take of salmon was more productive in 1870 than in 1869—attributed to unusual number of spawning fish that ascended the river in spawning season of '69, and to its being a favourable season for those operations, as no heavy floods occurred during incubation of the ova to destroy it, as some years happens.
3. From 3s. to 6d. per lb. 2s. 6d.	3. 3d. to 1d. 2s. 6d.	3. 2d. 1s. 6d. 6d.
4. Nearly all exported.	4. Nearly all exported.	4. Almost the entire capture.
5. Protection increased.	5. Considerably increased on the Erne. Reduced on some rivers.	5. The same amount of protection during the close season of 1870. No increase of water-bailiffs considered necessary.
6. Large increase.	6. Greater.	6. About the same.
7. November and December. December. Leitrim and Sligo.	7. Commence in November. Greatest in November and December. Over in January. The Arney, Swanlinbar, Maguire's-bridge, Killeshandra, Ballyconnell, and the Erne.	7. Middle of November and month of December. December to middle of January—some few run as far as middle of February. The important spawning-beds are from [illegible]-bridge above Lough [illegible] to upper sources of the River Leanan.
8. Sligo, December and January; other rivers, March and April. May. May. April and May.	8. Bundrowes, in February. June. April. April and May.	8. At first week in February when fishing opens. Some are taken first week in May. All gone by end of March. Month of April to 15th May.
9. Angling not prohibited.	9. Prohibited in the Erne only.	9. Angling is not prohibited. Angling is carried on by the very few permitted to fish, but no salmon-fry are destroyed.
10. August and September. Angling should cease about the 15th September.	10. End of August discolouring. Proper season in the Drowes from 1st February to middle of September; in the Erne from middle of May to middle of September.	10. Those taken in sea show a slight discolouration in month of August, those in fresh water as early as June, from boggy nature of river-water. Fish are heavy in spawn in month of November. The present season for angling is considered fair enough. Anglers have no chance till about middle of March.
11. No.	11. In the Erne a great many spent fish are taken by spoon baits under pretence of fishing for pike. Also some foul fish in October are taken in the same manner.	11. No spent fish are destroyed in February as fishing is not carried on till about middle of following month—and foul. Little or no angling for salmon is carried on in October in this district.
12. Early fish is the best in order.	12. Not aware of any change.	12. No change.
13. None.	13. A good deal of flax-water. It was complained that a great quantity of flax-sewers were thrown into the Drowes from the flax-mills at Mullinaleck.	13. Flax-water begins to find its way into the river about first week in August in every year.
14. Decreased.	14. Diminished.	14. Diminished. None of any moment for years.
15. Passes at Sligo and Ballisodare.	15. On the Olley carries have been lately built across the river at two or three mills, proving a total obstruction to salmon ever again getting up that (formerly) excellent spawning river.	15. One weir at Ramelton, and one at Tully, and one mill-dam also at Ramelton. No fish-ladders in any of them. The Ramelton passes, by Mr G. Kelly, about five years ago, but top of one of them is so [illegible] that fish cannot get up through it, they, however, freely get up in flood times over wings of this weir. The Tully weir cannot be ascended by salmon except in flood times also—it is built some seven or eight years; erected by Mrs Watt; is a great obstruction to fish ascending at any time.
—	16. At Ballycassidy, [illegible], and the Olley, very much wanted.	
17. Answered in Query 15.	17. Ballyconnell, Carreal Lock, and Skelia Lock, by Board of Works; Donegal, by Lord Arran; Pettigo, by Dr Shiel—it is now dry and useless.	
—	18. All specified in return of 24th of April last, and no change reported since then.	16. At Ramelton and at Tully both existing fish passes are imperfect, but during the summer months when the river is very low, I do not consider that any pass or ladder would enable fish to ascend.
19. Some at Ballisodare and Collooney.	19. Stated in the before-mentioned report.	17. No proper passes in almost any of the rivers. One ladder erected on the Gweedore River at expense of the proprietor, Lord G. A. Hill.
20. None.	20. Do not know of any.	18. Yes, at Ramelton and Tully gratings have been erected in head-races—not to tail-races. No apparent need for them as fish could not ascend by mill-wheels.
21. See Appendix.	21. See Appendix.	
22. Advantageous in all mills.	22. Would be advantageous at all the mills, both at head and tail.	19. At Ramelton as well as at Tully mill, there are no gratings to tail-races, but they are not required. These are the exceptions, many mills being without such.
—	—	20. None.
24. None.	24. One drift net was fished first time in the memory of man outside the mouth of the river Erne.	21. See Appendix.
—	25. 136.	22. None required.
26. Fifty-three.	26. Eight.	23. Nil.
27. Twelve and six months.	27. Yearly.	24. Nil. 25. Two in Letterkenny. Many others are appointed in the district, viz., at Ramelton, Gweedore, Lacka, Dochary Bridge, &c. 26. Two by private individuals.
28. From £15 to £8 10s.	28. From £7 to £1.	
29. Shortening the angling season, and opening the net fishing earlier in the Sligo river.	29. None.	27. Usually by the year. 28. From £9 14s. to £6 each. 29. I consider the fish-passes in mill-weirs most defective; and in some the fish cannot ascend the weirs except in floods, and even then with difficulty.

APPENDIX, No. 17.—ABSTRACT of

Substance of Queries issued to Boards of Conservators.	Replies received from Boards of Conservators. 15. LONDONDERRY.
1. What is the general state of the Salmon Fisheries in this District?	1. In a very fair state
2. Has the take of salmon throughout the district been more or less productive in 1870 than in 1869, and to what is attributed the increase or diminution?	2. The take in 1870 was not so great as in 1869, but was a fair average of preceding years
3. What was the average price obtained for salmon last year by the captors? (This has no reference to price obtained by the dealers in salmon.) What was the highest price given for salmon last season? What was the lowest price?	3. 7d per lb. 1s 6d per lb. 3½d. per lb.
4. What proportion of the salmon captured in your district is exported, and what proportion purchased for home consumption?	4. Nearly all exported.
5. What has been the amount of protection rendered during the present close season of 1870, as compared with preceding season of 1869?	5. Slightly increased.
6. Has the quantity of breeding fish observed in the rivers in your district been greater or less as compared with preceding year, 1869?	6. Greater.
7. About what period do the salmon commence to spawn in the several rivers in your district? What are the greatest spawning months? and when is spawning over? and generally where are the most important spawning grounds situated?	7. Commence to spawn in November. Greatest spawning months are December and January. Spawning over in February. The most important spawning grounds are—Rivers Derg, Strule, Glenelly, Finn, and Roe.
8. At what period of the year, in each river in your district, are the first clean fish taken? When do the grilse begin to run? When are the spent fish well out of the river? and when does the great bulk of the fry go to sea?	8. In the tideway of the Foyle in the month of May, and in some of the upper waters, viz., the Derg, Strule, and Finn in the beginning of June. First grilse caught last season on the 31st May. Spent fish are well out of the rivers by the end of March, and the great bulk of the fry go to the sea in the month of April
9. During the descent of the fry to the sea, is angling prohibited by any of the proprietors of fisheries, or is it carried on during these months, and does much destruction of fry take place?	9. There is no prohibition of angling during the time the fry are descending, and a great many are captured by small boys angling.
10. At what period of the year do the fish begin to be discoloured or to get heavy in spawn; and what is the general opinion as to the proper season for angling in your district?	10. At the end of August the fish in the Foyle are discoloured from lying in the brackish and flax-water, and full of spawn towards the end of September. The 15th October is the date most people would recommend for the close season for angling to commence, and end on the 15th March
11. Have you reason to suppose that many spent fish have been destroyed hitherto in the month of February, and full fish in the month of October by anglers?	11. In some seasons there is no doubt large quantities of spent fish are captured by anglers in the month of February, and full fish in the month of October.
12. Are you aware of any change having taken place in regard to the period of the season when the salmon in your district is in best order, whether earlier or later than heretofore? If so, state particulars.	12. I am not aware of any change.
13. Are there any poisonous or deleterious matter entering the rivers in your district? If so, state the particular cases.	13. Only flax-water.
14. Have offences against the Fishery Laws increased or diminished?	14. Less number of offences, but an increase in amount of penalties owing to some cases of illegal fishing in the open season
15. Give a list of the mill-weirs, or dams, or other obstructions in each river in your district, and specify where ladders or fish-passes have been built, when, and by whom?	15. The only fish pass in the district is at Slan Mills, constructed by the proprietors of the mills.
16. State where fish-passes would be practicable and advantageous?	16. At Mr. Irvine's weir, at Ballyarton on the Faughan River.
17. Give a list of all the fish-ladders or passes built in your district, whether under the provisions of the Fishery Acts, or by the Board of Works or private individuals; and specify each locality?	17. Slan Mills weir on Mourne River, erected by the proprietors of the mills.
18. Have gratings been attached to mill-heads, or other artificial channels, in conformity with the Act 32 Vic., cap. 9; and, if so, specify the particular cases.	18. In some cases the provisions of the Act have been complied with, and others have got exemption by the Inspectors, and several mill-owners have promised to erect them in a proper and sufficient manner
19. State the instances in which the provision has been partially carried out, specifying whether at the head or tail-race?	19. Some mill-owners have erected them on the head, and some on the tail-races, according to the decision of the Inspectors
20. State the instances and nature of precautions adopted at mills to prevent the destruction of fish, other than that prescribed by the late Act?	20. None, except extra watching by the bailiffs
21. State where and by whom fixed engines were used in 1870?	21. See Appendix
22. State any instances where head and tail gratings, either or both, would be advantageous (specifying which), if erected?	22. At the Inspectors' meeting in Londonderry, in February, 1871, Messrs. Ballantine, Brothers, were directed to erect gratings in the tail-race of their mills on the Faughan River, from 1st November till 15th January, and several other cases where the Inspectors have ordered them to be erected.
23. Can you give a list of the prosecutions instituted by the Conservators during the year 1870?	—
24. Are there any new modes of fishing for salmon adopted in your district? If so, describe them, and where used?	24. None.
25. Number of water-bailiffs employed by Conservators?	25. About 100.
26. Number employed in district by private individuals?	26. About ninety by the Lessees of the Irish Society's Fishery in the Foyle.
27. For what length of time employed?	27. Generally from November till April; in a few cases the whole year.
28. Rate of wages paid by the Conservators?	28. From £12 to £3.
29. Are there any suggestions or general observations with which the Conservators may be disposed to favour the Inspectors, with reference to the Salmon Fisheries in your district?	29. The Conservators would strongly recommend that the close season for angling be extended from 15th October to the 15th March.

STATEMENTS from Boards of Conservators.

Replies received from Boards of Conservators.		
15a. Coleraine.	16 Ballycastle.	17. Drogheda.
1 Progressing favourably.	1. In my opinion flourishing.	1. Improving
2 A little less productive in 1879 than in 1880 This is attributed to the long drought in the fishing season, or very low water.	2 Much the same in 1879 as in 1880	2 More in 1879 than in 1880, increase attributed to better protection
3. 1s. 4s. 9d.	3. 2s 6d. per lb. 2s. 4d. per lb. In Spring months 5d. per lb.	3 1s 8d. 2s. 9d. 5d.
4 More than two-thirds of the entire capture in this district is exported, the remainder is for home supply	4. Almost all exported.	4. About nine-tenths to Dublin, Belfast, and Liverpool.
5. The protection in this close season is considerably increased by that of 1880 Additional keepers are employed by the Board of Conservators, and a few temporarily engaged by the Inspector in places on the rivers where he considered it necessary for the protection of the fish.	5. Much the same as in the preceding year of 1880.	5 Improved.
6 Considerably greater as compared with 1880.	6. Considerably greater than in 1880	6. About the same
7. The salmon commence to spawn in November in some rivers. The greatest spawning months are November, and particularly December. The spawning is generally over in December The river Maine and its tributaries, also the Ballinderry and Claudy are the best spawning rivers.	7. 1st November From 1st November till 20th December 1st January. All River Bush contains good spawning ground	7. September September, October, November, and to end of December Spawning over early in January. Best spawning beds on the Boyne, at Rossnaree, Slane, and Trim.
8 Late in February and March. May and June Early in February April and May.	8. I believe a clean fish can be got in the Bush any day in the year 30th June 15th April During April and until 15th May.	8. February in Boyne, Dee, Glyde, and Annagassan June in the Fane. The middle of June In February March, April, and May
9 I am not aware that angling is prohibited by any of the proprietors of fisheries during the descent of the fry I think it is practised to a small extent, but without much destruction of fry.	9. It is prohibited in upper waters. Where salmon angling is let, little damage is done.	9. Angling is not prohibited Not much destruction of fry.
10 In September and October fish are discoloured, and begin to grow heavy From the 1st day of February to the last day in September is considered the proper season for angling	10 Fish don't become discoloured until they have been in river some time. They get heavy in spawn towards end of August The general opinion is angling is carried on too long	10 About the middle of August. Angling from 1st of February to 15th of September.
11 In my opinion few spent fish are destroyed in February, but many full fish are destroyed in October by anglers; and I am of opinion angling should be prohibited during the month of October	11 No, I have never known any spent fish, except by accident or mistake, being destroyed Full fish are often killed in October by legitimate anglers and poachers.	11. No.
12 I am not aware of any change having taken place in the period of the year that salmon are in good order I should say May, June, July, and August they are in good order. In September they are not so good as previously. In October they are quite discoloured.	12. Not to my knowledge.	12 No change.
13 Pollutions enter the Six-mile Water in several places from Ballyclare to Antrim; but it is too far east from the river Bann to be a good salmon river. In other rivers there are also pollutions, but little injury is done by them	13. Nothing except flax-water. Diminished.	13. Very much by flax-water.
14 Offences against the Fishery Laws have considerably diminished.	—	14 Diminished.
—	15. I don't think any are required.	—
16. An improvement made on the fish-ladder at Carnroe would considerably assist the salmon passing up the breeding river I consider an improvement there would be most necessary, fish cannot pass at low water It is now called by many the Club's Pound.	16 None necessary in this district.	16 Boyne river at Slane and Orinstown; White mill on Dee river; Jallinstown on same; Fane river; Channonrock, Philipstown, on the Philipstown river.
17 On the River Bann, at Portna, Movanagher, and Carnroe, fish-ladders were made by the Board of Works, during their drainage operations on the River Bann, and one was erected at Benburb by a private Fish Company	—	—
18. Lisnafillan, Hillmount, Funaghy; Drumcon, Race View, Culmady.	18 Yes, generally	18 On M'Cann's mill-lead on the Fane river; on Drumcar mill-lead on the Dee river, and tail-race of Dunmoe mill on Boyne river
19. The provisions of the Act have been carried out, generally speaking, at the tail-races.	19 None but gratings.	19. Same as No. 18.
20. No precaution used at mills to preserve fish unless where the gratings are erected.	20. None but gratings, as above.	20. None, unless gratings that have been put up in conformity with law, before the turbine wheels at Mr. Wetherall's, on the Mattock, and Mr. Chester's, on the Blackwater.
21. See Appendix.	21. All bag-nets and draft-nets, same as in 1880.	21. See Appendix
22 Grating would be necessary on the tail-race at Crevilly-valley, Kildrum, Ballyfinnick, Aghaboy, Randalstown, Moan, Tullywatery, Glasgow, Kells, and Claudy.	22. On all mill-races I should say.	22. A grating much wanted at Channonrock tail-race, and Mr. Spicer's Blackwater mill tail-race.
23 Total amount of fines received during the year 1879, £40 10s. 7d.	23. See Appendix.	—
24 Fixed draft nets used at Portstewart.	24. None	24. None.
25. Fifty.	25. On Bush, thirteen permanent, at some time as many as twenty-five during spawning season. On the Ballycastle sub-district, four permanent men and seven in spawning season.	25. Seventeen.
26. About sixteen.	26 The owners of Bush augment the funds to enable the number as stated to last query to be employed The owner of the Ballycastle estate employs one in spawning season.	26. Two.
27 Employed from 1st February to the 30th September and 31st October.	27. See above, No 25.	27. Six months.
28. From £4 to £40.	28 Permanent men from 7s to 10s. per week. Watchers at spawning season 10s. to 12s.	28. Six at £1 10s; eleven at £1.
29 In the month of October angling should be prohibited.	—	—

APPENDIX, Nos. 18 & 19.

APPENDIX, No. 18.

REGULATIONS for the ELECTIONS of CONSERVATORS of FISHERIES, 1870.

SALMON FISHERIES ACTS (IRELAND),

32 & 33 Vic., c. 92, and the Acts incorporated therewith.

NOTICE.

WHEREAS all existing Boards of Conservators will cease in the month of October next, and new Boards are to be elected, We, the Inspectors of Irish Fisheries, call the attention of the Boards of Conservators, and those interested in the Fisheries, to the following provisions and regulations in respect to such

ELECTIONS OF CONSERVATORS OF FISHERIES.

The elections for the district of   should be held so as to commence on the   day of October next.

1.—The Board of Conservators shall fix and publish notice of the *times* and *places for the meetings* of electors, *in each electoral division*, for the election of Conservators for the same, and the number of Conservators as already settled to be elected *for each electoral division*.

2.—*Two weeks' notice thereof shall be given by handbills and advertisements* in two or more newspapers circulating in the district.

3.—The meetings for elections *shall commence at the hour named in the notice to be published by the Boards of Conservators, and no votes shall be received after three o'clock in the afternoon of the day so fixed.*

4.—Every person shall be entitled to vote at such meetings who shall have paid licence duty for the current year, within the electoral division for which such meeting is held, and no others.

5.—Such person shall choose a Chairman to preside at such meeting, who shall receive the votes of the electors.

6.—No person shall be eligible for the office of Conservator in any electoral division in which he does not reside or possess real property.

7.—Every person shall produce their licences for the current year at the time of voting.

8.—Persons entitled as aforesaid to vote at such meetings shall be entitled to have a vote or votes thereat according to the following scale (that is to say) if the licence duty paid—

Shall not amount to £2, ... One Vote.
Shall amount to £2, and not amount to £5, Two Votes.
Shall amount to £5, " £10, Three Votes.
Shall exceed £10, ... Four Votes.

9.—Persons voting by proxy shall indorse upon their licence the name of the proxy whom they authorize to vote for them, and the said licence shall be produced at the time of voting by the said proxy, *such proxy being a qualified elector.*

10.—The Chairman of such Meetings respectively shall declare the persons who shall have received the greatest number of votes to be the elected Conservators, and shall certify under his hand the election of each Conservator, and furnish him with a certificate which shall be sufficient authority for him to act as such Conservator; *and shall also, within four days after such election*, cause a list of such Conservators, with a statement of the residence and post town of each, to be transmitted to our office, 12, Ely-place, Dublin, and *shall also publish the said list in one or more newspapers circulating in the district.*

11.—If in any district one or more persons shall possess a several or exclusive fishery or fisheries therein, as owner, lessee, or occupier, valued under the Acts for the more effectual relief of the destitute poor in Ireland at one hundred pounds yearly, or upwards, he or they shall be entitled to sit with the elected Conservators for such district, and shall be deemed ex-officio a Conservator or Conservators for the same, so long as he or they shall possess such fishery or fisheries, and shall have a vote in all matters, and have all the powers and privileges under the Act which the elected Conservators may individually possess; provided always, that when a fishery so rated shall be held by several persons as owners, lessees, or occupiers, one person alone shall sit and act as a Conservator as aforesaid in respect of such fishery.

12.—Magistrates paying licence duty, and being owners of land abutting on rivers or lakes in any district, may act and vote as ex-officio members of any Board of Conservators elected for any such district.

13.—The persons elected, as aforesaid, together with all the said ex-officio Conservators shall conjointly form a Board of Conservators of Fisheries for the District, and shall continue to hold office for three years from the time of their election, when a new Board shall be elected in like manner, and so in like manner at each Triennial Election.

Given under our hands this 15th day of June, 1870.

THOS. F. BRADY.
JOHN A. BLAKE.
JOS. HAYES.

NOTE to ¶ 10.—*Forms of Certificates will be furnished by the Inspectors to the different Clerks of the Boards of Conservators.*

APPENDIX, No. 19.

RETURN of FISH conveyed over the Line of the Waterford and Limerick Railway Company, year ending 31st December, 1870.

Stations.	Salmon and Trout.		White Fish.		Weight.			
	Boxes.	Baskets, &c.	Boxes.	Baskets, &c.	Tons.	cwt.	qrs.	lbs.
Limerick, ...	1,339	242	452	—		—		
Foynes, ...	2,559	—	—	—	240	1	1	0
Caher, ...	219	27	—	—	26	4	0	0
Clonmel, ...	20	—	—	—	3	11	0	12
Carrick, ...	—	—	—	—	7	13	1	0
Kilsheelan, ...	Nil.							
	4,337	269	452	—	277	9	2	12

APPENDIX, No. 19—*continued.*

RETURN of FISH conveyed by the Belfast and Northern Counties Railway Company during the year 1870.

	Boxes.	Baskets, &c.
Salmon and Trout,	5,546	206
White Fish,	3,115	725

RETURN of FISH conveyed by Irish North-Western Railway Company during the year 1870.

Co.	Stations.	Tons.	cwts.	qrs.	lbs.	Tons.	cwts.	qrs.	lbs.
I. N. W.	Strabane,	5	17	0	0				
	Porthall,	0	7	2	4				
	Saint Johnston,	0	11	0	2				
	Carrigans,	0	0	1	23				
	Londonderry,	8	10	0	0				
						15	6	0	1
F. V.	Clady,	0	17	2	0				
	Stranorlar,	12	16	0	0				
						13	13	2	0
E. B. & S.	Pettigoe,	1	2	2	0				
	Belleek,	39	16	2	0				
	Ballyshannon,	118	12	2	24				
	Bundoran,	8	4	3	3				
						167	16	1	27
	Total,					196	16	0	0

RETURN of FISH conveyed by Dublin and Belfast Junction Railway for year 1870.

Station.	Salmon.		White Fish.		Weight.			
	Boxes.	Baskets.	Boxes.	Baskets.	Tons.	cwts.	qrs.	lbs.
Dunleer,	65	4	—	—	7	16	0	24
Castlebellingham,	11	346	—	—	6	4	0	0
Dundalk,	19	30	—	13	1	14	1	26
					17	14	2	22
Drogheda,	—	—	Herrings. 468	10	59	0	0	0
Total,	95	380	468	23	76	14	2	22

RETURN of FISH conveyed by the Cork, Bandon, and Kinsale Railway Company, booked at Kinsale Station, for the year ending 31st December, 1870.

Description of Fish.	Tons.	cwts.	qrs.	lbs.	Description of Fish.	Tons.	cwts.	qrs.	lbs.
Salmon,	0	1	0	0	Mackerel,	977	18	0	0
Turbot,	0	16	3	0	Plaice,	0	17	2	0
Haddock,	0	14	2	0	Sprat,	29	5	2	0
Pollock,	0	4	0	0	Eels,	0	15	2	0
Hake,	78	13	2	0	Bream,	13	11	2	0
Pilchers,	60	18	0	0	Oyster	0	3	0	0
Herrings,	10	16	2	0	Hallibut,	0	6	2	0
Scad,	20	2	0	0					
Ling,	13	18	0	0	Total,	1,215	0	1	0
Cod,	5	14	1	0					

RETURN of the WEIGHT of all FRESH FISH conveyed over the Great Southern and Western Railway, and the Cork, Youghal, and Queenstown section, for the year ending 31st December, 1870.

Description of Fish	Tons.	Description of Fish.	Tons.
Salmon,	269	Flat-fish,	43
Cod,	5	Eels,	16
Haddock,	3	Sprats,	8
Herrings,	287	Fresh Fish, not named,	297
Shell-fish,	203		
Mackerel,	537	Total,	1,764
Hake,	9		

APPENDIX, No. 19—*continued.*

RETURN of FISH conveyed to Dublin by the trains of the Midland Great Western Railway Company of Ireland in year 1870.

Stations	Fine Fish		Coarse Fish		Weight.			
	Boxes.	Baskets.	Boxes.	Baskets.	Tons	cwts.	qrs.	lbs.
Galway,	471	41	—	—	30	18	3	20
Sligo,	194	44	—	—	23	0	2	0
Westport,	93	54	—	—	11	9	3	0
Athenry,	19	101	—	—	9	17	1	0
Ballysodare,	44	62	—	—	14	17	1	0
Ballina,	40	56	—	—	12	1	2	0
Foxford,	35	12	—	—	4	3	2	20
Castlebar,	42	81	—	—	6	0	0	12
Total,	938	453	—	—	122	17	3	24
Galway,	—	—	40	4,239	253	16	2	0
Sligo,	—	—	10	443	53	1	0	2
Ballysodare,	—	—	6	38	3	1	2	0
Castlebar,	—	—	12	20	2	3	3	2
Total,	—	—	68	4,740	312	2	3	4

RETURN of FISH conveyed by the Dublin, Wicklow, and Wexford Railway for the year ending 31st December, 1870.

Description of Fish.	Tons.	cwt.	qrs.
Fresh fish,	39	10	3
Herrings,	918	8	3
Oysters,	1,109	7	1
Salmon,	10	9	3
Total,	2,077	16	2

RETURN of FISH conveyed by the Dublin and Drogheda Railway Company in 1870.

Dates	Salmon and Trout.		White Fish.			Weight.			
	Boxes.	Baskets, &c.	Boxes.	Baskets, &c.	Barrels.	Tons.	cwt.	qrs.	lbs.
From 1st January to 31st December, 1870, per Goods Train,	—	91	1,500	156	1,443	314	16	0	0
From 1st January to 31st December, 1870, inclusive, per Passenger Train,	136	60	—	—	—	10	1	0	0

RETURN of FISH conveyed by the West Cork Railway Company in 1870.

Dates.	Salmon and Trout.		Shell Fish.		
	Boxes.	Baskets, &c.	Boxes.	Baskets, &c.	Barrels.
January,	2	8	—	—	11
February,	5	6	—	1	23
March,	7	17	—	—	—
April,	12	11	—	—	1
May,	3	2	—	—	—
June,	1	—	—	—	—
July,	144	34	—	—	—
August,	112	20	—	—	—
September,	16	3	3	10	7
October,	3	2	1	1	—
November,	4	2	—	34	2
December,	3	4	1	2	5
Total,	313	104	5	48	49

APPENDIX, No. 10—*continued.*

RETURN of FISH conveyed from Dublin to Holyhead by the Steamers of the London and North-Western Railway and Steam Packet Company, 1870.

Dates.	Salmon and Trout.		White Fish.	
	Boxes.	Baskets, &c.	Boxes.	Baskets, &c.
January,	1	—	575	12
February,	84	—	290	4
March,	106	—	381	5
April,	145	—	852	6
May,	97	—	661	1
June,	310	—	1,627	—
July,	482	—	1,041	2
August,	105	—	1,471	9
September,	17	—	1,781	7
October,	—	—	3,149	54
November,	—	—	884	28
December,	—	—	459	30
Total,	1,407	—	13,551	158

RETURN of FISH conveyed to Bristol by the Steamers of the Bristol General Steam Navigation Company, 1870.

Dates.	Salmon and Trout.		Herrings.	
	Boxes.	Baskets, &c.	Boxes.	Barrels.
June 21,	—	—	—	17
July 19,	—	—	—	18
,, 26,	—	—	16	26
Aug. 23,	—	—	—	7
Oct. 18,	—	—	—	19

RETURN of FISH conveyed to Glasgow by the Steamers of the Glasgow and Dublin Screw Steam Packet Company, in 1870.

Dates.	Salmon and Trout.		Herrings.	
	Boxes.	Baskets, &c.	Boxes.	Barrels.
March 31,	—	—	2	—
April 28,	—	—	3	—
May 5,	—	—	1	5
,, 19,	—	—	1	—
June 2,	—	—	7	—
,, 16,	—	—	1	—
,, 30,	—	—	9	—
Nov. 4,	—	—	—	19

RETURN of FISH conveyed to Glasgow and Greenock by the Steamers of the Dublin and Glasgow Company, 1870.

Dates.	White Fish.		Herrings
	Boxes.	Baskets, &c.	Barrels.
January,	2	3	2
February,	2	2	—
March,	11	6	2
April,	25	5	1
May,	20	2	1
June,	15	—	16
October,	—	2	802
November,	—	—	379
December,	—	8	61
	64	28	1,264

APPENDIX, Nos. 19—21.

APPENDIX, No. 19—*continued*.

RETURN of FISH conveyed to Liverpool by the City of Dublin Steam Packet Company's vessels for the year 1870.

Dates.	Salmon.				White Fish.			
	Boxes.	Baskets	Packgs	Weight.	Boxes	Baskets.	Packgs.	Weight.
				Tons. cwt. qrs. lbs.				Tons. cwt. qrs. lbs.
January, . .	23	—	—	2 2 2 0	—	—	—	—
February, . .	72	5	—	7 1 1 15	43	12	—	5 16 1 26
March, . . .	115	7	4	12 7 3 5	163	120	3	72 16 1 22
April, . . .	135	3	5	10 16 3 10	382	16	2	40 0 3 7
May, . . .	360	—	3	37 1 2 22	101	—	—	10 4 2 0
June, . . .	516	2	2	58 11 2 4	424	89	93	50 14 2 18
July, . . .	687	—	—	69 10 2 14	407	44	37	43 4 3 15
August, . .	169	—	—	17 14 2 16	1,068	33	33	94 17 2 19
September, . .	30	—	—	0 10 0 14	1,558	8	14	173 10 2 8
October, . .	—	—	—	—	1,025	3	1	103 14 2 0
November, . .	—	—	—	--	599	14	1	61 2 3 0
December, . .	—	—	—	—	182	30	3	21 10 2 1
	2,107	17	14	216 5 3 24	6,022	335	189	633 8 2 1

APPENDIX, No. 20.

ABSTRACT of the Quantity of SALMON, HERRINGS, MACKEREL, SHELL FISH, HOOK FISH, FRESH-WATER EELS, and TRAWL FISH, delivered at and sold in Dublin, consigned from the Irish Fisheries in 1870, as far as can be ascertained; with a computation of the value thereof.

			£	s.	d.
Salmon, 2,860 boxes and baskets, 112 lbs. average weight,	at 1s. per lb., . .		16,128	0	0
Herrings, 19,920 mease, ...	at £1 per mease, . .		19,920	0	0
Mackerel, 4,900 boxes and baskets, . . .	at £1 per basket, . .		4,900	0	0
Shell Fish (Lobsters, Crabs, Cockles, Shrimps, &c.), .	. . . .		1,500	0	0
Hook Fish (Haddock and Cod), 3,000 packages, .	at £2 per package, . .		6,000	0	0
Eels (fresh water), 1,000 packages, . . .	at £1 10s. per package, .		1,500	0	0
Trawl Fish, 2,304 hampers, prime, . . .	at £3 per hamper,	£6,912			
,, 8,856 hampers, offal, . . .	at £1 per hamper	8,856			
			15,768	0	0
Total, .			£65,716	0	0

APPENDIX, No. 21.

ABSTRACT of the Quantity of SALMON delivered and sold in Billingsgate Market, consigned from the Irish Fisheries in 1870.

9,211 boxes.—Each box weighs, on the average, 120 lbs., which, at the average price of 1s. 4d. per lb., represents, *en gros*, £73,088 sterling.

ABSTRACT of the Quantity of SALMON, HERRINGS, MACKEREL, and COD, delivered at and sold in the following places, consigned from the Irish Fisheries in 1870, as far as can be ascertained; with a computation of the value thereof.

PLACES.	SALMON.		HERRINGS		MACKEREL.		COD.		TOTAL.
	No. of Boxes.	Value.	No. of Boxes and Barrels	Value.	No. of Boxes and Barrels.	Value.	No. of Boxes and Baskets.	Value.	
		£		£		£		£	£
Nottingham, .	250*	1,750	2,000	3,000	1,000	1,800	150	325	6,875
Wolverhampton, .	300*	2,100	2,000	3,000	1,500	2,250	200	500	7,850
Bradford, . .	600*	5,000	6,000	7,500	2,000	3,000	300	450	16,630
Sheffield, . .	800*	5,600	8,000	12,000	2,000	3,000	500	800	21,400
Leeds, . . .	1,000*	7,000	8,000	12,000	2,000	3,000	500	800	22,800
Birmingham, .	2,000*	14,000	12,000	18,000	4,000	6,000	600	1,900	39,900
Manchester, . .	3,500†	24,500	15,000	22,000	6,000	9,000	1,000	2,350	57,850
Liverpool, . .	–	–	20,000	30,000	8,500	17,000	2,000	5,000	
Billingsgate Market,	–	–	23,350	48,277‡	12,700	25,800	400	1,000	75,077

* At £7 per box. † Each box 120 lbs., at 1s. 2d. per lb. = £7 per box.

‡ The average price Irish Herrings realized during the season was about £2 1s. per box. They arrive usually before the English fisheries open and rate high in this market. The same observation applies to other English markets.

RETURN of SALMON consigned to and sold in Billingsgate Market, for 1869 and 1870.

	Boxes.	
	1869.	1870.
Scotch, ...	20,474	20,648
Irish, ...	8,800	9,211
Dutch, ...	637	626
Norwegian, ...	686	852
English and Welsh, ...	1,843	3,120

Appendix No. 22.

Appendix, No. 22.

Digest of the Principal Sections in the Acts of Parliament relating to the Irish Fisheries, with Appendices. Compiled by Thomas Francis Brady, Inspector of Irish Fisheries.

5 & 6 Vic., c. 106; 7 & 8 Vic., c. 108; 8 & 9 Vic., c. 108; 9 & 10 Vic., c. 114; 11 & 12 Vic., c. 92; 13 & 14 Vic., c. 88; 24 & 25 Vic., c. 96; 26 Vic., c. 10; 26 & 27 Vic., c. 114; 32 Vic., c. 9; 32 & 33 Vic., c. 92; and 33 & 34 Vic., c. 33.

The following extracts from the Acts of Parliament in force in Ireland, for the regulation and protection of the Fisheries, are published chiefly for the guidance of Persons empowered to enforce the provisions of the Acts of Parliament, and with the view of pointing out the particular powers they possess under the Statutes, which being extensive, should, at all times, be carried out temperately, yet firmly and strictly.

There are some provisions referred to applying to the Fresh Water portions of Rivers and Lakes which do not properly come under the cognizance of the Coast Guard. They should confine their duties exclusively to the enforcement of the Laws in the Sea, Sea Coast, and Tidal Waters of Rivers.

Particular attention should be paid to the enforcement of a strict observance of the Close Seasons, both Annual and Weekly, amongst all classes of Fishermen.

1st January, 1871. T. F. B.

☞ Note.—In case of seizure of any Net or other Engine by any person duly authorized to seize same, care should be taken that such Net or other Engine should be brought before the Magistrates at the next sitting of the Petty Sessions Court, as directed by the 102nd section of the 5th & 6th Vic., c. 106—see No 63.

No power under the Fishery Laws to seize Boats, save only on second offence against Annual or Weekly Close Season—see Nos. 10 & 30.

No power to seize Fish caught during Weekly Close Season. This power is confined to the Annual Close Season.

No power to seize Black, Foul, or Unclean Fish during the Open Season.

No power to Arrest save in cases pointed out by Nos. 5 & 6.

Coast Guard, Constables, Powers of, &c.

1. It shall be lawful for such Officers and Petty Officers belonging to the Cruisers of Her Majesty's Navy, and for such Officers and Men of the Coast Guard Stations as shall be thereunto authorized by the Commissioners of Her Majesty's Customs, at such times and in all such places, and subject to such directions and regulations as the said Commissioners of Customs shall from time to time think fit to prescribe, to go on board any Vessel employed in Fishing and examine the certificate of Registry and nets of such Vessel, and whether the regulations of Act have been complied with, and whether the Master and other Persons on board such Vessel are carrying on the said Fishery in the manner required by law, and to seize any illegal Nets or Engines, or any Nets or Engines used contrary to the Provisions of Act, or to any of the Orders, Regulations, or Bye-laws; and lawful for the Officers and Men employed in the Coast Guard Service in Ireland to execute for the purposes of Act on Sea or on Land the Warrants of any Justice as fully and effectually as any person authorized and empowered to execute Warrants of any Justice in Ireland, may now execute the same on Land within their respective Districts; and to do all such other acts on Sea or Land in relation to the preservation of peace among Persons engaged in fishing, and the enforcement of the Provisions of Act as any Constable may lawfully do within his jurisdiction.—*See* also Nos. 32 and 85.

[Margin: Officers and Men of Her Majesty's Cruisers, and Officers and Men of Coast Guard Service empowered to enforce Provisions of Act. 5 & 6 V. c. 106, s. 86. Coast Guard empowered to act as Constables.]

Note.—The Coast Guard should confine themselves to the enforcement of the Law in the Sea, Sea Coast, and Tidal Waters of Rivers, and should not incur any expenses, *unless in cases of emergency*, without the sanction of the Inspectors of Irish Fisheries. All accounts of expenses incurred should be forwarded for payment as soon as possible through the District Captain, to the Accountant-General of the Navy, and, if correct and duly authorized, will be paid.

[Margin: Coast Guard special powers. Expenses incurred.]

2. The enforcement and observance of the Annual Close Seasons for Salmon, Trout, Eel, and Oyster Fisheries respectively; the free passage of Fish during such Annual Close Seasons, and requiring for that purpose the making and maintaining of openings and removal of obstructions—the Weekly Close Seasons for Salmon and Trout—the prohibition of taking, selling, purchasing, or having in possession the Spawn, Smelts, or Fry of Salmon, or Eels, or wilfully obstructing the passage of such, or injuring or disturbing the Spawn or Fry, or any Spawning Bed, Bank or Shallow where same may be, or wilfully taking, killing, destroying, exposing to sale, or having in possession any red, black, foul, unclean, or unseasonable Salmon or Trout, or placing, laying, setting, or drawing any net, grate, creel, or other Engine or Device whatsoever (save and except Rod and line only), in any Mill-pool, or Mill-dam, or in any Works appurtenant to any Mill or Factory, or in any Water-courses leading the Water to or from such Mill or Factory for the purpose of taking or obstructing Salmon or other Fish, or the Fry thereof; or the taking any Salmon, or Trout, or Fry thereof, or spent Salmon in any Eel-weir; or having or using between sunset and sunrise any light or fire, spear, gaff, strokehaul, or other such instrument, with intent to take Salmon or other Fish in or on the Banks of any Lake or River, or chasing, injuring, or disturbing Spawning Fish, or Fish on Spawning Beds, or attempting to catch Fish in such places (except with Rod and Flies only within the lawful period), or damming, or teeming, or emptying any River or Mill-race, for the purpose of taking or destroying any Salmon, or Trout, or the Fry thereof.—*See* also 32 and 85.

[Margin: Powers of Constables, 7 & 8 V. c. 108, s. 1.]

For Seasons for Salmon and Trout—*see* Appendix.

For Seasons for Oyster Fisheries—*see* Special Book of Instructions on the subject.

3. Every Water Bailiff shall be empowered to exercise the power and authorities of a Constable for the enforcement of the provisions of Act, and shall be at liberty, at all times and seasons, without any let or hindrance whatsoever, to enter into and pass through or along the banks or borders of any

[Margin: Powers of Water Bailiffs. 5 & 6 V. c. 106, s. 64.]

APPENDIX, No. 23.

Lakes or Rivers, frequented by Salmon or Trout, or of the Tributaries thereof, for the protection of the Fisheries whereof he shall be so appointed, and with Boats or otherwise to enter upon all and every such Lakes or Rivers, and to enter upon and examine all Weirs, Sluices, Mill-dams, Mill-races, and Watercourses, communicating therewith, and to pass along the same, and to enter any boat or boats engaged in fishing, and to examine all standing, floating, or other Nets whatsoever, and to seize all illegal Nets, Engines, Instruments, and Devices whatsoever, and all and every other Nets, Engines, and Instruments whatsoever, when used illegally, and to do all such other acts and things as he shall be required to do; and the production of his Certificate of Appointment shall be sufficient Warrant for such Water Bailiff so acting in any of the cases aforesaid. Provided always that nothing herein contained shall be construed to authorize any such Water Bailiff to enter any Garden enclosed with a Wall or Paling, or any Dwelling-house, or the curtilage thereof (except where the ordinary Road or Passage to any Weir, Dam or Dyke shall be through any such Garden or curtilage as aforesaid), save when thereunto authorized by the Warrant of a Justice of the Peace as hereinafter provided.—*See* also 85.

Justices may grant a Warrant to enter excepted Places. 5 & 6 V. c. 106, s. 85.

4. It shall be lawful for any Justice of the Peace, upon information on oath, that there is probable cause to suspect any breach of the provisions of this Act to be committed within any of the before-excepted Grounds and Premises, by Warrant under his Hand and Seal, to authorize and empower by name any Water Bailiff to enter the said excepted Premises for the purpose of detecting such Offence, at such time or times, in the Day or Night, as in such Warrant may be mentioned. Provided that no such Warrant shall continue in force for more than One Week from the date thereof.

Offenders may be apprehended if they refuse to tell their Names. 5 & 6 V. c. 106, s. 87.

5. When any Person shall be found at Sea, or on Rivers, Lakes, or other Waters, or on Land, offending against any of the Provisions of Act, by the Use of any illegal Net, Engine, or Device whatsoever, for the taking of Fish, or by the use of any Net, Engine, or Device prohibited at such time, or in any other Manner, it shall be lawful for any Officer or Person herein-before empowered to enforce the Provisions of Act, or for any Person interested in the Fishery in which such illegal act may be committed, to require the Person so found offending forthwith to desist from such Offence, and also to tell his Christian Name, Surname, and Place of Abode; and in case such Person shall, after being so required, refuse to tell his real Name or Place of Abode, or shall give such a general Description of his Place of Abode as shall be illusory, for the purpose of Discovery, or shall wilfully continue such Offence, it shall be lawful for the Officer or Person so requiring as aforesaid, and also for any Person acting by his Order and in his Aid, to apprehend such Offender, and to convey him or cause him to be conveyed, as soon as conveniently may be, before a Justice of the Peace, to be dealt with according to Law. Provided always, that no Person so apprehended shall, on any pretence whatsoever, be detained for a longer period than Twenty-four Hours from the time of his Apprehension before he shall be brought before some Justice of the Peace; and that if he cannot, on account of the Absence or Distance of the Residence of any such Justice of the Peace, or owing to any other reasonable Cause, be brought before a Justice of the Peace within such Twelve Hours as aforesaid, then the Person so apprehended shall be discharged, but may, nevertheless, be proceeded against for his Offence by Summons or Warrant, as if no such Apprehension had taken place.

But not to be detained in Custody longer than 24 hours.

Penalty on Persons using Violence. 5 & 6 V. c. 106, s. 88.

6. Where any Persons, to the number of Three or more together, shall be found by any Water Bailiff or Peace Officer, by Violence, Intimidation or Menace, impeding or obstructing, or attempting to impede or obstruct, any other Person or Persons in the lawful prosecution of any Fishery, it shall be lawful for such Water Bailiff or Peace Officer so requiring, and also for any Person acting by his Order or in his Aid, to apprehend such Offenders, and to convey them before a Justice of the Peace, to be dealt with according to Law; and every Person so offending by such Violence, Intimidation, or Menace as aforesaid, and every Person then and there aiding or abetting such Offender, shall, upon being convicted thereof, forfeit, and pay for every such Offence such Penalty, not exceeding Twenty Pounds, as to the convicting Justice shall seem meet, together with the Costs of the conviction, which said Penalty shall be in addition to and independent of any other Penalty to which any such Person may be liable for any other Offence against Act.

ASSAULTING OR RESISTING.

Penalty on opposing or assaulting. 5 & 6 V. c. 106, s. 90.

7. If any Person shall assault, resist, or obstruct any of the Commissioners, or any Person acting by their authority, or any Officer of Her Majesty's Navy or Coast Guard, or any Person acting under him, or them, or any Water Bailiff in the execution of any of the Powers conferred on him by Act, or by any Rule, Order, or Bye-law to be made in pursuance of Act, or if the Master of any Fishing Vessel shall refuse to produce his Certificate of Registry when thereunto required, every Person so offending shall for every such Offence forfeit and pay any Sum not exceeding Ten Pounds.

Penalty for obstructing any Person fishing in a legal manner. 5 & 6 V. c. 106, s. 89.

8. If any Person shall resist or obstruct any Persons lawfully engaged in Fishing, or proceeding to Fish, or in returning from Fishing, or shall wilfully and maliciously place any Net or other Engine with the intent and design to prevent Fish from entering the Nets of Persons set or placed in a legal manner, he shall for every such Offence, pay a Penalty not exceeding Five Pounds; and every Net or other Engine so placed shall be forfeited.

Discharging Ballast in improper places. 5 & 6 V. c. 106, s. 14.

BALLAST.

9. No Person shall throw out, or unlade, from any Vessel the Ballast thereof, or any part thereof, within any Estuary, Harbour, or Place, unless where the same may be allowed by the Commissioners, or by the Local Regulations of such Harbour or Place—Penalty not exceeding Ten Pounds.

Appendix, No. 22.

Bye-Laws.

10. Copies of Bye-Laws obtained from the Office of Clerk of the Peace, or Clerk of Petty Sessions, and certified by him to be true copies, are legal evidences of the existence of such Bye-Laws, and the due publication thereof—*See* Abstract of Bye-Laws in Appendix.

Evidence of. 5 & 6 V. c. 106, sec. 93.

Close Seasons.

11. For Annual Close Seasons in the different Districts in Ireland—*see* Appendix.

12. The Close Season for Trout fixed to be the same as that for Salmon Fishing.—*See* Appendix.

For Trout, 13 & 14 V. c. 88, s. 43.

Note.—By 21st Section of 26th and 27th Vic., cap 114, the Annual Close Season shall not comprise fewer than 168 days in each Fishery.

13. Annual Close Season for Angling with Single Rod and Line was fixed by 23rd section 26th and 27th Vic., c. 114, to be uniform over Ireland from 1st November to 1st February. This Season has since been changed in some Districts.—*See* Appendix.

Note.—The Inspectors of Irish Fisheries are now empowered to alter Close Season for Angling, under 32nd and 33rd Vic., cap. 92, sec. 16.—For the changes made see Appendix.

14. Any Person taking or fishing for, or aiding or assisting in taking or fishing for Salmon or Trout during the Close Season, is liable to a Penalty of any sum not exceeding Ten Pounds for every such Offence, and Forfeiture of Fish and Engine by which the same may have been taken. And any Person buying, selling, or exposing for Sale, or having in his possession any Salmon or Trout, or any part thereof, so caught in the Close Time, shall forfeit such Fish and a Sum not exceeding Two Pounds for each fish; and having in possession shall be *prima facie* evidence of the fish having been caught in Close Season. And any Person placing or hanging any Coghill, or Eel Net, or Basket, or other Fixed modes of catching fish in the Eyes, Gaps, or Sluices of Eel or other Weirs, within prohibited periods, shall be liable to a penalty of Ten Pounds, and forfeiture of such Net, &c., and proof that such person is the occupier of Weir shall be *prima facie* evidence that such Nets were set by him.—Not liable to any penalty on account of using Eel Nets in the Eyes or in Gaps of Weirs, if only hung in four-fifths in number of the Eyes or Gaps of such Weir. And any Person dredging for, taking, catching, or destroying, having in his possession, selling, or buying Oysters or Oyster Brood within the Close Season for Oysters, shall forfeit such Oysters, and pay a sum not exceeding Five Pounds for each Offence. *See* also Nos. 18 and 21. Minimum of Penalties in any of the foregoing cases Ten Shillings.

Fishing for Salmon or Trout in Close Season. 5 & 6 V. c. 106, s. 30. Having in possession. 13 & 14 V. c. 88, s. 35. 5 & 6 V. c. 106, s. 36. Sec. 37. Appendix. Oysters. 11 & 12 V. c. 92, s. 42.

15. Nothing shall apply to any person who shall catch, or have in his possession Salmon or Trout for the purpose of Artificial Propagation, or other scientific purposes.

Exception for Scientific Purposes. 26 & 27 V. c. 114, s. 22.

16. If it be proved to the satisfaction of the Justices that any Boat, Cot, or Curragh, found on or near Waters frequented by Salmon or Trout, has been used for the capture of Salmon or Trout during any part of the Annual or Weekly Close Time, the persons who shall be proved to have used such Boat, Cot, or Curragh for the capture of Salmon or Trout during the Annual or Weekly Close Time, shall for the first offence be subject to a penalty not exceeding Five Pounds—and for second or any subsequent offence in addition to penalty, Boat, Cot, or Curragh may be seized and Forfeited. Boat not to be Forfeited, if used by some person other than the Owner, and the Owner proves it was so used without his knowledge or consent.

Forfeiture of Boat in illegal Fishing. 26 & 27 V. c. 114, s. 18.

Note.—Boat also liable to Forfeiture for being used in Fishing for Salmon or Trout in Fresh Water between Eight o'clock Evening and Six o'clock Morning, except so far as the same may have been used before 1864, within limits of a Several Fishery next above Tidal Flow, and held under Grant or Charter, or by immemorial usage.—*See* No. 72 "Inland Rivers."

26 & 27 V. c. 114, s. 24.

17. Any person in whose possession any part or portion of a Salmon or Trout shall be found or exposed for sale during the Close Season liable to penalty not less than Ten Shillings and not exceeding Two Pounds for each such Fish; and all persons empowered to enforce the provisions of Act, are authorized to seize all such Salmon or Trout, or any such portion thereof, when found in possession of any person, or exposed for sale during the Close Season. (*See* also No. 14.)

Having in possession part of a Salmon or Trout during Close Season. 13 & 14 V. c. 88, s. 36. 11 & 12 V. c. 92, s. 42.

18. During the Close Season for Salmon every Occupier or Farmer of any Fishery shall remove and carry away or cause to be removed and carried away, from such Fishery, and the Weirs, Dikes, and Dams connected therewith, and from the River or Stream in which such Weirs, Dikes, or Dams are placed, and from the Landing Places adjoining thereto all and every Engine, Spear, Hand Net, or other Net, Inscale, Hecks, and Rails of all Cruives, Boxes, or Cribs, used for the purpose of taking or killing Salmon, and the tops of such Cruives, Boxes, or Cribs, and all Planks and temporary Engines and Fixtures used and required for the fishing of the same; and that all and every Obstruction to the free Passage of the Fish in and through each and every such Cruive, Crib, or Box, be wholly removed and carried away, within Thirty-six Hours after the Expiration of the Open Season, and shall not be again placed or allowed to be placed or to remain therein until within Thirty-six Hours of the commencement of such Open Season; and in case any such Occupier or Farmer shall omit or neglect so to remove all and every such Net, Engine, or other Tackle, and every Contrivance or Obstruction as aforesaid, he shall forfeit all such Nets, Engines, or other Tackle or Contrivance as aforesaid, and shall for every such Offence forfeit and pay a Sum not exceeding Fifty Pounds, and shall also for every Day during which he shall suffer such Obstacles and other Things to remain and be unremoved beyond the time prescribed by Act, pay a Sum not exceeding Five Pounds: Provided always, that nothing shall be construed to render liable to

All Machinery, Nets, and Tackling for the taking of Salmon, &c. in Salmon Weirs, or other fixed Engines, shall be wholly removed during Close Seasons. 5 & 6 V. c. 106, s. 27. Penalty for Neglect. Proviso.

APPENDIX, No. 22. any Penalty any person who shall be prevented by Floods, Storm, or Stress of Weather from removing any such Net, Engine, or Tackle during the continuance of such prevention; and provided also that the Proprietor or Farmer of any Salmon Weir, now legally entitled by Patent, Charter, or otherwise, to a Right of Fishing for Eels in such Weir, and who has exercised such Right previous to the passing of Act (1842), shall not be liable to any Penalty on account of his placing, hanging, or using Coghill or Eel Nets or Baskets in the Eyes or Gaps of such Weir, if such Coghill or Eel Nets or Baskets be only used in conformity with the provisions of Act, and be only hung in Four-fifths in Number of the Eyes or Gaps of such Weir, and the other One-fifth of such Eyes or Gaps, in addition to the Queen's or Free Pass, be kept open and unobstructed for the free Passage of all Kinds of Fish; and provided also, that nothing herein contained shall be construed to exempt such Proprietor or Farmer from Liability to the Penalties by Act directed in case any Salmon or Trout shall be killed, taken, or caught in such Weir, during Close Season, or in case he shall not keep open and unobstructed, according to the provisions of Act, One-fifth in Number, as aforesaid, of the Eyes or Gaps of the said Weir. The Inscales of every Box, Crib, or Cruive shall be wholly taken out during the Close Season, so that the space within the Box shall present no obstruction or obstacle whatever to Salmon passing through such Box, &c.

Storm, Stress of Weather, &c. — Eels. — 5 & 6 V. c. 106, s. 58.

All Bag, Sole, Fly, or Stake Nets and other Engines for catching Salmon in the Tideway shall be removed during Close Season. 5 & 6 V. c. 106, s. 38. — 19 During the Close Season for Salmon, every Proprietor, Lessee, or other Person who shall be engaged in fishing for Salmon by means of Fixed Engines, shall remove and carry away, or cause to be removed and carried away, from the Poles or Fixtures to which they shall be attached, all Stake Nets, Bag Nets, Sole Nets, Fly Nets, or other Devices or Engines used for the purpose of taking Salmon, except where such Nets, Devices, or Engines shall be formed of Wood, Iron, Copper, or other rigid Substance, in which case a clear Opening of Four Feet in width shall be made and maintained in and completely through the Pouches, Traps, or Chambers, of all such Nets, Devices or Engines, from the Top to the Bottom of such Pouches, Traps, or Chambers, and in the Eyes of Flood and Ebb Weirs, commonly called Head Weirs, so as to allow the free passage of Salmon and other Fish through the same, and effectually to prevent the catching or taking of any Fish therein; and in case any such person shall omit or neglect to remove or carry away all such Nets and Engines, or, as the case may be, to make and maintain free from all Obstruction such Openings as aforesaid, during the Times aforesaid, he shall forfeit all such Nets or Engines, and shall forfeit and pay a sum not exceeding Fifty Pounds, and shall also for every Day during which such Nets or Engines shall remain and be unremoved beyond the period prescribed by Act forfeit and pay a sum not exceeding Five Pounds: Provided always, that nothing herein contained shall be construed to render liable to any Penalty any Person who shall be prevented by Storm or Stress of Weather from removing such Nets or Engines, or making such Openings as aforesaid, during the continuance of such prevention.

Forfeiture. — Penalty. — Stress of Weather.

Nets to be removed, &c. 13 & 14 V. c. 88, s. 34. 5 & 6 V. c. 106, s. 66. — 20. Every Proprietor, Lessee, or other Person who shall be engaged in Fishing for Salmon by means of Nets of any kind, shall remove and carry them away during the Yearly Close Season under a penalty of not less than Two Pounds and Forfeiture of Nets. Penalty for fishing with any Nets whatever except Eel Nets, in Inland Waters during the Salmon Close Season, Ten Pounds.

Fixed Engines for Eels not to be set between 10th January and 1st July. 5 & 6 V. c. 106, s. 21. — 21. Not lawful for any person between the 10th day of January, and 1st day of July (except in such places where the Season may have been altered), to hang or fix any Coghill, Eel or other Net or Basket, or Basket-work, in the Eye, Gap, or Sluice of any Eel or other Weir in any River, or to make use of any other Fixed Engine for taking Eels—or between the 1st July and 10th January, to keep or leave such Net, Basket, or other Engine, Set or in the Water in the Eye, Gaps or Sluices of such Eel or other Weirs between Sunrise and Sunset; and taking, or suffering to be taken, in any
s. 77. Eel Weir any Salmon, or Trout, or Fry thereof—penalty, Ten Pounds.—For Seasons for fishing for Eels with fixed Nets, see Appendix.

Angling. 5 & 6 V. c. 106, s. 69. — 22. Any person Angling for Salmon or Trout during Close Season liable to penalty not exceeding Five Pounds.

NOTE.—Power in certain persons to Open Passage Shut during Close Season.—See 8 & 9 V., c. 108, s. 10. No. 32.

CLOSE TIME—WEEKLY.

Weekly. 26 & 27 V. c. 114, s. 20. — 23 Weekly Close Time, between Six of the Clock on Saturday Morning, and Six of the Clock on Monday Morning

5 & 6 V. c. 106, ss. 40, 66. 13 & 14 V. c. 88, s. 33. 5 & 6 V. c. 106, s. 66. — 24 No person shall Lay, Draw, or Fish with any Nets whatever for Salmon or Trout, or take any Salmon or Trout in any Crib, Box, Cruive, Eye, or Gap, in any Salmon, Eel, or other Weir, or in Fresh Water portions of Rivers use any Net whatever for any kind of Fish (except Nets for taking Eels) during the Weekly Close Season.—See 27 & 28.

25. All Fishing for Salmon and Trout, save with Single Rod and Line excepted, prohibited during Weekly Close Season.

Weekly Close Season. 5 & 6 V. c. 106, s. 40. — 26. During such time in each Stake, Flood, Ebb, or Head Weir and Stake Net, a clear opening of at least Four Feet in width shall be made, and kept from Obstruction in the Pouches, Traps, Chambers, or Eyes of the same from Bottom to Top thereof, so as effectually to allow of the free passage of Salmon and other Fish, and the Netting of the Leader of every Bag, Fly, Sole, or other Fixed Net shall be raised and kept out of the water; and in all Rivers, Lakes and Tideways, all other Nets and Baskets whatsoever, except those used for the taking of Eels, shall be wholly removed and taken out of the water for the space of time above-mentioned; and the Inscales or Gates, and Rails, or Framework of all such Cribs, Boxes, or Cruives, for the catching of Salmon, &c., shall be removed out of, or opened in each such Crib, &c., in every Salmon and other Weir wherein Salmon may be caught, in such a manner that a clear opening of not less than Four Feet in width from the Bottom to the Top shall be left therein, and a free, direct, and uninterrupted space or opening of said width shall be effectually secured for the passage of Fish of all kinds, both up and down through such Cribs, &c.—*See* also 5 & 6 V. c. 106, s. 58, No. 53.

APPENDIX. No. 22.

27. Penalty for non-observance, or for using any means or device to prevent the Free Passage, or Frightening or Scaring, or attempting to Frighten or Scare any Salmon from passing, or taking any Salmon during the time specified—not less than Ten Pounds, and not exceeding Fifty Pounds: Provided such person shall not be prevented by Floods, Storm, or Stress of Weather from removing such Leaders, or making such Openings. *See* also 28.

Penalty for non-observance. 13 & 14 V. c. 88, s. 46.

28. In addition to the Penalty provided by the Salmon Fishery Acts, any Net or other Instrument, or the Inscales or Gates and Rails of any Crib, Box, or Cruive used between the times aforesaid, shall be Forfeited; and also when any Salmon or Trout is taken at any Fishing Weir during the times aforesaid, or when any Box is left unopened or not in conformity with the Acts, the Penalty shall be payable in respect of each Box or Crib, &c., in which any fish is so illegally taken, or which is left unopened or not in conformity with Acts.

Further Penalty by 26 & 27 V. c. 114, s. 20.

29. Any person Scaring, Impeding, or Obstructing the Free passage of Salmon or Trout during the Times aforesaid, shall incur a Penalty not less than Two Pounds, and not exceeding Ten Pounds, with Forfeiture of any Fish taken by him, and any Net or Instrument used by him.

This Section does not apply to any Person who takes Fish legally by the Single Rod and Line, during the Weekly Close Season.

Scaring or obstructing Fish during Weekly Close Season. 26 & 27 V. c. 114, s. 25.

30. If it be proved to the satisfaction of the Justices that any Boat, Cot, or Curragh found on or near Waters frequented by Salmon or Trout, has been used for the Capture of Salmon or Trout during any part of the Annual or Weekly Close Time, the persons who shall be proved to have used such Boat, Cot, or Curragh for the Capture of Salmon or Trout, during the Annual or Weekly Close Time, shall for the first Offence be subject to a Penalty not exceeding Five Pounds, and for second or any subsequent Offence in addition to Penalty, Boat, Cot or Curragh, may be seized and forfeited. —*See* also No. 16.

Forfeiture of Boat in illegal Fishing. 26 & 27 V. c. 114, sec. 18.

31. During the Weekly Close Season, the sluices which admit the water to the wheels of all Mills or Factories and all Waste Gates shall at all seasons of the Year be kept shut for twenty-four consecutive hours in each week, between six o'clock on Saturday afternoon, and six o'clock on Monday morning, so that the water may be allowed to flow freely through any existing Gap in such Weir, or any Fish Passage formed therein, or where no Gap or Fish Pass, through the waste gate on the up-stream side of the wheel sluices of such mill, and the Waste Gates shall in such latter case be kept open. *See* 13 and 14 V., c. 88, s. 39—and 5 & 6 V., c. 106, s. 63.—*See* also 41, 42, 43.

Sluices of Mills to be kept shut, &c. 5 & 6 V. c. 106, s. 63 and 13 & 14 V. c. 88, s. 39.

32. It shall be lawful for Constabulary and Coast Guard, and any person acting under authority of the Commissioners (now Inspectors), when and as often as they or any of them shall, in any Fishing Weir, Net, or Contrivance, during the Weekly or other Close Season, find any Passage shut, closed, or obstructed, or during such Close Time in any place find any Net or other Contrivance placed or used where the same are now by Law, or may be prohibited by the Commissioners, or shall at any time find any Obstruction in the Queen's Share or Free Gap, through or over any Fishing or other Weir, or in the Sluice Passages appurtenant to any Mill or Factory, at any time when the Sluice Gate of same shall be open, then and so often to Open such Passages and remove all such Obstructions, doing no unnecessary damage; and to seize and remove all Nets and parts of Nets which may be found so Placed or used contrary to Provisions of Act. Nothing to exempt any person from the Penalties and Forfeitures prescribed by Act, in respect to any of the matters aforesaid—not liable for any damage caused by Opening such Passage, or removal of Nets or Obstructions.

Constabulary and Coast Guard empowered to open passages during Close Season. 8 & 9 V. c. 108, s. 10.

COMPLAINTS.

33. All Offences against Act, or any By-law, &c., may be determined on in a summary way by one or more Justices, on the complaint, verbal or otherwise, of any person.

Offences. 5 & 6 V. c. 106, s. 94.

EEL FIXTURES.

See Nos. 14, 18, 19, 20, 21, 24, 26, 63, 71, 75, 76, 95.

ENTERING LANDS.

34. If any person or persons shall enter upon any Lands or Premises, for the purpose or under the pretence of fishing or angling in any Lake, River, Stream, Pond, or Water, without Authority in Writing, from the Proprietor or Occupier of such Lands or Premises, every such person shall forfeit and pay a sum not exceeding the sum of Two Pounds for every such Offence.

See also "Private Waters."

Penalty on Persons entering Lands without permission. 5 & 6 V. c. 106, s. 71.

M

Appendix, No. 22.

Fishing near Mouths of Rivers.

Fixed Nets not to be placed in Narrow Channels. 5 & 6 V., c. 106, s. 22.

Or within One Mile of Mouth of River, &c. Ib.

35. Not lawful for any Person, save the Proprietor of a Several Fishery in the whole of the Estuary and River, to erect any Fixed Net in such part of any Estuary, or Tidal part of any River frequented by Salmon, where the breadth of the Channel at Low Water of Ordinary Spring Tides is less than Three Quarters of a Mile Statute Measure; unless in cases where the Engine was erected for Twenty Years previous to 1842, or for Ten Years within the limits of a Several Fishery; and not lawful for any Person, save the Proprietor of a Several Fishery within the limits thereof, to erect any Fixed Net within One Mile of the Mouth of any River frequented by Salmon, where the breadth of such Mouth is less than Half a Mile at Low Water of Ordinary Spring Tides. Penalty, not exceeding Thirty Pounds, and forfeiture of Net.

Stretching Nets across mouths of rivers, &c. 5 & 6 V. c. 106, s. 27. 5 & 6 Vic. c. 106, s. 27, and 13 & 14 V. c. 88, s. 44.

36. Not lawful for any person, save and except the Proprietor of a Several Fishery in the whole of a river and its tributaries, to shoot, draw, or stretch Nets entirely across the Mouth or across any other part of any River. Penalty not exceeding Ten Pounds. Nor lawful for any person, save and except the Proprietor of a Several Fishery, within the limits thereof at any time to use Nets for taking Salmon at the Mouth of any River where the Breadth of such Mouth shall not exceed Quarter of a mile Statute Measure; or within Half-a-mile from the mouth of any River, such Mouth to be defined by the Commissioners. Penalty not exceeding Ten Pounds, nor less than One Pound, and a further Penalty of Five Shillings for every Fish taken, and forfeiture of Net.

Or so as to be injurious to free passage of Fish. 13 & 14 V. c. 88, s. 44.

37. Not lawful for any person, save the Proprietor of a Several Fishery in the whole of a River and its Tributaries to Shoot, Draw, Stretch, or use Nets at the Mouth, or any other part of any River in such wise as in the judgment of the Commissioners to be injurious to the Free Passage of Fish, and which they shall have prohibited by Bye-Law. Penalty not exceeding Ten Pounds, nor less than One Pound, and a further Penalty of Five Shillings for every Fish taken; and forfeiture of Net.

Note.—For Mouths of Rivers defined—see Appendix.

Prohibition of Bag Nets in certain places. 26 & 27 V. c. 114, s. 3.

38. No Bag Net shall be placed or allowed to continue in any River, or the Estuary of any River, as such River or Estuary has been defined by the Commissioners, or shall be defined by the Commissioners, or within a distance of less than Three Statute Miles from the Mouth of any River, as defined But where Owner of Bag Net within Three Miles of the Mouth of any River, has the exclusive right of catching Salmon in the whole of such River, and all Tributary Rivers and Lakes on its course, foregoing Provision as to Three Miles shall not apply.

Penalty 26 & 27 V. c. 114, s. 3.

39. Any Bag Net placed in contravention of foregoing Provision may be taken possession of or destroyed, and any Salmon taken therewith shall be forfeited.—Penalty not less than Five Pounds, and not exceeding Twenty Pounds for every Day Bag Net so placed.

Fish Passages.

Fish Passes. 5 & 6 V. c. 106, s. 61.

40. All Dams, Weirs, Dykes, or other Erections which shall after the passing of Act (1842), be placed in or across any River frequented by Salmon, shall be so built as to permit the free run or migration of Salmon and other Fish at all periods of the year, and at the expense of person forming such Weir, &c., and in such manner as the Commissioners shall approve.

Existing Weirs. 5 & 6 V. c. 106, s. 61.

41. In all Weirs, Dams, or Dykes at present (1842) erected in or across such Rivers, lawful for the Commissioners, on the application of one or more persons interested in the Fishing of such River, and at the Costs and Charges of such persons to direct such alterations to be made therein, or such additional work to be added thereto, as shall in the opinion of the Commissioners be necessary and desirable for the purpose of affording a free and uninterrupted passage to Fish.—Not to impair Navigation or lessen or impair the effective working power of Mill or Factory. And where such means of migration of Fish, (or Fish Passes) have been built in Weirs, the Owners or Occupiers of all such Mills or Factories are required at any time during which such Mill or Factory shall not be at work, or where the Water-wheel or Water-courses thereof shall not be undergoing such repairs as shall require the Water above such Mill to be run off, to stop and close up in dry seasons all other Waste Gates or Overfalls, so as to direct and force the surplus Water of such River or Stream through the Fish Passage: Penalty for non-observance, any sum not exceeding Five Pounds.

Penalty.

Further provisions. 13 & 14 V. c. 88, s. 39.

42. The Waste Sluices, Waste Gates, or Overfalls, shall at all seasons of the year, when and during the time the Mills or Factories shall not be used for Milling Purposes, be kept open, if no passage for Fish be provided; and when such passage provided, the Sluices which admit the Water, and the Waste Sluices, Waste Gates, and Overfalls, shall be kept down and shut to force the water through such passage for Fish. Penalty for neglect not less than Two Pounds, nor more than Ten Pounds for every offence.—No injury to be done by the Opening or Shutting of such Sluices, to the Machinery or Water Power.

During Weekly Close Season. 5 & 6 V. c. 106, s. 62.

43. During the Weekly Close Season the Sluices, &c., shall at all seasons of the year be kept shut up for Twenty-four consecutive hours in each week, so that the water may be allowed to go freely through any existing Gap or Passage in such Weir, &c.

Fishing at or near Fish Passages.

44. It shall not be lawful for any person to take, kill, or destroy any Salmon or other Fish, or hang, fix, use or set in such Fish Passage made through natural obstructions, Mill Dams, Weirs, or other similar Works, any Net, Basket or other Engine or Contrivance whatsoever for the taking

APPENDIX. No. 22.

of Fish, or to place any Obstacle or Contrivance of any kind soever, in or near thereto, in order to deter Fish from freely entering or passing up and down through the same, at all periods of the year, but the Fish Pass shall be kept and preserved free from every Obstruction, and all such Obstructions shall be removed in like manner as in the case of Free Gaps and Queen's Shares in Fishing Weirs. Penalty any sum not exceeding Twenty Pounds.—If offence committed by person in employment or under control of Owner or Occupier of Mill, or with the knowledge or connivance of Owner or Occupier or Person in charge of Mill, or through default of reasonable precaution on the part of the Owner or Occupier to prevent offence, then Owner or Occupier liable to penalty.

5 & 6 V. c. 106, s. 64. Penalty.

45. No fishing (Rods and Lines only excepted) allowed within Two Hundred Yards of a Milldam, unless such right has been exercised for Twenty Years before passing of Act, (1850).—Penalty not less than Two Pounds nor more than Ten Pounds, and Forfeiture of Net—nor within Fifty Yards of a Milldam, unless there be attached thereto a Fish Pass approved by the Commissioners, nor unless it shall have constantly running through it such a Flow of Water as will enable Salmon to pass up and down it. *See also No. 93.*

Fishing near Milldams. 13 & 14 V. c. 88, s. 37. 26 & 27 V. c. 114, s. 14.

46. Salmon Passes and Fish Ladders shall be at all Times open to the Inspection of the Commissioners, and the Conservators of the District, and of any Person duly authorized by them or any of them.

To be open to Inspection. 26 & 27 V. c. 114, s. 31.

Fishing Weirs.

47. Within Twelve Months after the commencement of this Act (Act dated 28th July, 1863), Free Gaps shall be made in all Fishing Weirs according to the following Regulations:—Penalty not less than Five Pounds and not exceeding Fifty Pounds for every Day after the expiration of such period of Twelve Months, during which Free Gaps are not made:—

Free Gaps in Fishing Weirs. 26 & 27 V. c. 114, ss. 9 & 12.

- The Free Gap shall be situate in the deepest part of the Stream: *Sec. 9.*
- The Sides of the Gap shall be in a Line with and Parallel to the Direction of the Stream at the Weir:
- The bottom of the Gap shall be level with the natural Bed of the Stream above and below the Gap:
- The Width of the Gap in its narrowest Part shall be not less than One-tenth Part of the Width of the Stream: Provided always, that such Gap shall not be required to be wider than Fifty Feet, and shall not in any case be narrower than Three Feet: and provided also, that no existing Gap in any Weir shall be reduced in Width, or a Gap of less Width substituted in lieu thereof, or any Alteration made therein so as to reduce the Flow of Water through such Gap:
- Where a Free Gap has been made in a Weir, but the same is not maintained in accordance with Act, the owner of such Weir shall incur a Penalty not exceeding Five Pounds a Day for each Day he is in default: *Sec. 12.*
- No alteration shall be made in the Bed of any River in such manner as to reduce the Flow of Water through a Free Gap: If it is, the person making the same shall incur a Penalty not less than Five Pounds and not exceeding Fifty Pounds, and a further Penalty of One Pound a Day until he restores the Bed of the River to its original State:

48. No person shall place any Obstruction, use any Contrivance, or do any Act whereby Fish may be scared, deterred, or in any way prevented from freely entering and passing up and down a Free Gap at all Periods of the Year, or shall use any Nets or other Engines within Fifty Yards above or below any Free Gap; and any person placing any Obstruction, using any Contrivance, Net or Engine, or doing any Act in contravention of the Regulation lastly herein before contained, shall incur a penalty not less than Five Pounds and not exceeding Twenty Pounds for the First Offence, and not less than Ten Pounds and not exceeding Fifty Pounds for each subsequent Offence. *See also No. 50.*

Obstructing or deterring Fish from Entering. 26 & 27 V. c. 114, s. 12.

49. In any case where the Breadth of the River where any Chartered or Patent Fishing Weir now exists shall not exceed Forty Feet, and it might be inexpedient to require a Free Gap to be made therein, the Commissioners may, if they think fit, instead thereof, direct by their Order the Extension of the Weekly Close Time for a Period of Twenty-four Hours.—(*See* Appendix.)

Extension of Weekly Close Season, where Gap inexpedient. 26 & 27 V. c. 114, s. 11.

50. No person shall Fish with Rod and Line, or in any other manner, in any Part of the Free Gap or Queen's Share, in any Weir in any River, or hang, fix, set, or use, within the space of Fifty Yards above or below any part of such Weir, any Net, Basket, or other Engine for the taking of Fish or in order to deter or prevent Fish from going up or down the same, or place any obstruction, or throw any Gravel, Clay, Stones, or other matter into the same, nor shall beat the Water, or place or set any bridge, board, cloth, or any other thing in, over, or across the same, save a temporary bridge or board during the time only when the person engaged in fishing said Weirs shall be passing over the same, nor shall in any manner prevent the free and uninterrupted passage of Fish through the same, at all Periods of the Year; Penalty for every Offence, a sum not exceeding Thirty Pounds; and all such Obstructions shall be removed at the expense of such person upon the Order of the Justices imposing penalty; proof that such person is the Occupier or Owner of such Weir shall be taken as prima facie that such Obstructions were placed by him.

No obstructions to be placed near Queen's share nor shall any person fish in or near same. 5 & 6 V. c. 106, s. 57.

Appendix. No. 22

Boxes and Cribs. 26 & 27 V. c. 114, sec. 10.

31. The following Rules shall be observed in relation to the construction of Boxes and Cribs in Fishing Weirs and Fishing Milldams.—

The Upper Surface of the Sill shall be level with the Bed of the River:

The Bars or Inscales of the Heck or Upstream side of the Box or Crib shall not be nearer each other than Two Inches, and shall be capable of being removed, and shall be placed perpendicularly:

The Boxes, Cribs, or Cruives shall not be built over, or in any other manner hidden from public Inspection.

Note.—Power in Commissioners to authorise the lessening of the width between the bars where the principal or a considerable part of the value of any Weir has consisted in catching Trout. 5 & 6 V., c. 106, s. 58—Appendix.

Penalty

32. Penalty for not making Boxes and Cribs in conformity with foregoing regulations not less than Five Pounds, and not exceeding Twenty Pounds for every day of failure in complying with these Provisions; and not less than One Pound, and not exceeding Five Pounds for every day failing to maintain Boxes accordingly.

Further Regulations as to Boxes in Weirs. 5 & 6 V. c. 106, s. 58.

33. During the Weekly Close Season the Inscales of every Box, Crib, or Cruive, used for the taking of Salmon, shall be opened to the full width of Four Feet, and the Upstream Rails shall be entirely removed or taken out, or so opened and fastened back that a Space of Four Feet shall be completely free and clear in each such Box, Crib, or Cruive. *See also* 56.

Spur and Tail Walls. 5 & 6 V. c. 106, s. 54.

34. It shall not be lawful to construct or attach to, or permit to remain if already constructed or attached to any Cruive Weir or Cruive Dam used for fishing in any river any Spur or Tail Wall, Leader or Outrigger, of any kind or description whatever, of a greater length than Twenty Feet, from the Upper or Lower side respectively of the Walls or Piers of such Weir or Dam, except the Wall or Leader connecting the Cribs of such Weir or Dam with the Bank of the River; nor shall any such Wall, Leader or Outrigger, be so built or constructed as to narrow up or prevent the ingress or discharge of the water through or from the Free Opening or Queen's Share in River or Stream; nor shall any Island or natural formation in any River be so made use of as to secure the proprietor of any Fishery the same advantage which such proprietor would have obtained by the erection of a Tail Wall of greater length than Twenty Feet; nor shall any such Walls or Leaders be constructed or suffered to remain in Narrow Rivers or other places of a greater length than the Commissioners upon application made to them for that purpose, shall determine and approve. —Penalty not exceeding Twenty Pounds and Five Pounds a Day.

5 & 6 V. c. 106, s. 55.

Not to extend to Weirs, Banks, or Heads used for sustaining Mills and Navigation, if such shall not be made use of for the purpose of taking Fish.

Boxes or Nets not to be used within Fifty Yards of Milldam. 26 & 27 Vic., c. 114, s. 16.

35. No Box, Crib, Cruive, Net or other Instrument (Rods and Lines only excepted), shall be used at or within Fifty Yards of a Milldam, unless there is attached thereto a Fish Pass approved by the Commissioners, and which shall have constantly running through it such a Flow of Water as will enable Salmon to pass up and down it. *See also* 93.

During Weekly Close Season. 26 & 27 V. c. 114, s. 16.

36. Any Net or other Instrument, or the Inscales or Gates and Rails of any Crib, Box, or Cruive used during the Weekly Close Season to be Forfeited; and when any Salmon or Trout taken during such time, or when any Box, Crib, or Cruive is during such time left unopened, the penalty shall be in respect of each Box, &c., in which any Fish is so taken or is left unopened.

For Fishing Weirs in Ireland, *see* Appendix.

Fixed Nets.

Prohibition of Bag Nets in certain places. 26 & 27 V. c. 114, s. 3.

37. No Bag Net shall be placed or allowed to continue in any River, or the Estuary of any River, as such River or Estuary has been defined by the Commissioners, or shall be defined by the Commissioners, or within a distance of less than Three Statute Miles from the Mouth of any River, as defined. But where Owner of Bag Net within Three Miles of the Mouth of any River, has the exclusive right of catching Salmon in the whole of such River, and all Tributary Rivers and Lakes of its course, foregoing provisions with respect to Three Miles does not apply. No Bag Net allowed within any Estuary of a River as defined.

Penalty. 26 & 27 V. c. 114, s. 3.

38. Any Bag Net placed in contravention of foregoing provisions may be taken possession of or destroyed, and any Salmon taken therewith shall be forfeited. Penalty not less than Five Pounds, and not exceeding Twenty Pounds for every Day Bag Net so placed.

Penalty on new Fixed Nets. 26 & 27 V. c. 114, s. 4.

39. No Fixed Net that was not legally erected for catching Salmon or Trout, during the open Season of One thousand eight hundred and sixty-two, shall be placed or used for catching Salmon or Trout. Any Net placed or used contrary hereto may be taken possession of or destroyed; and any Salmon taken forfeited, and the Owner thereof is liable to a Penalty not less than Five Pounds, and not exceeding Twenty Pounds for each Day of so placing or using the same.

Regulations as to 5 & 6 V. c. 106, s. 20.

40. No engine formed of Wood, Iron, or other rigid material having Meshes or Openings of less width than Three Inches on each side of the Square, and where no Meshes or Openings of the nature of reticulations shall be used of less width between the Bars than Two Inches, shall be used on any part of the Coast, or in any Bay, Estuary, or Tideway, save by the Proprietor of the whole of the Fishery of the River flowing into such Bay, or from the Mouth to the Source thereof including Tributaries. Penalty not exceeding Ten Pounds. Power in Commissioners to alter Meshes.—*See* Appendix.

APPENDIX. No. 22.

61 Not lawful for any Person, save the Proprietor of a Several Fishery in the whole of the Estuary and River, to erect any Fixed Net in such parts of any Estuary, or Tidal part of any River frequented by Salmon, where the breadth of the Channel at Low Water of "Ordinary" Spring Tides is less than Three Quarters of a Mile Statute Measure; and not lawful for any Person, save the Proprietor of a Several Fishery within the limits thereof, to erect any Fixed Net within One Mile of the Mouth of any River frequented by Salmon, where the breadth of such Mouth is less than Half a Mile at Low Water of "Ordinary" Spring Tides. Penalty, not exceeding Thirty Pounds, and forfeiture of Net.

Fixed Nets not to be erected in Narrow Channels. 5 & 6 V., c. 106, s. 22. 26 & 27 V. c. 114, s. 19

62. Stake Nets shall not extend further than from High to Low Water Mark of Ordinary Spring Tides, save and except in the case of Ebb and Flood Weirs commonly called Head Weirs; nor shall any such Weir be so constructed as to be capable of taking Young or Unsizeable Fish. The Netting of all Fixed Nets shall be extended evenly, so that the Meshes shall be stretched to their full opening. Bag Nets shall be so placed that the Leaders can be kept and raised out of the Water. Stake Nets shall be so placed that clear openings of at least Four Feet in width shall be made and kept from obstruction in the Pouches, Traps, Chambers, or Eyes of the same, from the Bottom to the Top, so as effectually to allow the free passage of Salmon and other Fish through such Pouches, Traps, Chambers and Eyes during the Weekly Close Time.

Stake Nets not to extend beyond low water mark 5 & 6 V c. 106, s. 26. Ordinary 26 & 27 V. c. 114, s. 13 5 & 6 V c. 106, s. 36.

NOTE.—By the 44th Section 26th and 27th V. c. 114, a "Head Weir" is now included under the expression "Fixed Net."

5 & 6 V. c. 106, s. 44.

63. Fixed Engines for Eels not to be used between 10th January and 1st July, save where Season may be altered—or between 1st July and 10th January between Sunrise and Sunset. For Places where this Season has been altered, *see* Appendix. And any Person taking, or suffering to be taken, in any Eel Weir, any Salmon, or Trout, or Fry thereof, liable to Penalty of Ten Pounds.

For Eels 5 & 6 V. c. 106, s. 31. S. 77.

64. Any person who shall Fish with, make use of, or erect any Fixed Engine for the capture of Salmon, without having obtained a Certificate for same, shall Forfeit such Fixed Engine and incur a penalty of Fifty Pounds and a further Penalty of Twenty Pounds for every day during which it shall have been erected, used, or fished with; and any person authorised to enforce provisions of Acts, may seize and take possession of such Fixed Engine.
For Certificates issued, *see* Appendix.

Penalty for Fishing with Fixed Engine for Salmon without Certificate. 32 & 33 V. c. 92, s. 16

65 In all cases where any person has any right of Appeal against any Judgment, Order, Proceeding, or Conviction for placing, erecting, maintaining, or using any Fixed Net or Engine, or any part thereof, such Appeal shall be to the next going Judges of Assize at the Assizes to be held for the County, or for the City or place where such Judgment, &c., shall have been given, or such alleged offence shall have been committed; provided that such Assizes shall be held at any time not less than Twenty-one Days after the time such Judgment, &c., shall have been given; and in case such Assizes shall be held within Twenty-one Days from the time of such Judgment, &c., such Appeal shall be to the going Judges of Assizes to be holden next but one after such Judgment, &c.—and no such Appeal shall be allowed unless the party appealing shall within Ten Days next after, or if the Court appealed from shall think fit so to require it, immediately on the pronouncing of such Judgment, &c., enter into a recognizance with Two sufficient Sureties in a Sum not less than £50, to appear at the said Assizes, and abide the Judgment of the said Judges there, and to pay such costs and expenses as the Judges at Assizes may award against him.
For Mouths of Rivers defined, *see* Appendix.
For Fixed Nets in Ireland, *see* Appendix.

Appeal against Convictions for erecting or using any Fixed Net. 13 & 14 V. c. 88, s. 51.

FRY.

66. If any person shall wilfully take, sell, purchase, or have in his possession, the Spawn, Smolts, or Fry of Salmon or Trout, or of Eels, or in any way, or by any Device wilfully obstruct the Passage of the said Smolts or Fry, or injure or disturb any Spawn or Fry, or any Spawning Bed, Bank, or Shallow where the same may be, such person shall forfeit and pay a sum not exceeding Ten Pounds for each and every such Offence, and all Nets, Engines, and Devices, used in the taking of the same, or whereby any such injury shall be caused shall be forfeited. Nothing shall apply to having in possession Salmon or Trout for Artificial Propagation or other Scientific Purposes—nor prejudice the right of any owner to take materials from any stream.

Penalty for having, taking, or attempting to take Fry and Spawn of Salmon, Trout or Eels, 5 & 6 V. c. 106, s. 72. 26 & 27 V c. 114, s. 22.

67. The word "Salmon" shall extend to and include Grilse, Peale, Sea Trout, Samlets, Par, &c., and the Spawn and fry thereof.

13 & 14 V. c. 88, s. 1.

68. And the words "Jenkin," "Gravelling," are deemed to be Salmon.

26 & 27 V. c. 114, s. 14.

ILLEGAL NETS.

69 In case any officer or person authorized and empowered to seize Illegal Nets or Engine, or Nets or Engines of a legal form and size, when used contrary to the Provisions of Act or any of the Bye-Laws to be made in pursuance of Act, shall seize the same, it shall and may be lawful for him to retain the same in his custody until the next sitting of the Petty Sessions Court, or any adjournment thereof, in the District where the same shall be seized, and at such Petty Sessions Court it shall and may be lawful for the Justices to order and direct the same to be Forfeited, and in case the same shall be such as cannot be legally used according to the provisions of Act, to order the same to be

Illegal Nets shall be brought before Magistrates at Petty Sessions, and destroyed. 5 & 6 V c. 106, s. 103.

Appendix, No. 22.

And Legal Nets when used Illegally shall, when forfeited, be sold.

destroyed, and in case the same shall be such as may be legally used according to the provisions of Act, that then and in such case it shall be lawful for such Justices to order the same to be sold, and the money arising therefrom to be applied in the same manner as the penalties imposed for violation of the provisions of Act are directed to be applied. *See* No. 105.

Boats. 26 & 27 V. c. 114, s. 18.

70. Boats may also be forfeited in certain cases for breach of Annual or Weekly Close Season.—*See* Annual and Weekly Close Seasons, Nos 16 and 30.

Inland Rivers.

Taking Salmon in Inland Rivers. 5 & 6 V. c. 106, s. 65.

71. In the Inland and Fresh Water portions of Rivers and Lakes in Ireland, no person, save the Owner of a Several Fishery within the Limits thereof, shall, at any period of the year, lay, draw, make use of, or fish with Haul, Draft, Seine or other Net, for the taking of Salmon or Trout, unless in cases where a general public Right of Fishing for Salmon with such Nets, in the nature of a common of Piscary,* has been enjoyed for a space of Twenty Years next before the passing of Act; and if any person shall offend contrary hereto, such person so offending shall forfeit all such Nets so used, and shall also forfeit and pay a sum not exceeding Ten Pounds. Penalty for fishing with any Nets whatsoever, except Eel Nets, in Inland Waters, during the Salmon Annual or Weekly Close Season, not exceeding Ten Pounds.

5 & 6 V. c. 106, s. 66.

* Note.—The claim of the right in the public to fish in Fresh Water Rivers cannot be sustained.—Murphy v. Ryan, C. P. 1868.

Nets during certain hours in Rivers prohibited. 26 & 27 V. c. 114, s. 24.

72. No person shall use any Net except a Landing Net, for the capture of Salmon or Trout in the Fresh Water portion of any River, as defined by the Commissioners, between the hours of Eight o'clock in the Evening and Six o'clock in the Morning, except so far as the same may have heretofore been used within the limits of a Several Fishery, next above the Tidal Flow, and held under Grant or Charter, or by immemorial usage. Penalty not exceeding Ten Pounds, and forfeiture of all Boats, Nets, and Gear.

For Tidal and Fresh Water Limits—*See* Appendix.

Fishing with Nets near Milldams. 26 & 27 V. c. 114, s. 16.

73. No person shall use any Box, Crib, Cruive, Net, Instrument, or Device for taking Fish (save and except Rods and Lines only), at or within Fifty Yards either above or below a Milldam, unless there is attached to such Milldam a Fish Pass of such Form and Dimensions as may be approved by the Commissioners, nor unless such Fish Pass has constantly running through it such a Flow of Water as will enable Salmon to pass up and down it.—Penalty not less than Five Pounds, and not exceeding Twenty Pounds.

See also No. 93

Turbines or other Machines. 26 & 27 V. c. 114, s. 20.

74. Where Turbines or similar Hydraulic Machines are used, the person owning or using same shall, during the descent of Salmon, or Young of Salmon to the Sea, provide a Grating or other efficient means to prevent such Salmon or Young of Salmon passing into such Machine. Penalty not exceeding Fifty Pounds, and Five Pounds a Day.

Fishing with False-bottomed Nets, or Nets one behind the other, &c., &c. 5 & 6 V. c. 106, s. 08.

75. No person shall make Use of or Fish with any Net formed with a False Bottom (except Nets for the taking of Eels), or shall place Two or more Nets, one behind the other, or use any Nets covered with Canvas, Hide, or other Substance, for the purpose of taking Small Fish, or shall affix, or keep up continued Nets stretched across any River; or place, affix, or attach any Nets to any Stakes, Bridges, Sluices, Lock-gates of Canals, or other such fixed erections. Penalty forfeiture of Net, and any sum not exceeding Ten Pounds.

Note.—As to Cross Lines in—see No. 93.
As to Meshes of Nets in—see No. 88.

Licences.

Engines for Salmon &c., to be Licensed. 11 & 12 V. c. 92, s. 8. 26 & 27 V. c. 114, s. 26

76. All Engines, Nets, Instruments, or Devices whatsoever, used for the taking of Salmon, Trout, Pollen, or Fish of the Salmon and Trout kind, or for the taking of Eels, and all fixed Salmon, Trout, or Eel Fisheries within any District, or on or off the Sea Coast thereof, shall, before the same be used in any year, be duly licensed and rated, upon payment of the Licence Duty or Rate, as the case may be. For amount of Licence Duty—*see* Appendix.

Saving for Trout, &c. 11 & 12 V. c. 92, s. 31.

77. Rods used singly for taking Trout, Perch, Pike or other Fish, save and except Salmon, shall not be subject to any Licence Duty.

White Trout. 13 & 14 V. c. 88, s. 1.

78. Rods used for taking White Trout subject to Licence Duty—*see* definition of "White Trout."

11 & 12 V. c. 92, s. 30.

79. If any person shall have paid a Licence for a Rod within any District, such person shall not be liable to pay an additional sum for a Licence in any other District, by reason only of Angling with a Rod in any other District.

11 & 12 V. c. 92, s. 31.

80. But no Licence confers on the holder any right to fish, not otherwise possessed.

Licences for Angling not transferable. 32 & 33 V. c. 92, s. 17.

81. Every Licence to fish with Single Rod and Line shall have the name and address of the person to whom the same shall be sold written thereon in clear and legible characters, and such Licence shall not be transferred to or available to any person except the person named therein. Penalty for breach, same as for fishing without Licence.—*See* 84-86.

82. Cross Lines for any description of fish liable to Licence Duty.

83. Not lawful for any person (save the proprietor of a Several Fishery, or any person duly authorized by him, in writing), to use Cross Lines for the capture of Salmon or Trout in any River—Penalty not exceeding Five Pounds.

Cross Lines prohibited, &c. 5 & 6 V. c. 106, s. 70.

84. Penalty for using Engines subject to Licence Duty without the same being duly Licensed for such year, not less than double nor more than treble the Licence Duty which the Engine would for the time be subject to, and Forfeiture of Engine, such Engine to be sold or otherwise disposed of as the Magistrates shall deem fit, and the entire proceeds thereof shall be added to the general funds of the District in which the same shall be used or erected.

Using Engines without Licence. 11 & 12 V. c. 92, s. 22. 13 & 14 V. c. 88, s. 12.

85. Persons using Engines for fishing, or having the same erected or in Fishing Order, or found with the same in his possession in or near any Fishing Place, required to produce Licence to any Commissioner, Conservator, Inspector, or Officers or Men of the Navy, Coast Guard, or Constabulary, or Water Bailiff, when demanded. Penalty same as in No. 84.

Forfeiture to be applied to District. Licences to be produced. 11 & 12 V. c. 92, s. 29.

86. Licences to be printed, and stamped with the Seal of the Board of Conservators of the District from which it was issued; and the year for which such Licence shall issue, and a name, number or letter describing the District and the Electoral Division, and the name of the Engine for which same shall be issued shall also be printed thereon in clear and legible characters—such Licence only good and valid for the year and purpose for which it shall be issued.

Licences to be printed, &c. 11 & 12 V. c. 92, s. 28.

LIMITATION OF ACTIONS.

87. No person shall be convicted of any Offence committed against the provisions of Act, unless the prosecution shall be commenced within Six Calendar Months from the time of the commission of such Offence.

Actions 5 & 6 V. c. 106, s. 110.

MESHES OF NETS.

88. Nets for the capture of Salmon and Trout (or for any kind of Fish in the Inland or Fresh Water portions of Rivers), to be of not less size than one and three-quarter inches from knot to knot, measured when the Net is Wet.

Size of Meshes of Nets. 8 & 9 V. c. 108, s. 11.

NOTE.—Commissioners of Fisheries (now Inspectors), are empowered to alter the size of Meshes of Nets by any Bye-Law.—For alterations made, see Appendix.

MILLS AND SLUICES.

89. The Waste Sluices, Waste Gates, or Overfalls of the Weirs of any Mill or Factory deriving their supply from Rivers frequented by Salmon, shall, at all Seasons of the year when and during the time such Mills or Factories shall not be used for Milling purposes, be kept open if no passage for Fish be provided; and when such passage for Fish shall be provided then the Sluices which admit the Water to such Mills or Factories, and the Waste Sluices, Waste Gates or Overfalls shall be kept down or shut to force the Water through such passage for Fish, as provided by 5 & 6 Vic., c. 106; and if the Owners of any such Mill or Factory, not used for Milling purposes as aforesaid, shall omit to keep any such Sluice or Sluices, Waste Gates, or Overfalls shut as aforesaid, or open as aforesaid, he shall forfeit and pay a sum not less than Two Pounds, nor more than Ten Pounds for every such Offence: Provided always, that the opening or shutting of such Sluices, Waste Gates or Overfalls, shall not in any way injuriously interfere with the Machinery or Water Power of any Mill or Factory.

Mill Sluices to be opened or shut as by Law required at all times when Mills are out of use. Fish Passes 13 & 14 V. c. 88, s. 30.

90. Where Turbines or similar Hydraulic Machines are used, the person owning or using same shall, during the descent of Salmon, or Young of Salmon to the Sea, provide a Grating or other efficient means, to prevent such Salmon, or Young of Salmon, passing into such Machine: Penalty not exceeding Fifty Pounds and Five Pounds a Day.

Turbines, or other Hydraulic Machines. 26 & 27 V. c. 114, s. 30.

91. The exemption from compliance with the 76th section of the 5th & 6th Vic., c. 106, which directs, that in all Water-courses, Cuts, Channels, or Sluices for the purpose of conveying water from any River frequented by Salmon, there shall be placed and fixed by the occupier, at their points of divergence from and return to such River, and below such Sluices, a Grating or Lattice (the space between the bars whereof shall not exceed two inches in any place), extending across the whole width of such Water-courses, &c., shall extend only to such cases in which and for such periods during which it shall be proved to the satisfaction of the Inspectors of Irish Fisheries, that such exemption is necessary for the effective working of any machinery.

This section includes a Wire Lattice or Net-work to be stretched over such Grating during the time when the Fry of Salmon or Trout shall be descending, and the exemption above refers to such Network.

Gratings to be placed in all Water-courses. 32 & 33 V. c. 9, s. 4, and 5 & 6 V. c. 106, s. 76.

MILLDAMS AND WATER-COURSES.

92. If any person shall, at any Season of the Year, in any Mill Pool or Milldam, or in any Works appurtenant to any Mill or Factory, or in any of the Water-courses leading the Water to or from such Mill or Factory, place, lay, set, or draw any Net, Grate, Creel, or other Engine, or use any Means or Device whatsoever (save and except Rod and Line used subject to the provisions of Act), for the purpose of taking, destroying, or obstructing any Salmon or other Fish, or the Fry thereof, every such person so offending shall for every such offence forfeit and pay a sum not exceeding Ten Pounds, and shall also forfeit such Nets or other Engines; and in case the person who shall have actually committed any such Offence shall not be known or found, and if such Offence shall

Penalty for any Person taking or attempting to take Fish or the Fry of Fish, in Works appurtenant to Mills or

APPENDIX. No. 32.

Factories, or in Water-courses diverted from Rivers for such purposes. 5 & 6 V. c. 106, s. 73.

have been committed by means of shutting down or closing any Gate or Sluice which is under the exclusive power of the Occupier of any Mill or Factory, or if such Offence shall have been committed under such circumstances as shall appear to the Justice or Justices before whom any Complaint thereupon shall be made, to afford reasonable grounds for believing that such Offence was committed by some person in the employment or under the control of the Owner or Occupier of such Mill or Factory, or that it was committed with the knowledge or connivance of such Owner or Occupier, or the person in charge of such Mill or Factory, or through the default of reasonable precaution on the part of such Owner or Occupier to prevent such Offence, then and in every such Case such Owner or Occupier of such Mill or Factory shall be deemed and taken to be liable to and shall incur the Penalty and Forfeiture aforesaid, as if such Offence had been actually committed by him.

Taking Fish near Weirs. 13 & 14 V. c. 88, s. 37.

Proviso.

Taking with Nets near Milldams. 26 & 27 V. c. 114, s. 16.

93. No Net, Instrument or Device, for taking Fish (save and except Rods and Lines only), shall be used within Two Hundred Yards of any Weir used for supplying Water to Mills, &c., or for Navigation, either above or below the same.—Penalty for every such offence not less than Two Pounds nor more than Ten Pounds, and Forfeiture of Net, &c. Where such right has been exercised in any such place by any person lawfully possessed of a Several Fishery therein, for Twenty Years next before passing of Act, he shall not be subject to the penalty provided. But such person shall not use any Engine (save and except Rods and Lines only), at or within Fifty Yards above or below a Milldam, unless there be attached to such Milldam a Fish Pass of such Form and Dimensions as may be approved by the Commissioners, and that such Fish Pass shall have constantly running through it such a flow of Water as will enable Salmon to pass up and down it—penalty not less than Five Pounds and not exceeding Twenty Pounds.

Definition of "Fishing Milldam." 26 & 27 V. c. 114, s. 44.

94. "Fishing Milldams" shall mean a Dam used, or intended to be used, partly for the purpose of catching or facilitating the catching of Fish, and partly for the purpose of supplying Water for Milling or other purposes.—See also "Fishing Weirs."

NETS.

Regulations as to. 5 & 6 V. c. 106, s. 66.

95. No person shall, in the fresh-water portion of any inland River or Lake, make use of or Fish with any Net formed with a false bottom (except Nets for taking Eels), or shall place two or more Nets one behind the other, or use any Nets covered with canvass, hide, or other substance, for the purpose of taking small Fish, or shall affix or keep up continued Nets stretched across any River, or shall Fish with any Nets within the limits of a Several Fishery without a Licence in writing from the Owner or Renter of such Fishery (see 110)—or shall place, affix, or attach any Nets to any stakes, bridges, sluices, lock-gates of Canals, or other such fixed erections.—Penalty not exceeding Ten Pounds.

Regulations as to Sea Net. 5 & 6 V. c. 106, s. 6.

96. No Net or other Engine covered with Canvas, Hide, or other Material, by which unsizeable and Young Fish may be taken or destroyed, shall be used on the Sea Coast, or within any Estuary, except for the purpose of dredging for Shell Fish—Penalty not exceeding Ten Pounds, and forfeiture of Net.

No Herring or other Nets, save as herein provided, to be shot or left floating in the day time. 5 & 6 V. c. 106, s. 7, 7 & 8 V. c. 108, s. 7.

97. No Person shall at any Time between sunrise and sunset, set, either in the Sea or within the Tideway in any Estuary, any Sea Net for the catching of Herrings, or any Trammel Net, or leave any Drag or other Net in the Water between sunrise and sunset, except Stake or Fixed Nets for the catching of Salmon, and save also Seines or Drift Nets for Pilchards or Herrings, provided such Stake or Fixed Nets, and such Seines or Drift Nets, be used at such times and places as may not be prohibited by any Bye-law—Penalty not exceeding Ten Pounds, and forfeiture of Net.

Penalty for not hauling up Nets. 5 & 6 V. c. 106, s. 8.

98. Every Person who shall, between sunset and sunrise, have set, either in the Sea or within the Tideway in any Estuary, any such Net as is prohibited from being left set, or in the Water between sunrise and sunset, shall before sunrise haul up and remove such Net or Nets—Penalty not exceeding Five Pounds, and forfeiture of Net. Proviso as to being prevented by Storm or Stress of Weather.—See Appendix for places where Trammel Nets are allowed during daytime.

Trawl or Trammel Nets. 5 & 6 V. c. 106, s. 9.

99. Every person who shall use any Trawl or Trammel Net at any Season, or any Place, either in the Sea or within the Tideway in any Estuary, when, or where the use of the same shall have been prohibited by any Bye-law, shall forfeit such Net, and pay a Penalty not exceeding Twenty Pounds.—See Appendix for Bye-laws relating thereto.

Nets or Lines not to be set or laid contrary to Bye-laws. 5 & 6 V. c. 106, s. 10.

100. No person shall set any Net, at or across the entrance of any Bay or Estuary, in any place, or at any Time, which shall be prohibited by any Bye-law—Penalty not exceeding Five Pounds.

Stake Nets not to extend further than from High to Low Water Mark. 5 & 6 V. c. 106, s. 26. 26 & 27 V. c. 114, s. 12. Leaders of Bag Nets to be raised.

101. No Stake Weir, Stake Net, nor any Leader, Out-rigger, or other work of any kind whatsoever connected therewith or adjacent thereto, shall be placed, or erected, or suffered to remain in such a manner as that it shall extend to a greater distance than from High water to Low water mark of ordinary Spring Tides, save and except in the case of Ebb and Flood Weirs, commonly called Head Weirs, not fished by means of a fixed Net; nor shall any such Weir be so constructed as to be capable of taking young or unsizeable fish;—and the Nets made use of in the formation and construction of Stake Nets, and of the Leaders of all Bag, or other fixed Nets, shall be extended evenly in such a manner that the Meshes shall be stretched to their full opening;—and all Bag Nets shall be so placed and erected as that the Netting of the Leaders can be raised and kept out of water, and that clear openings can be made in all Stake Nets, &c.—Penalty not exceeding Ten Pounds.—See also paragraphs "Fixed Nets," "Meshes of Nets," and "Illegal Nets."

For Bye-Laws, see Appendix.

OYSTER FISHERIES.

102. See Special Book of Instructions on this subject. — *Appendix, No. 22.*

NIGHT.

103. If any person shall, between sunset and sunrise, have, or use any Light or Fire of any kind, or any Spear, Gaff, Strokehaul, or other such instrument, with the intent to take Salmon or other Fish in or on the banks of any Lake or River, or if any person shall be found at any Time chasing, injuring, or disturbing Spawning Fish, or Fish on the Spawning Beds, or attempting to catch Fish in such places (except with Rods and Flies only, within the lawful period) or damming, or teeming, or emptying any River or Mill Race, for the purpose of taking or destroying any Salmon or Trout, or Fry thereof, every person so offending in any of the cases aforesaid, shall also forfeit all such Instruments, and shall also forfeit and pay any sum not exceeding Ten Pounds. — *Penalty for attempting to take Salmon, Trout, &c., at Night in Inland Rivers, &c., or using Light, &c., for such Purposes. 5 & 6 V. c. 106, s. 78.*

104. No person shall use any Net except a Landing Net, for the capture of Salmon or Trout in the Fresh Water portion of any River, as defined by the Commissioners, between the Hours of Eight o'clock in the Evening and Six o'clock in the Morning, except so far as the same may have heretofore been used within the limits of a Several Fishery, next above the Tidal Flow, and held under Grant or Charter, or by immemorial usage.—Penalty not exceeding Ten Pounds, and Forfeiture of all Boats, Nets, and Gear. — *Nets during certain hours in Rivers Prohibited. 26 & 27 V. c. 114, s. 24*

See also "Private Waters."

PENALTIES—APPLICATION OF

105. One-third of every sum of money levied as a fine, penalty, or forfeiture, shall be paid to the person who shall be the means of bringing to justice any person committing any offence against any of the Provisions of Acts, and the remainder shall be paid to the Board of Conservators of the District in which the offence was committed, or their authorized officer. — *32 & 33 V. c. 92, s. 19*

POISONING RIVERS.

106. Any person found on the Bank of or near any River, with any deleterious Matter in his possession, under such circumstances as shall satisfy the Court before whom he may be tried that such person had employed, or was about to employ, such deleterious matter for the capture or destruction of Fish, the said Court is empowered to inflict on such person a penalty not less than Five Pounds, nor more than Ten Pounds; and any person found taking Fish from any River or Lake where it shall be proved to the satisfaction of any Justice that such Fish has been willfully poisoned, shall be subject to a penalty of not less than Ten Shillings nor more than Five Pounds. — *Poisoning Rivers for purpose of taking Fish. 13 & 14 V. c. 88, s. 36*

POISONOUS MATTER.

107. No person shall throw, empty, or cause to run or flow into any River or Lake, any Dye-stuff or other deleterious or poisonous Liquid, or shall throw into such River or Lake any Lime, Spurge, or other deleterious or poisonous matter, or shall steep in such River or Lake any Flax or Hemp; and if any person shall so offend, he shall forfeit and pay for every such offence any sum not exceeding Ten Pounds: Provided always, that nothing in Act contained shall extend or be construed to render any person liable to the Penalties hereby imposed for casting into any River or Stream any Dye-stuffs or other Materials which are not of a deleterious Nature, or which are not in a state poisonous to Fish or other Animals using the Waters thereof. — *Allowing poisonous matter to flow into Inland Rivers. 5 & 6 V. c. 106, s. 90.*

POLLEN.

108. Close Season for Pollen by Trammel Nets in Lough Neagh, 29th September and 1st March. — *8 & 9 V. c. 108, s. 26.*

Bye-Law made by Commissioners PROHIBITING DRAFT NETS for Pollen in Lough Neagh.

PRIVATE WATERS.

109. Unlawfully and wilfully taking or destroying any fish in any water running through, or being in any land adjoining or belonging to the Dwelling-house of any person being the Owner of such water, or having a right of Fishing therein, a misdemeanour; and doing so in any water, not being such as before-mentioned, but which shall be private property, in which there shall be any private right of Fishing, penalty of Five Pounds over value of Fish taken. — *Fishing in Private Waters. 24 & 25 V. c. 96, sec. 24.*

110. Nothing to extend to any person angling between the beginning of the last hour before sunrise and expiration of first hour after sunset; but any person angling between hours mentioned in any such water as *first* mentioned, liable to penalty of Five Pounds; and in any such water as last mentioned, liable to penalty of Two Pounds.

111. If any person found Fishing against provisions of this Act, the Owner of ground, water or Fishery, his servant, or any person authorised by him, may demand from Offender any Rod, Line, Hook, Net, or other Implement then in his possession, and if not immediately delivered up, he may seize and take the same for the use of such owner. — *Engine may be seized 24 & 25 V. c. 96, s. 26*

112. Any person angling against the provisions of this Act between the hours mentioned, from whom any Implement used by Anglers shall be taken, or by whom it shall be delivered up, exempted from any Damages or Penalty for such Angling. — *24 & 25 V. c. 96, s. 25.*

Appendix, No. 22.

Fishing in Several Fishery without permission in writing. 5 & 6 V., c. 106, s. 86. 11 & 12 V., c. 92, s. 41.

113. No person shall lay, draw, make use of, or fish with any Nets within the limits of any Several Fishery, without a Licence in writing from the Owner or Renter of such Fishery—Penalty forfeiture of Net, and any sum not exceeding Ten Pounds.

114. Entering in, or upon a Several Fishery, for the purpose or under the pretence of killing Fish therein, or taking Fish therefrom—Penalty not less than Ten Shillings nor more than Five Pounds. *See also* "Inland Rivers."

Registry of Fishing Vessels.

115. Regulations for the Lettering, Numbering, and Registering of British Sea-Fishing Boats, under Part II. of the Sea Fisheries Act, 1868 (31 & 32 Victoria, Chapter 45).

[Note.—The Regulations approved by Her Majesty in Council on the 4th day of February, 1869, are REVOKED by the Order in Council of the 18th day of June, 1869, and the following Regulations are now in force.]

1. The following Regulations shall be in future observed by owners and masters of all British boats or vessels hailing from or belonging to any port or place in the United Kingdom, the islands of Guernsey, Jersey, Alderney, Sark, or Man, of whatever size, and however propelled or navigated, which find any portion of their ordinary employment in sea fishing, or oyster or mussel dredging, for purposes of sale; subject, however, to the following qualifications:—

(1.) Yachts, vessels, or boats not usually employed in fishing or dredging for purposes of sale shall not be subject to the following Regulations when they are not so employed:

(2.) If a boat or vessel employed in fishing or dredging for purposes of sale is also used as a pilot boat, and is marked and numbered as such, under any laws or regulations governing such pilot boats, such boat or vessel shall not be subject to the following Regulations.

(3.) Boats employed in the pilchard seyn fishery on the coasts of Cornwall shall, if otherwise duly marked to the satisfaction of the officers of Customs or Coast Guard, be exempt from the necessity of having letters and numbers painted on their sails, bows, or sterns as required by the following Regulations.

2. Every sea fishing vessel or boat, whether registered under any other Act or not, shall, except as hereinbefore provided for, be lettered, numbered, and have a certificate of registry, and shall for that purpose be entered or registered in a Register of Sea Fishing Boats to be kept at the principal office of Customs in each collectorship. Applications, as hereafter prescribed, for letters, numbers, and certificates of Registry shall be made by all owners of fishing boats to the Officer of Coast Guard or Fishery Officer in charge of the Station at or near the place where the boat may for the time being be employed. In any case where a boat belongs to a place situated at a distance from a Coast Guard Station, such application may be delivered to the principal Officer of Customs or to any Fishery Officer at the creek or station at or nearest to the place to which the boat belongs, or at which she may be temporarily employed in fishing. And such application, upon being received by any such Officer, shall be forthwith forwarded to the Collector of Customs of the Port in which the place to which the boat belongs is situated, who, upon the receipt of such application, shall cause the boat to be registered and numbered, and grant the certificate of such registry, and forward the same to the Officer through whom the application was received, who is to deliver such certificate to the applicant.

3. The port or place at which any British vessel or boat is registered under the provisions of "The Merchant Shipping Act, 1854," (17 & 18 Vict., c. 104) shall be considered the port or place to which she belongs.

4. In Scotland the Officers of the Board of British White Herring Fishery shall assist the Officers of Customs and of Coast Guard in the performance of the duties imposed by these Regulations; and shall, in places where there are no Coast Guard, themselves discharge the duties hereby imposed upon the Coast Guard.

5. If, in the opinion of the Collector of the Port to which any boats belong, or of the Inspecting Commander or Divisional Officer of the District, it is desirable, from local circumstances or otherwise, that the mode of application prescribed in the second article of these Regulations should be partially modified or altered, such Collector, Inspecting Commander, or Divisional Officer shall make a special report to the Board of Trade, setting forth the reasons for and particulars of such modification or alteration.

6. There shall be series of numbers and distinguishing letters for the boats belonging to each collectorship of customs.

7. For purposes of numbering, lettering, and registration, boats shall be divided into three classes, as follows.—

1st Class.—Boats of 15 tons burthen and upwards.

2nd Class.—Boats of less than 15 tons burthen, navigated otherwise than by oars only.

3rd Class.—Boats navigated by oars only.

Provided that the officer to whom the application to register is made may, if he think proper, place any small boat occasionally navigated or propelled by sail in the third instead of the second class.

8. For boats of the above classes the positions and dimensions of the letters and numbers shall be as follows:—

1st Class.—For the hulls, 18 inches in height, and 2½ inches in breadth, and for the sails one-third larger every way.

2nd Class.—For the hulls, 10 inches in height, and 1½ inches in breadth, and for the sails one-third larger in every way.

3rd Class.—Three inches at least in height, and half an inch in breadth.

Provided that in boats that have a "bend piece" or "rubbing streak" the letters and numbers shall be as high as the space above the "bend piece" or "rubbing streak" will admit. In boats where the space between the gunwale and water-line is not sufficient in size for the prescribed letters and numbers, the letters and numbers shall be as high as the size of the boats will admit.

9. In boats of the 1st and 3rd class the number will follow, and in those of the 2nd class precede, the distinguishing letter or letters.

10. When vessels carry, or have attached to them, small boats as tenders or otherwise, such boats must be marked with the same numbers and letters as the vessels to which they belong. Such numbers and letters may be of the size appropriate to the class to which the boat would belong according to its own size and means of propulsion, but in position and precedence according to the class of the vessel to which the boat is attached.

11. In sailing boats, and boats navigated by the occasional use of sails, the letters and numbers shall be placed on each bow, three or four inches below the gunwale, and on each side of the mainsail, except for lug-sail boats, in which the letters and numbers may be placed on the foresail or mizen instead of the mainsail. For boats of the third class, the letters and numbers shall be placed on the outside of the stern of the boat immediately under the name. On the hulls all letters and numbers shall be painted in white oil colour on a black ground; and on sails, in black oil colour on white or grey sails, and in white oil colour on tanned or black sails. Except in the case of vessels only occasionally engaged in fishing for purposes of sale, hereinafter in the thirteenth article of these Regulations specially provided for, the letters and numbers of sails shall be painted on each side of the cloth forming the substance of the sail, and not upon any cloth or other thing sewn or otherwise attached to it; and shall be placed on each side of the centre cloth or cloths of the mainsail, clear of and immediately above the close reef, and so as to be at all times conspicuous whether the sail be reefed or not.

12. All boats of whatever class shall have their names, and those of the ports to which they belong, painted in white oil colour on a black ground on the outside of the sterns, in letters which shall be at least 3 inches in height and ½ an inch in breadth.

13. In the case of any vessel or boat only occasionally engaged in fishing for purposes of sale, and not usually so employed the letters and numbers prescribed by these Regulations may be temporarily affixed, by pieces of canvas or board attached to the mainsail and bows, but of the same dimensions as those specified in the eighth article of these Regulations.

14. The letters, numbers, and names placed on boats and on their sails shall not be effaced, covered, or concealed in any manner whatsoever.

15. All the buoys, barrels, and principal floats of each net, and all other implements of fishery, shall be marked with the same letters and numbers as the boats to which they belong, so as to be easily distinguished. The owners may further distinguish them by any private marks they think proper. Provided that this Regulation shall not apply in the case of boats employed,

(1) In the Scotch herring fishery;
(2) In the drift net and seyn fisheries in Cornwall;
(3) In such other drift net and seyn fisheries (if any) as the Board of Trade may direct

In the above-mentioned cases it will be held sufficient that the nets and buoys be so marked, so as to identify their true owners; but in all cases of doubt it will devolve upon the masters of buoys and nets to satisfy Sea Fishery officers, (as defined by the 8th section of the Sea Fisheries Act, 1868,) that the said buoys and nets properly form part of the train of the boat with which they may be found, or that they belong to the fishermen of other boats temporarily fishing in it.

16. The owner and master of any boat not having all its nets, buoys, and other implements duly marked in the manner above directed, shall be liable to a penalty not exceeding five pounds.

17. A register of sea-fishing boats, in the form contained in Table A. hereto annexed, shall be kept by the Collector of Customs at each collectorship, which shall contain the date of registry, name of the vessel or boat, and of the port or place to which she belongs, names of owner and master, description of her rig and of her ordinary mode of fishing, her registered number, class, tonnage, and length of keel, and number of crew usually employed.

18. Certificates of Registry in the above register shall be issued by the respective Collectors of Customs, on application being duly made as directed by the second article of these Regulations; and such certificate shall be in the form contained in Table B. hereto annexed, and when necessary shall be transmitted to the Officer of Coast Guard or Customs or other Fishery Officer through whom the application may have been transmitted for delivery by such Officer to the owner. The Certificates of Registry shall contain the name of the collectorship and the distinguishing letters, the name and description of boat, the name of the owner and master, the registered number and class, and the date of entry.

19. All applications for letters, numbers, and registration of fishing boats must be in writing, and according to the form contained in Table C. hereto annexed, and in duplicate if they are to be forwarded from a distant station as provided by the second article of these Regulations; and the duplicate copy is to be retained and filed by the Officer of Coast Guard or Customs at the station to which the boat belongs.

20. Whenever the owner of any registered vessel or boat proves to the satisfaction of the proper Officer of Customs or Coast Guard or any Fishery Officer that he has lost or been deprived of any Certificate of Registry already granted to him, the proper Officer may cause a copy of such Certificate of Registry to be made out and delivered to such owner; and such copy, duly certified by the proper officer, shall have all the effect of the original.

21. Once in every year the owner of every boat shall submit his Certificate of Registry for examination, either at the head office in each collectorship or at the station through which it was originally obtained, and the proper officer shall sign his name on the back of the said Certificate, together with the date of examination, as a record of its authenticity and correctness.

22. In the first week of every year each officer of Customs or of Coast Guard and each Fishery Officer shall forward to the Collector of Customs of the district a list, showing the numbers and classes of all boats whose Certificates of Registry have been presented for examination and endorsed in the preceding year; and a notation of all inspections of Certificates shall be made in the Register against the name of each boat. On a change of ownership, or on removal to another collectorship, of any boat registered under these Regulations, a fresh Certificate of Registry must be applied for, and the former Certificate be given up, in order that the same, together with the former Registry, may be cancelled; and on *a change of Master* due notice shall be given of such change, which shall be duly noted in the Register, *and be endorsed on the Certificate of Registry*.* A failure on the part of the owner of any boat to comply with these Regulations shall subject the owner and master to the same penalties that they would have incurred if the Certificate of Registry had never been applied for.

23. If any boat required to be registered, lettered, and numbered in pursuance of these Regulations, and not being so registered, lettered, and numbered, in the manner prescribed, is used as a fishing boat, the owner and the master shall each be liable to a penalty not exceeding twenty pounds. Any Sea Fishery officer may seize and detain such boat, and prevent it from going to sea and from sea fishing until it is duly registered, lettered, and numbered, and may for that purpose, if it is at sea, take it back into the nearest or most convenient British port. Such boat shall not be entitled to any of the privileges or advantages of a British Sea Fishing Boat, but all obligations, liabilities, and penalties with reference to such boat shall be the same as if it had been duly registered.

24. The master of every boat registered under these Regulations shall have on board his boat at all times the Certificate of Registry hereby required to be obtained; and any master not having such Certificate shall, in the absence of any reasonable cause for the same, (proof whereof shall lie on him,) be liable, together with his boat and crew, to be taken by any Sea Fishery officer, without warrant, summons, or other process, into the nearest or most convenient port and there to be ordered by the Court, on any proceeding in a summary manner, to pay a penalty not exceeding twenty pounds. Provided that the masters of boats employed in the pilchard fishery in Cornwall, or in such other fishery (if any) as the Board of Trade shall direct, shall be exempt from this Regulation.

25. After registration no change shall be made in the name of any Sea Fishing Boat.

* Note.—Where a change of Master occurs, the Lords of the Admiralty, by letter dated 11th April, [illegible], have authorized officers of the Coast Guard in Ireland, in all cases where they feel satisfied that delay in Fishing would be caused by forwarding the Register for endorsement to the Collector and waiting till it is returned, may themselves make the endorsement, notifying the same as early as possible to the Collector at the Head Port of Registry.

TABLE A.

SEA FISHERIES ACT, 1868, 31 & 32 Vict. Cap. 45.

Port of ____________________

REGISTRY of VESSELS and BOATS ENGAGED in FISHING.

Date of Registry.	Name of Vessel.	Port or Place to which belonging.	Name of Owner.	Name of Master.	Description.		Registered No.			Size.		No. of Crew usually employed.		Remarks.
					Of Vessel or Boat, how rigged, what floats used, &c.	Ordinary Mode of Fishing.	1st Class.	2nd Class.	3rd Class.	Tonnage.	Length of Keel.	Men.	Boys.	

TABLE B.

SEA FISHERIES ACT, 1868.—31 & 32 Vict. Cap. 45.

Port of ————

CERTIFICATE OF REGISTRY

of ————, named ————

of ————

Owner ————

Master ————

Registered No. ——— of ——— Class ————

Signature of Registering Officer ————

Date ————

TABLE C.

SEA FISHERIES ACT, 1868.—31 & 32 Vict. Cap. 45.

Application to Register a Vessel or Boat.

Port of ———— Letter ————

The ————

Port or place to which belonging ————

Owner ————

Master ————

Description of vessel or boat, how rigged, what sails used, &c. ————

Mode of fishing ————

Tonnage ————

Length of keel ————

No. of men ———— } usually employed.
No. of boys ———— }

Signature of applicant - ————

Residence ————

NOTE.—The Act does not require that Boats *engaged exclusively* in Salmon Fishing should be registered; but the 81st section of 5 & 6 V. c. 106, *further directs that every Boat, Cot, or Curragh, shall have, upon some conspicuous place thereof, the Name of the Owner, or of one of the Owners, where more than one, and of his Place of Residence, painted in clear, legible characters or letters, of not less than Two Inches in length. Penalty for non-compliance, Two Pounds.*

SEVERAL FISHERY.

Taking Fish from Several Fisheries. 11 & 12 V. c. 92, s. 41.

116. If any person or persons not being authorized by the Owner, Lessee, or Occupier of a Several Fishery, shall enter into or upon such Several Fishery for the purpose or under the pretence of killing Fish therein, or taking Fish therefrom, or shall kill Fish therein, or take Fish therefrom, he or they shall, for every such offence forfeit and pay a sum not less than Ten Shillings nor more than Five Pounds, the same to be recoverable in a summary way before a Justice or Justices.—*See also* "Private Waters;" and 5 & 6 V. c. 106, s. 66, No. 113, which imposes a penalty of Ten Pounds for using Nets in Several Fishery, without leave in writing from Owner or Renter.

Definition of Several Fishery. 13 & 14 V. c. 88, s. 1.

117. The words "Several" Fisheries shall mean and include all Fisheries lawfully possessed and enjoyed as such under any Title whatsoever, being a good and valid Title at Law exclusively of the public, by any person or persons whether in Navigable Waters or in Waters not Navigable, and whether the Soil covered by such Waters be vested in such person or persons, or in any other person or persons.—*See also* "Private Waters."

SPEARS, &c.

Otters, Spears, &c. prohibited. 13 & 14 V. c. 88, s. 40.

118. It shall not be lawful in any Fresh Water River or Lake at any Season of the year, to use for the purpose of taking Fish, any Otter, Lyster, Spear, Strokehaul, Dree Draw, or Gaff (except when the latter Implement may be used solely as auxiliary to Angling with Rod and Line, or for the purpose of removing Fish from any legal Weir or Box by the Owner or Occupier thereof,) under penalty of not less than Four Pounds nor greater than Ten Pounds.

NOTE.—This does not extend to Eel Spears.

SUMMONS.

How to be served. 5 & 6 V. c. 106, s. 94.

119. To be served personally, or left at or on board the Vessel, or posted on the known residence of the person for whom intended.—For Witnesses, to be served personally.

UNCLEAN FISH.

Penalty for having, taking, or offering for Sale, any unclean or spent Fish. 5 & 6 V. c. 106, s. 74.

120. If any person shall at any Time wilfully take, kill, destroy, expose to sale, or have in his possession, any red, black, foul, unclean, or unseasonable Salmon or Trout, such person shall forfeit and pay any sum not exceeding Two Pounds for every such Fish so taken, killed, destroyed, exposed to sale, or in his possession; Provided always, that if any Person shall take or catch any such Fish accidentally, and return the same immediately to the Water without injury, such person shall not be liable to the penalty aforesaid.

Artificial propagation, &c. 26 & 27 V. c. 114, s. 32.

121. Nothing shall apply to any person who shall Catch, or have in his possession Salmon or Trout for the purpose of Artificial Propagation, or other Scientific purposes.

Export of Salmon. 28 V. c. 10, s. 11, and 33 & 34 V. c. 33.

122. No unclean or unseasonable Salmon, and no Salmon caught during the time at which the sale of Salmon is prohibited in the District where it is caught shall be Exported or entered for Exportation from any part of the United Kingdom, to parts beyond Seas.—Penalty, forfeiture of Salmon, and Five Pounds for each Salmon; and the burden of proving that any Salmon entered for Exportation from any part of the United Kingdom to parts beyond Seas between the 3rd September and 30th April following, is not so entered in contravention of Act, shall lie on the person entering same.

VESSELS, BOATS, &c.

Taking or using Boats without permission. 5 & 6 V. c. 106, s. 79.

123. Any Person removing, taking, using, or employing any Vessel, Boat, Cot, or Barge, without permission of the Owner thereof, liable to penalty of Two Pounds.

WASTE SHORES.

Fishermen may use Waste Shores for purpose of fishing. 5 & 6 V. c. 106, s. 8.

124. Lawful for all Fishermen and Persons employed by them to enter upon all such Beaches, Strands, and Wastes, on or adjoining the Sea-shore, or any Estuary as may be necessary for the purpose of carrying on any Herring or other Sea-fishing, and also to draw up and spread their Nets, and land their Fish upon any such Beach, Strand, or Waste; Provided that they shall not erect any Fixtures or fixed Nets thereon.

Appendix, No. 22.

Or for watching for fish. Ib., s. 4.

125. And lawful for all Watchmen, Directors, and Guiders of Fishermen, and all such Fishermen themselves, and such other Persons as shall necessarily attend the Nets or Fishings, at the times of fishing for Herrings, Pilchards, and other Sea Fish, to enter and go into and upon any Lands, which lie or adjoin near unto any Fishing Place, fit, convenient, and necessary to watch and to draw or carry the Fish on Shore, and there to watch for the said Fish, and to direct and guide the said Fishermen, which shall be upon the Sea and Sea-coasts for the taking of the said Fish; Provided that no Person shall be empowered or authorized to enter in or upon any enclosed Garden, or any tillage Land with a growing Crop thereon.

Penalty for obstructing Fishermen in using such Shores. Ib., s. 4.

126. If any Person shall persist or forcibly obstruct any Fisherman or Person employed by him in entering upon and using in the manner and for the purposes aforesaid, the said Beaches, Strands, Wastes, and other Lands, save Gardens and Lands with a growing Crop, he shall for every such Offence pay a Penalty not exceeding Five Pounds.

Water Bailiffs.

11 & 12 V. c. 92, s. 19. Board of Conservators empowered to appoint Water Bailiffs.

127. It shall be lawful for the Board of Conservators for each district, to appoint as many Inspectors and Water Bailiffs as may be necessary for the protection of the Fisheries in the District, and for generally enforcing the Fishery Laws within the same.

Proprietors of Fisheries may appoint Water Bailiffs. 5 & 6 V. c. 106, s. 82. 8 & 9 V. c. 108, s. 13.

128 Lawful for any person interested in the preservation of the Fish of any river or lake, or for any persons who shall have united themselves into a society for the preservation of said Fisheries, or for the Owner of any Fishery in any river or lake, or the proprietor of any Salmon Fishery on the Sea Coast to appoint Water Bailiffs. No such Bailiff empowered to act until his appointment shall have been approved and confirmed by two or more Justices assembled in Petty Sessions in the District in which the Bailiff is to act. The Warrant under which any such Bailiff acts must bear a Five Shilling Stamp.

11 & 12 V. c. 92, s. 36

129 The appointment of a Water Bailiff under the 11th & 12th Vic. c. 92, by a Board of Conservators, is not subject to Stamp Duty, nor does it require the approval of the Justices at Petty Sessions, as in the case of appointments under the 5th & 6th Vic. c. 106.

11 & 12 V. c. 92, s. 34. Powers of Inspectors and Water Bailiffs

130. Such Inspectors and Water Bailiffs as shall be appointed under the provisions of Act shall have for the enforcement of Acts, the power of Constables, and all the powers and authorities conferred on Water Bailiffs, or officers, or men of the Constabulary force, or Coast Guard, or Navy. *See* also No. 3.

White Trout.

Definition of 13 & 14 V. c. 88, s. 1.

131. The word "Salmon," shall extend to, and include Grilse, Peal, Sea Trout, Samlets, Par, and all other Fish of the Salmon Kind, and the Spawn and Fry thereof.

Jenkins, &c. 26 & 27 V. c. 114, s. 19.

132 "Jenkin," and "Cravalling," are deemed to be "Salmon."

Note.—The Appendices in this Digest are not reprinted in this Report, but are substantially the same as appear in the Schedules to Report.

INDEX.

	Paragraph
Actions: Limitation of,	87
Angling:	
Close season for,	13
During close season,	22
Permitted during weekly close season,	25
Entering lands without permission for purposes of,	34
Not prohibited near mill dams,	58–93
Rods for taking salmon and white trout liable to Licence duty—but not if used singly for taking perch, pike, and other fish, save salmon and white trout—Regulations as to,	76–85
Cross lines for any fish liable to Licence Duty,	82
Cross lines in rivers, save in a Several Fishery, not legal,	82
Exception in favour of, near mill-dams,	73, 93
In private waters without permission, liable to penalty or forfeiture of rod,	108–114
Gaff as auxiliary to, only permitted,	118
Annual Close Season: See "Close Season."	
Appeal against Order relating to Fixed Nets,	65
Arrest: Power to, only in certain cases,	5, 6
Artificial Propagation: Persons having in possession salmon or trout during close season for such purposes not liable to penalty,	15, 66, 121
Assaulting:	
Any person assaulting, resisting, or obstructing any officer or any person acting under him,	7
Or any person lawfully engaged in fishing,	8

	Paragraph
Bag Nets: See "Nets," or "Fixed Nets"	
Ballast: Not to be thrown out within estuary, harbour, or place, unless where same may be allowed by Commissioners or the Local Regulations,	9
Boats:	
Persons using for capture of salmon during annual or weekly close season, liable to penalty for first offence,	16, 30, 70
And may on second offence be forfeited,	16, 30, 70
Liable also to forfeiture in certain cases for fishing in fresh waters between eight o'clock, P.M., and six o'clock, A.M.	72, 106
Registry of,	115
Engaged exclusively in salmon fishing need not be registered,	115
To have name of owners painted thereon. (See 5 & 6 V. c. 106, s. 81),	115
Using without permission of owner,	123
Bridges: Nets not to be attached to,	75, 95
Buying salmon or trout during close season,	14
Bye Laws: Copies from Clerks of Peace or Clerks of Petty Sessions—evidence,	10
Close Season:	
Observance of annual and weekly,	3
Annual,	11
For trout same as for salmon,	12
For angling,	13

Appendix, No. 22.

	Paragraph
Close Seasons—continued.	
Fishing for or aiding in taking salmon or trout during,	14
Buying, selling, or having in possession during,	14
Having in possession salmon or trout during, *primâ facie* evidence of fish having been caught in,	14
Placing any coghill, eel-net, or basket, or other fixed modes of catching eels during times prohibited. (See "Eels"),	14
Nothing in Act to apply to any persons having in possession salmon or trout for artificial propagation, or other scientific purposes,	15
Any person using any boat, cot, or curragh for capture of salmon or trout during annual or weekly close season, liable to penalty,	16
And forfeiture of boat on second offence,	16
Any person having in possession any part of a salmon or trout during annual close season, liable to penalty,	14, 17
And such fish may be seized,	17
All machinery, nets, inscales, hecks, and cruives of weirs to be removed and carried away from the fishery within thirty-six hours after expiration of open season, and not be placed therein until within thirty-six hours of commencement of open season,	18
Exception as to eel fishing in certain cases,	18
Proviso as to storm or stress of weather,	18
All bag, sole, fly, stake nets, or other engines to be removed in like manner,	19
Nets of every kind for salmon shall be removed and carried away during the annual,	20
Penalty for fishing with nets, except eel nets, in inland waters during,	20
Angling for salmon and trout during,	22
Constabulary or Coastguard empowered to make openings and remove obstructions during,	33
For pollen,	108
Coastguard:	
General powers of,	1
May go on board any vessel,	1
And examine Certificate of Registry,	1
May seize illegal nets, or legal nets used illegally,	1
May execute warrants,	1
Not to incur expenses without authority,	1
Expenses, how to be furnished,	1
Assaulting or resisting,	7
May seize all salmon or trout found in possession of any person during annual close season,	17
Empowered to make openings and remove obstructions during close season,	33
Complaints: See "Offences."	
Conservators may appoint Bailiffs, &c.,	127-130
Constabulary:	
Powers of,	2
Empowered to make openings and remove obstructions during close season,	33
Cross-lines for any description of fish liable to Licence Duty,	82
In rivers, save in a Several Fishery, not legal,	83
Eels:	
Provisions as to use of fixed nets for, during salmon close season,	14, 18, 19
Fixed nets for, not to be used within certain periods or hours,	21, 63
Nets for, may be used during weekly close season,	24
Taking, selling, purchasing, or having in possession the fry of,	66
Taking salmon or trout, or fry thereof, in eel weirs,	21, 63
See also "Eel Fixtures."	
Entering lands under pretence of fishing,	34
Exportation of salmon between 3rd September and 30th April,	122
Factory: See "Mills."	
Fish Passes to be made in all erections placed in rivers since 1842,	40
May be made by Commissioners in all erections placed in rivers before 1842,	41
Regulations as to,	41, 42, 43
Fishing in such, or obstructing the free passage of fish through,	44
To be open to inspection of Commissioners and Conservators,	46
Fishing Weirs:	
All machinery, nets, inscales, hecks, and rails, cruives, &c., to be removed from fishing within thirty-six hours after expiration of open season, and not to be placed therein until within thirty-six hours of commencement of open season,	18
Taking salmon therein during weekly close season,	24
Openings to be made of four feet during weekly close season,	26, 53
Inscales, rails, and hecks forfeited, if box used during close season,	28
And penalty in respect of each crib in, by which any salmon caught during close season,	28
Constabulary and coast guard empowered to make openings, and remove all obstructions during close season,	33
Regulations as to free gaps, and fishing near,	47-50
Do. as to boxes and cribs in,	51, 52, 53
Do. as to spur and tail walls,	54
Inscales, &c., to be removed during weekly close season,	53
Fishing within fifty yards of, by nets,	50
Boxes in, used during weekly close season, to be forfeited, and penalty in respect of each box left unopened during,	56
Fixed Nets:	
For eels not to be used within certain times and hours,	21
Four feet openings to be made in all during weekly close season, &c.,	26
Leaders of bag nets to be removed during weekly close time,	26
Not to be used within one mile of mouth of river where breadth of mouth less than half a mile, except by proprietor of Several Fishery,	35, 61
Or placed in narrow channels,	35, 61
Bag-nets not to be placed in estuaries, or within three miles of mouths of rivers,	36, 37, 38
No fixed net not legally erected in 1862 legal,	39
Regulations as to meshes of,	60
Stake nets not to extend further than low water of ordinary spring tides—Regulations as to,	62, 101
For eels not to be used between 10th January and 1st July, save where season altered, or between 1st July and 10th January, between sunrise and sunset,	63
Not to be made use of without a certificate from Commissioners or Inspectors,	64
Appeal against judgment or order, &c., to Judge of Assize,	65
Fly Nets. See "Nets," or "Fixed Nets."	
Free gaps in fishing weirs:	
Regulations as to—or obstructing passage of fish through,	47, 48, 50, 51
Using nets within fifty yards of,	48, 50
Frightening or scaring salmon during weekly close season,	27, 29
Fry:	
Taking, selling, purchasing, or having in possession the spawn or fry of salmon, trout, or eels, &c.,	66
Salmon shall include grilse, smolts, par, peals, sea-trout, &c.,	67
Jenkin, gravelling, deemed to be salmon,	68
Gaff, spear, or strokehaul prohibited,	103, 119
Gaps: See "Free Gaps,"	102, 119
Gravelling,	68, 132
Grilse,	67, 131
Harbours: See "Ballast."	
Illegal Nets to be destroyed,	69
Inland Rivers:	
Penalty for using nets, except eel nets, in, during salmon close season,	20
Regulations as to fishing in,	71-75, 104
Meshes of nets for all descriptions of fish in,	80
Intimidation: See "Offenders."	
Jenkins,	68, 133
Justices may grant warrant to enter suspected places,	4
Legal Nets when forfeited to be sold,	69
Licences:	
Engines for taking salmon, trout, eels, or pollen liable to Licence Duty,	76

Appendix, No. 22.

www.ingramcontent.com/pod-product-compliance
Lightning Source LLC
Chambersburg PA
CBHW031411160426
43196CB00007B/970
* 9 7 8 3 7 4 1 1 0 4 7 5 6 *